The Natives of British Central Africa

WOMEN CARRYING WATER-JARS, CHIROMO

The Native Races of the British Empire

THE NATIVES

OF

BRITISH CENTRAL AFRICA

BY

A. WERNER

WITH THIRTY-TWO FULL-PAGE

ILLUSTRATIONS

LONDON

ARCHIBALD CONSTABLE

AND COMPANY, LTD.

1906

189093

Edinburgh: T. and A. CONSTABLE, Printers to His Majesty

IN MEMORIAM

J. R. W.

ELMINA, AUGUST 16, 1891

. . . '*Desiderio* . . .
Tam cari capitis. . . .'

EDITOR'S PREFACE

INTEREST in the subject races of the British Empire should be especially keen in the Mother Country, where there are few families but send into our dependencies some member, be it as Government official, soldier, or colonist. Anthropological text-books are at once too technical and too bulky to attract the ordinary reader, who wishes for no more than a sketch of habits and customs, accurate but readable, in which matter too abstruse, or otherwise unsuitable for general consumption, is omitted. The present series is intended to supply in handy and readable form the needs of those who wish to learn something of the life of the uncivilised races of our Empire; it will serve the purpose equally of those who remain at home and of those who fare forth into the world and come into personal contact with peoples in the lower stages of culture.

Unless otherwise stated the contributors to the series will be anthropologists who have personal knowledge of the tribes of whom they write; references to authorities will be dispensed with, as unnecessary for the general reader; but for those who desire to follow up the subject a bibliography will be found at the end of each volume.

The present series may perhaps do more than

merely spread a knowledge of the dark-skinned races beneath the British flag. Germany awoke years ago to the importance of the study of native races from a political and commercial, no less than from a scientific point of view. In twenty-five years the Berlin Museum has accumulated ethnographical collections more than ten times as large as those of the British Museum, and the work of collection goes on incessantly. England, with the greatest colonial empire which the world has ever seen, lags far behind. Money will perhaps be forthcoming in England for work in anthropology when savage life and savage culture has disappeared for ever from the earth before the onward march of so-called civilisation. If, one hundred years hence, English anthropologists have to go to Germany to study the remains of those who were once our subject races, we shall owe this humiliation to the supineness of England at the end of the nineteenth and beginning of the twentieth century. The past, once lost, can never be recovered; we have before us, in the subject races of our Empire, a living memorial of the past, and if England does her duty, she will lose no time in organising an Imperial Bureau of Ethnology, and thus enable English anthropologists to hold up their heads before their more fortunate German and American brethren.

NORTHCOTE W. THOMAS.

LONDON, *November 22, 1906.*

CONTENTS

ERRATA

Page 42, line 23, *for* fourth, *read* first.

„ 100, line 12. The illustration referred to has not been
           included in the volume, but the same type of square
           house may be seen in Plate 16.

„ 192, last line. This illustration has not been included.

„ 199, last line, *for* Pl. 23, *read* Pl. 18.

LIST OF PLATES

THE NATIVES OF
BRITISH CENTRAL AFRICA

CHAPTER I

INTRODUCTORY

Geography. Botany : bush-fire. Climate. Fauna :
beasts, birds, fish, insects.

WHEN you steam up the Shiré, you pass on the first,
second, or some subsequent day (according to the state
of the river and the capabilities of your craft), after
turning out of the Zambezi at Chimwara, a tree on the
western bank. This tree bears a notice-board which
marks the beginning of the British Central Africa
Protectorate.

But the globe-trotter who is anxious to record in his
diary the precise hour and minute of all momentous
events of a monotonous voyage may easily overlook
the all-important tree. The most eager inquirer may
find his experiences pall upon him when for hour after
hour he sees nothing but level shore, and a foreground
of green *bango*-reeds festooned with dull magenta con-
volvulus. In fact, the reason why the boundary had
to be marked by a board affixed to a tree, is because
this particular angle of alluvial land is so level and
devoid of natural features that, in the rainy season,
there is usually one navigable channel, if not more,

A

cutting it off into an island, by connecting the Shiré
and Zambezi. On the eastern bank we have left Mount
Morambala behind—a massive ridge, extending over
several miles and reaching a height of 4000 feet. Beyond the flats in the north-east you see the strangely
shaped cone of Chinga-Chinga Mountain against the
sky, and later on other ranges come into view; but
just here the river valley is a marsh (some parts of it
an actual lake) in the wet season, and a dusty plain at
the end of the dry.

The Portuguese territory on the eastern bank extends
a little farther north till it reaches a more tangible
boundary in the river Ruo, which rushes down from
Matapwiri's Mountain in the north-east, throwing itself
over a fall of 200 feet, and then, winding through the
same sort of plain as that already described, enters the
Shiré through a sort of miniature delta, by the reedy
island of Malo and the 'lip' of land where now stands
the British township of Chiromo.

I have spoken all along of the Shiré River; and it
is not now to be expected that Europeans will ever
call it anything else; but it is perhaps unnecessary to
say that no native, unless thoroughly accustomed to
Europeans and their ways, would ever know it by that
name. To him it is the *Nyanja*, or, if he happens to
be a Yao, the *Nyasa*—a word which means any large
body of water, whether river or lake. To those living
near Lake Nyasa, it is the lake which is Nyanja or
Nyasa, as the case may be; it is only European usage
which has stereotyped the Yao word on our maps.
Chiri, in the Mang'anja language, means ' a steep bank,'

and was misunderstood (by the Portuguese, probably, as it seems to have been in use before Livingstone penetrated the country) as the name of the river; since a native would say, 'I am going to the *bank*,' where we should say, 'I am going to the *river*.' As Sir H. H. Johnston has remarked, the Zambezi is the only one of the four great African rivers which bears a name given by, or even known to, the people dwelling on it.

Roughly speaking, the British Protectorate, to which we have been referring, comprises the basin of Lake Nyasa and its outlet, the Shiré. This general statement, of course, requires some qualification. The north end of the lake (the British boundary is the Songwe River, running out in about 10° of S. latitude) and nearly half the eastern side are German; south of that, *i.e.* from 11° 30' S. to Fort Maguire, is Portuguese. From Fort Maguire, the border-line runs south-east to the small lake called Chiuta, then south, by the salt lake Chilwa and Mlanje Mountain to the Ruo.

The western frontier of the Protectorate is an irregular line, following more or less the watershed between the streams that flow into the lake and those that flow into the Luangwa (a tributary of the Zambezi which, unlike most tributaries, goes up-stream to join its river—in this case in a south-westerly direction), and meeting the Portuguese border about 14° S. Thence it keeps on to the south-east, as far as the point on the Shiré already mentioned, where the notice-board is affixed to the tree.

Measurements in square miles convey little or nothing to my mind, as a rule, and I shall abstain as far as possible from inflicting them on the reader; but it may as well be noted here that the area of the Protectorate is estimated at 40,980.

West of the territory thus defined, and between the Zambezi and the upper waters of the Congo, lies a vast region known officially as North-east Rhodesia, and reaching up to the south end of Lake Tanganika. We shall have something to say about the tribes living in this part of the country; some of them, indeed, are identical with those in the Protectorate proper; but it is with the latter that we shall chiefly have to do.

We have seen that British Central Africa is a land of lakes and rivers; it is a land of mountains also. 'Before the discovery of Lake Ng'ami and the well-watered country in which the Makololo dwell,' said Livingstone, 'the idea prevailed that a large part of the interior of Africa consisted of sandy deserts into which rivers ran and were lost.' His great journey of 1852-56 dispelled this idea, and 'the peculiar form of the continent was then ascertained to be an elevated plateau, somewhat depressed in the centre, and with fissures in the sides by which the rivers escaped to the sea.' The great lakes all lie on this central plateau, and the rivers which drain them to the sea escape over its edge in the cataracts which for so many centuries, by interrupting navigation, have prevented the exploration of the interior. The Zambezi first throws itself into a huge crack in the earth in the Victoria Falls, and afterwards, between Zumbo and Tete, come the Kebrabasa Rapids.

Lake Nyasa is a narrow trough, 360 miles long,

between mountain-ranges which hem it in closely on
the west (sending down, during the rains, innumerable
small torrents from their steep slopes), and retreat
somewhat from it on the east, leaving room for a few
larger, but still inconsiderable streams, such as the
Songwe, the Rukuru, the Bua, and one or two more.
The Shiré is the lake's only outlet, flowing through
a level alluvial valley (something like a delta reversed)
till, a little below Matope, it comes to the edge of the
plateau and plunges over in a series of falls known as
the Murchison Cataracts. These extend over forty
miles of river, and make a difference in its level of some
1200 feet, though none of them, individually, are of
any great height.

The level of the lake, and consequently of the river
which it feeds, is very different at different seasons of
the year. During the rains, and for some time after,
steamers can go to the foot of the Murchison Cataracts
—the usual terminus is Katunga's, about twelve miles
below them. In the dry season they cannot always
come within sight of Chiromo, and, during the great
drought of 1903, the natives of that place were hoeing
their maize-gardens far out in the channel of the river.
The salt Lake Chilwa, east of the Shiré, disappeared
almost, if not quite, at that time, but reappeared with
subsequent rains. It is thought, however, that there
is a continuous fall in the level of Nyasa, which is
unaffected by the rise and fall of successive seasons,
In some places a series of old beaches can be traced.
ascending like terraces from the lake-shore to the foot-
hills.

This fall is attributed to several causes—the wearing away of the outlet channel, allowing more water to escape; the disappearance of the forests and consequent diminution of the rainfall; and the raising of the ground by volcanic action. There are not now any active volcanoes in the country, but earthquakes are common in the neighbourhood of the lake, and there are hot springs near Kotakota, and also on Mount Morambala (Lower Shiré). Mlanje Mountain is of volcanic origin; in the German territory, north of Nyasa, there are numerous extinct volcanoes and crater-lakes.

The district called the Shiré Highlands proper is enclosed between the Shiré, the Ruo, and Lake Chilwa. It was so named by Livingstone, and others besides him have noticed the similarity to the Scottish mountains, in these rugged peaks and crags of quartzite and grey granite, especially in the dry season, when the brown grass is very nearly the colour of the dead heather and bracken. Sochi, near Blantyre, is, in general outline, not unlike Ben Cruachan. The highest of these mountains are Mlanje and Zomba—they are ranges rather than mountains; or, more precisely still, Mlanje is an isolated mass, a plateau with peaks rising from it like buttresses—the highest point 9680 feet. The plateau has a height of 6000 feet, and a temperate climate—cool enough for hoar-frost at night. From these mountains the land sinks in a series of irregular undulations, to the Shiré, covered sometimes with bush, sometimes with the thick, coarse grass so feelingly described by all travellers, which is really more like canes. After it is burned, as it is every year, it is a greater nuisance than ever, for the larger stalks (about as thick as one's finger) never get quite consumed, and neither stand up nor lie flat, but lie across each other at every conceivable angle—too high to step on and too low to push one's way under. Other mountains are Chiperone, Chiradzulo and Tyolo, Nyambadwe and Ndirande—the two latter close to Blantyre. It is difficult to make out their relation to each other. At a bird's-eye view—as from the top of Nyambadwe, or some point on Ndirande—they look like a confused sea of peaks and ridges; but they are more or less continuous to Zomba, and are separated from Mlanje by the Chilwa plain and the valley of the Tuchila, which runs into the Ruo. West of the Shiré we have the Kirk Mountains, running north and south, with some striking peaks—Dzonze, a collection of rounded humps; Mvai, a rocky pyramid, with a three-cleft peak; Lipe-pete; and, far to the north, Chirobwe, with a sharp rock pointing from its summit like a finger.

These mountains are mostly granite and quartzite. West of the lake and the Shiré, there are outcrops of sandstone, and this part of the country also contains coal. Iron ore is abundant almost everywhere, especially the form called hæmatite—a soft, red stone, known to the natives as *ng'ama* or *kundwe*, and used by them as paint, and as medicine; lumps of this can be picked up in the beds of all the mountain streams. Graphite, or black lead, is found in the same way, and is used by the women for colouring their pottery, to which it gives an effect exactly like stove-polish. I think these are the only minerals of which they themselves take much account. Gold exists in the quartz in some places, and Sir Harry Johnston says : 'In the valleys of the rivers flowing south to the Zambezi (in Mpezeni's country), gold really does exist, and was worked at Misale by the half-caste Portuguese,' in the eighteenth century, and even later. But the Mang'anja and Yaos only know it through their dealings with Portuguese and Arabs, and have no word for it in their languages. *Ndalama*, which, with the addition of 'red,' means gold, and of 'white,' silver, and by itself='money,' is, I fancy, a borrowed word—the Arabic *dirhem*. I once bought (in the West Shiré district) a bangle of pure copper, which was vaguely said to have been obtained from a place to the north-west, but where it had been worked, I could not ascertain. The brass which is fashioned by native craftsmen is always bought from traders.

There are no deserts in this part, neither are there any dense forests of huge trees, such as we usually think of when Central Africa is mentioned, and such as are really to be found in the Upper Congo basin, on the Gold Coast, and elsewhere. Two Yao boys, who had served in Ashanti with the King's African Rifles, spoke of the West African forest with the same sort of surprise and wonder as any English rustic might have done. Both, independently, answered the question, 'What is that country like?' with the same expression—'*Palibe kuona*, one cannot see!' adding that the trees were high—very high (with an upward gesture of hands and eyes)—away up above one's head.

CARRIERS RESTING IN THE BUSH

Large trees, growing close together, are just what one does not find, as a rule, in the country we are thinking of. The Bush (*tengo*, or *chire*) usually consists of small trees, thinly scattered, with tufts of grass, small bushes, and various herbaceous plants growing between them, and here and there a large tree standing by itself—perhaps a baobab, or a wild fig, or a silver-thorn acacia, covered with bright golden blossom. Or we have the kind of scenery described by travellers as park-like—open glades, covered with short grass (which, however, never makes turf; you can see the soil between the separate tufts), and dotted with clumps of scrub and small trees, singly or in groups. This is the kind of place where the zebras come to graze—not that I ever had the luck to see any. The small boys who had held out hopes of this treat, said, when we passed the place early in the afternoon, that it was still too hot—the *mbidsi* were all hidden in the bush, resting in the shade; they would come out to feed on the *dambo* when it grew cooler. When we returned along the same path the sun was declining, but there were still no *mbidsi*—a party of natives on their way to the village we had left had scared them.

Where there are no trees or bushes, the grass is usually of the tall, coarse-growing kind already referred to, which is used in hut-building, and has to be burned off at the end of every dry season—otherwise it would become an impenetrable jungle. The grass-fires serve a double purpose—that of clearing the ground and manuring it—but they nearly always spread to the bush, even if it is not fired purposely, to clear a space for new gardens, or accidentally, by some travellers' camp-fire. These fires cause the scarcity of large trees, which, as a rule, are only found either in deep ravines along watercourses, which have always escaped the flames, or in the burying-grounds (the sacred groves called *nkalango*), where the people carefully beat out the fire before it reaches them.

These fires have from the earliest ages formed one of the characteristic features of African travel. One of the oldest records of exploration—the *Periplus* of Hanno—describes them, with other phenomena, in a weird and mysterious passage which fascinated my youth, and has not lost its charm even when the marvels are resolved into tolerably commonplace occurrences :—

'Having taken in water, we sailed thence straight-forwards, until we came to a great gulf, which the interpreters said was called the Horn of the West.' (This must have been somewhere near Sierra Leone, since the farthest point reached by the expedition seems to have been Sherbro Island.) 'In it was a large island, and in the island a lake like a sea, and in this another island, on which we landed; and by day we saw nothing but woods, but by night we saw many fires burning, and heard the sound of flutes and cymbals, and the beating of drums, and an immense shouting. Fear came upon us, and the soothsayers bade us quit the island.'

Evidently the people were 'playing,' as the Anyanja say—and their dances last sometimes from dark to daylight, even now—or there was a lyke-wake on. Or else, maybe, they were well aware of the presence of the strangers, and kept out of sight by day, and the effect of the drums and flutes on the Carthaginian soothsayers was that desired by the performers.

'Having speedily set sail, we passed by a burning country full of incense, and from it huge streams of fire flowed into the sea; and the land could not be walked upon because of the heat. Being alarmed, we speedily sailed away thence also, and going along four days, we saw by night the land full of flame, and in the midst was a lofty fire, greater than the rest, and seeming to touch the stars. This by day appeared as a vast mountain, called the Chariot of the Gods. On the third day from this, sailing by fiery streams, we came to a gulf called the Horn of the South.'

This, though the uninitiated would think it referred to a volcanic eruption, is really a very good description of a bush-fire on a large scale. On a moonless night in September, perhaps, you will see the black hills seamed with curved and zigzag lines of fire, as the blaze advances. Here and there a clump of dry scrub, or a dead tree, will burst into a sheet of flame, lighting up the dense white clouds of smoke. The heated air within the hollow stalks of grass and reeds expands till they burst with a sound like the firing of guns, which rises above a roar loud as that of the traffic of a great city. The smoke, rising from several points at once, hangs in the air and collects into a dense canopy of cloud, making the heat still more stifling, till, at last, sheet-lightnings begin to play about it, followed by low growls of thunder, and, perhaps, by the blessed relief of a shower. I have seen this happen more than once, though some writers appear to doubt it.

While these fires are going on, the air is full of black particles, which come floating down like an unnatural kind of snow, and the ground is covered with charred, crunching vegetation and grey ashes. The native name for this burning, or rather burnt stuff, is *lupsya*, and the early rains, which wash it away, are called *kokalupsya*, 'that which sweeps away the *lupsya*.' These rains are usually expected in October, and are a kind of prelude to the real rains, which should begin in November, but are sometimes delayed another month or even longer. While they last there may be continuous, soaking rains for three days together; but, more commonly, after a fine morning, the clouds begin to gather about 2 P.M., then a more or less heavy thunderstorm comes up, and the rain which follows continues into the night. By morning it is fine again, and then follows a half-day of the most exquisite weather, when you can almost feel things growing—till the thunderstorm comes up again as before. This will go on, day after day, till you get one without rain, as a change, or maybe a spell of steady rain, as aforesaid. There is usually a break of a few weeks about the end of the year— then the rains begin again, and last till March or April. Then begins the 'hungry time,' when the old food is done and the new crops are not yet ripe; it is some-times a time of real scarcity, as the supplies barely last out the year, and leave no margin for emergencies. This is not so much from improvidence as from the difficulty of preserving the stores from mice and weevils. But some relief comes before long when the pumpkins, gourds, and cucumbers—many of which may be gathered wild—are ready, and they help to bridge over the time before the first ears of green maize can be plucked, though there is always a good deal of more or less serious illness at this season. About May the crops are ripe, and the dry season has fairly set in. There are occasional cold showers in June and July, and sometimes in the hills a week's rain in August. At this time a chilly wind blows from the Indian Ocean, bringing with it heavy clouds, which, on some days, hang low, drifting along the slopes of the hills, and hurrying away to the west. Now and then, too, there is a thick white mist, like a sea-fog. But the sunny days, in the cold season, are bright and exhilarating. On such a day the difference between the temperature at noon and at night may be as much as 30°; and the dews are very heavy; a walk through long grass in the early morning drenches one like heavy rain. After this the air gets hotter and drier every day, and when the fires begin, it becomes still more oppressive. The most trying time of the year is the three or four weeks when the earth and all that is on it are 'waiting for the rains.' Curiously enough, the trees burst into leaf—with a greater variety of colour than our own in autumn—just *before* the rain comes, when the ground is so baked and hard that any growth seems impossible.

The variety of trees and plants growing in this country is very great, though it is somewhat difficult to give any clear idea of them, for most have no names except native ones, which are pretty, but convey nothing to the reader, and botanical ones, which are

ugly, and in most cases convey not much more. Such
a general term as 'palms,' for instance, is of little use ;
still, every one knows, to a certain extent, what the
different kinds of palms are like. We have several, all
growing on the lower levels ; none are to be found so
high as Blantyre, unless cultivated, except the wild
date, which grows beside the streams. The tall, graceful
fan-palms (*Borassus* and *Hyphæne*) are very abundant
in the plains. I remember quite a forest of them near
Maparera, on the Shiré. When you descend from the
hills either towards the river or towards Lake Chilwa,
baobabs and fan-palms make their appearance and
remind you that you are leaving the temperate heights
behind and entering the hotter zone of the low country.

Ferns are numerous—from the tree-fern, growing in
the gorges of Mlanje, to the smallest and most delicate
species of maiden-hair, to be found in the damp crevices
of rocks, and beside the streams. The asparagus and
parsley ferns, and a beautiful kind of large hart's-tongue,
with the tip of the frond cleft in two, are among the
more noticeable forms.

Though, as we have seen, there are no forests on a
large scale, a fair number of fine timber-trees are to
be found. There is the *mbawa*, a kind of mahogany,
and the *mpingo*, or ebony, both of large size and handsome growth, and the Mlanje cedar (really a *Widdring-
tonia*), the only indigenous conifer, and growing nowhere
but on that mountain. Its wood is pale red, smooth,
and deliciously scented. Most of the native wood
which can be used at all is hard and heavy, and somewhat difficult to work ; but the result, especially in the

case of the cedar, is worth the trouble. Another useful timber-tree, whose wood is never attacked by the destructive borer-beetle, is the *msuku* (*Napaca Kirkii*), only found at a height of over two thousand feet, and very common on the hills about Blantyre. It bears the favourite wild fruit of the natives, consisting of a skin and a quantity of large seeds, with a little sweet pulp, and a moderate allowance of juice; what there is of it is so good that it would be well worth cultivation. Other wild fruits are not so attractive to the European palate. There is one about the size of an orange, with a hard shell, and seeds embedded in a juicy pulp, slightly bitter, slightly acid, and slightly sweet, and at the same time not unpleasant in flavour. I believe the tree is a kind of *Strychnos*, consequently one would expect the fruit to be poisonous, yet native children eat any quantity, and seem none the worse.

The *myombo*, with leaves like our ash, is a very common tree, and the one from which bark-cloth is usually obtained. The bark of the wild fig is used for the same purpose.

The thorn-trees—acacias and mimosas—are among the most characteristic plants of the country, and some of them have very handsome flowers. The *mlungusi*, which has particularly vicious, hooked thorns, is sometimes planted in hedges. Another tree which makes a very effectual hedge is the cactus euphorbia. Of the same family (Spurges) are the weird candelabrum euphorbia, growing in the hills, and a leafless, fleshy, pale-green kind, often found in the villages, whose acrid, milky juice is used for stupefying fish.

There is no season of the year quite without flowers, and no place in which some kind or other is not to be found ; but, of course, the best time is the first few weeks of the rains. It would be hopeless to attempt a description, or even a mere enumeration, of the lovely and wonderful forms to be found side by side with familiar home growths, such as buttercups, penny-royal, and self-heal. Some slight idea of what is to be seen in the Shiré Highlands, and especially on Mlanje, where you pass from tropical to temperate, and even to Alpine, vegetation, may be gathered from the botanical chapter in Sir H. H. Johnston's *British Central Africa.*

We must say a few words about the *fauna* of British Central Africa, not only because it is interesting in itself, but because it plays an important part in the life and thought of the people. Elephants are less numerous than they were forty years ago, when herds of them haunted the marsh to which they have given their name ; but they are still frequently seen between Chikala and Mangoche, north-east of Lake Chilwa, and since they have been protected by Government, have even been returning to the banks of the Shiré. In 1877 the late Consul Elton saw a herd of over three hundred near the north end of Lake Nyasa.

The hippopotamus is found in the Shiré and Lake Nyasa, and indeed almost in any stream or lake where the water is deep enough to cover him. The rhino-ceros is known, but not very common. There are many Cape buffaloes in the plains and marshes of the Shiré, and the solitary bulls, driven out of the herd on

CHINGOMANJE STREAM, MLANJE

account of bad temper or other defects, are sometimes extremely savage. Such an animal, in 1894, charged out of the long grass on a party of carriers, near Chiromo, and knocked down, gored and trampled on, one man, who was rescued from him with difficulty. This man, a Tonga named Kajawa, when treated at Blantyre, was found to have seventeen wounds about him, but ultimately recovered.

Of other large animals, we have already mentioned the zebra; and the eland, though not very common, is also met with. There are several kinds of smaller antelopes, and, in the mountains, the beautiful little creature called the klipspringer, or, by the natives, the *gwapi*, which is something like a chamois.

Of monkeys, there are baboons, which go about in troops and plunder the growing crops, when they get a chance, and several smaller kinds.

The curious ant-eater called *Manis* or 'Pangolin,' and by the natives *nkaka*, is three or four feet long, shaped like a lizard and covered with lozenge-shaped brown scales, more like those on a fir-cone (the long, thin-scaled cones of the Norway spruce) than anything else I can think of. With his powerful claws he digs his way into the hills of the white ants on which he feeds, catching them on his sticky tongue, as he has no teeth wherewith to eat them. He is a slow-moving, nocturnal creature, and seldom seen, unless dug out of his burrow.

Another underground creature who ventures out by night is the porcupine, whose black and white quills are sometimes picked up in the bush and brought for sale by natives. It is fond of pumpkins and other vegetables, and often comes to feed on the crops at night.

Of beasts of prey we have the lion, the leopard, several smaller kinds of cats, the spotted hyena (disgusting in habits and contemptible in character, but interesting from his place in native folk-lore), jackals, and wild dogs (*mimbulu*), which hunt in packs like wolves.

Lions are common enough to be a plague. Thirteen years ago they were looked on as a thing of the past at Blantyre, though even then they were met with a few miles out on the Matope road, and I have heard, though not seen, them in the Upper Shiré district. (The roaring we heard two or three times, on stormy nights, came, we were assured, from the banks of the Kapeni, six miles away.) But the mysterious disease among the wild buffaloes, antelopes, and other game, which in 1894 spread westward to the lakes and then southward, and when it attacked the cattle in South Africa was known as rinderpest, deprived them of their food, and drove them to invade the more settled districts. Twelve were shot within a few weeks on one plantation, and a planter in the neighbourhood of Zomba, who was riding a bicycle, was chased for some miles by a lion, but ultimately escaped. In some parts, as, for instance, on the low ground near the Shiré, below the Murchison Cataracts, the natives build their huts on raised platforms so as to be safe from lions at night. Leopards also are apt to be dangerous; they prowl about habitations by night, usually in the hope of

HUT, NEAR SHIRÉ RIVER

getting into the goat-kraal, or picking up some stray
dog unlucky enough to have been left outside, and
are by no means above carrying off the miserable
fowls to be found in native villages, one of which can
scarcely be a mouthful. But they frequently attack
human beings; and at one village a leopard had
made a habit of waiting in the grass beside a certain
path along which the women went to fetch water from
the river, and had killed several before he was shot.
Wizards are supposed to take this shape, among others.

Domestic animals are not numerous, but we shall
come back to them in a later chapter.

British Central Africa, says Sir H. H. Johnston, 'is
a country singularly rich in bird life.' On the Shiré
we have a wonderful variety of water-birds—flamin-
goes, herons, cranes, ducks, geese, plovers—and, to
mention no more (these two are among the first
noticed by the new comer), the handsome black-and-
white fishing-eagle, and the tiny kingfisher, 'like a
flash of blue light.' Among the hills we have strange
forms, like the hornbill, and gorgeous colouring, as in
the plantain-eaters and rollers and some of the fly-
catchers, and familiar home birds, and their near
relations—swallows, thrushes, larks, woodpeckers (the
native name for the latter, *gogompanda*, is very
expressive). As to singing-birds, I may quote again
from Sir Harry Johnston: 'Both Mr. Whyte and
myself have remarked with emphasis at different times
on the beauty of the birds' songs in the hilly regions
of British Central Africa. The chorus of singing-birds
is quite as beautiful as anything one hears in Europe,

thus quite disposing of one of the numerous fictions circulated by early travellers about the tropics, to the effect that the birds, though beautiful, had no melodious songs, and the flowers, though gorgeous, no sweet and penetrating scents. The song of the Mlanje thrush is scarcely to be told from that of the English bird.' This entirely accords with my own experience. A bird which often sang at night sounded just like a thrush.

As to reptiles, crocodiles abound in the Shiré and the lake, and are so dangerous that in many places the women draw water from the top of a high bank by means of a calabash attached to a long pole, instead of going down to the edge of the stream, as they would naturally do. Though accidents are so frequent, the crocodile can hardly be called a habitual eater of human flesh. His staple food is fish, and 'it is only a rare incident for them to capture a mammal of any size; an incident which, given a number of crocodiles in any stream or lake, can only occur to each one at most once a year on an average.'[1] The natives (women sometimes do take the precaution I have mentioned) are strangely reckless in venturing into the water; they provide themselves with 'crocodile medicine' in whose efficacy they firmly believe; and if any bather comes to grief notwithstanding, it is presumed that his 'medicine' was not of the right kind, or had lost its power. But it seems that the crocodile will only seize a solitary person; consequently, if a whole party go into the water together, as usually

[1] Sir H. H. Johnston, *British Central Africa*, p. 355.

happens, and make a great splashing, they are comparatively safe.

Of other reptiles, we shall have to notice the iguana and the tortoise (of which there are several kinds) in connection with folk-lore. There are also several kinds of chameleon and some small lizards, very beautifully coloured. Snakes, venomous and non-venomous, are of all sizes, from the python downward to the harmless little *mitu iwiri* or 'two-heads,' silver-grey, and not much thicker than a pencil. It is a kind of slow-worm, and gets its native name from the bluntness of its tail, which makes it difficult to see which end is which.

Fish are numerous, but as yet insufficiently studied.

As for the insects, volumes might be written on them; though the beetles and butterflies are, on the whole, less gorgeous in colouring, and the objectionable insects less execrable than in other tropical countries. It is curious that, while the native languages have a word for 'butterfly' (usually more or less expressive of the peculiar movements of its flight —*chipuluputwa* in Yao, *peperu* and *gulugufe* in Nyanja), they never seem to distinguish between different kinds. Every kind of beetle, on the other hand, has its own name, but I could never get hold of a designation for beetles as a class. Perhaps this is the outcome of a severely practical turn of mind—beetles can be utilised, and therefore compel a certain degree of individual attention—butterflies, so far as I know, are not. Some beetles are eaten, for instance a glossy dark-green one, about an inch and a half long, called *nkumbutera*, and another kind is manufactured into a snuff-box ; and the useful ball-rolling beetles (all related to the sacred scarab of Egypt) have been observed and named accordingly.

Archdeacon Woodward assures me that the natives at Magila (Wa-Bondei and Wa-Shambala) absolutely refused to believe, till convinced by ocular demonstration (which must have taken time and trouble), that the butterfly came from the caterpillar. I did not ascertain whether this was the case at Blantyre ; on the whole, the people seemed fairly good observers of insects and their ways.   But, on consideration, it seems probable, for there are names for many different kinds of caterpillars ; and the reason for this closer observation is similar to that in the case of the beetles—some destroy man's food (as the *mpesa* which eats the young maize), and others are food for him—notably a green and yellow striped kind which is roasted on the equivalent for a hot shovel.

Ants, of course, abound—those that get into the food, those that eat you (or would if they got the chance), and those (only, properly speaking, they are not ants at all) that build mounds and destroy wood-work, besides others, which seem to do nothing in particular.   The hill-building termites vary their erections according to locality—the huge, conical mounds are chiefly found on low land liable to floods. Sometimes they build curious erections like irregular chimneys. The chapter devoted to these in the late Professor Drummond's *Tropical Africa* shows that they do an important work in the economy of

Nature; but it is a mistake to suppose that there are no earth-worms in Africa, though they are not so common as with us. I do not know, however, if the Nyasaland ones are ever as large as one I measured in Natal, which was 22 inches long, and except for its size, just like those in our gardens. Bees make their nests in hollow trees, or in boxes hung up for them; mason-wasps build tiny clay nests the shape of the common native water-jar, about the length of one's finger-nail. One must not conclude even the most imperfect review without a glance at the locusts (of which we shall have something to say later on), grass-hoppers, and the extraordinary group of insects which look like leaves and sticks, and are comprehended under the name of Mantis.

Having now taken a hasty survey of the country in its main outlines, of the vegetation which clothes it, and the wild creatures which (in their various ways) enliven it, let us see, in the next chapter, who are the people that live there.

CHAPTER II

INHABITANTS

Classification of tribes. Physical characters. Keloids
and tribal marks. Ear ornaments. Tooth-chipping.
Hair.

THE principal tribes inhabiting British Central Africa
are as follows:

In the Protectorate proper:—

1. The Anyanja, or Mang'anja.
2. The Yaos (Wayao or Ajawa).
3. The Alolo.
4. The Awankonde.
5. The Batumbuka.
6. The Angoni.

The Angoni are placed last, as being the most
recent arrivals in the country. They are, as will be
explained later on, rather a ruling caste than a distinct
race. The Makololo, as we shall see, cannot be
counted as a tribe; neither can the Achikunda of the
Middle and Lower Zambezi, 'compounded of the old
slaves of the Portuguese, brought from many different
parts of Eastern and Central Africa,'[1] who, moreover,
scarcely come into British Central Africa, though
some of them are to be found on the Shiré.

Of the above, 1 and 6 extend beyond the Pro-

[1] Sir H. H. Johnston.

tectorate into North-eastern Rhodesia, where we find, in addition,

The Awemba (Babemba).

The Alunda.

The Alungu.

The Batonga—above Zumbo on the Zambezi.

The Anyanja extend, under several different names, from the Shiré valley to the Luangwa, and as far north as the middle of Lake Nyasa. At one time they seem to have occupied this country continuously, but they have been displaced and broken up by intrusions of strange tribes. The Makalanga (of whom the Mashona are a subdivision) appear to have formed a powerful kingdom in the sixteenth century, and they are nearly related to the Anyanja, if not actually the same people. Their language so closely resembles Anyanja that a European, who had acquired the latter at Likoma, could make himself understood without difficulty in Mashonaland. The languages called by some writers 'Sena,' and 'Tete' (Nyungwe) are dialects of Nyanja, and the following tribes may all be reckoned as closely united branches of the same stock: Achewa, Achipeta (Maravi), Basenga, Makanga, Badema (north bank of the Zambezi, near Kebrabasa Rapids), Anguru, Ambo, and Machinjiri, the last-named in Portuguese territory, between the Ruo and the coast.

Livingstone first came across these people under the name of the Maravi, when he descended the Zambezi from Linyanti in 1855. 'Beyond Senga,' he says, 'lies a range of mountains called Mashinga, to which the Portuguese in former times went to wash for gold, and beyond that are great numbers of tribes which pass under the general name Maravi.' A little above Zumbo, he first came across women wearing the characteristic lip-ring (*pelele*), and adds : 'This custom prevails throughout the country of the Maravi.' It is now more prevalent among the Yaos—the Anyanja, from whom they adopted it, having more or less disused it. Between Kebrabasa and Zumbo there were two independent Anyanja chiefs, Mpende and Sandia ; all the rest were subject to these. 'Formerly all the Mang'anja were united under the government of their great chief, Undi, whose empire extended from Lake Shirwa (Chilwa) to the river Luangwa ; but after Undi's death it fell to pieces, and a large portion of it on the Zambezi was absorbed by their powerful southern neighbours, the Banyai.'[1]

These are the people marked on the Portuguese maps as '*Mang'anja d'alem Chire*' (beyond the Shiré).

In attempting to describe the physical type of this people, one finds that there is so much variety as to make it difficult to fix on any one as specially characteristic. This is not to be wondered at, when we remember how the various tribes have been blended together in the course of the wars and migrations to which we shall come back in a later chapter. I think I may say I have noticed three well-marked varieties of physique among Anyanja, or men reckoned as such. Before considering these, it may be well, however, to

[1] Livingstone, *The Zambesi and its Tributaries*, p. 198.

glance at the characteristics possessed in common by the people with whom we have to do in this book.

They all belong to the 'Bantu' family of African natives, which, as regards *language*, is sharply distinguished from the ' Negro' peoples of West Africa and the Soudan. In other respects, it is more difficult to draw the line. As long as our ideas of the 'Negro' were taken from degraded and exaggerated types found in the unhealthy Niger delta and the slave-trading ports of the Guinea coast, it was easy to say that the Bantu were altogether on a higher level, and attribute the difference to some hypothetical admixture of Arab or other Asiatic blood. A better acquaintance with the inland peoples of the Guinea region shows that the difference is not so great as one had supposed. But the question which was the main stock whence the other parted off, and that as to the exact nature of the difference between them, need not be discussed here, as our concern is entirely with the Bantu.

Perhaps it is scarcely necessary to explain that this word, or something very like it, means 'people,' in the language of (roughly speaking) every tribe from the Cape of Good Hope to Lake Victoria and the great loop of the Congo, with the exception of the Kora and Nama (Hottentots), the Bushmen, and the Masai. It was adopted as a convenient designation when Bleek had shown how closely these languages were inter-related, and has never been superseded by any other.

The Bantu, then, are brown (not black), and have woolly hair, growing continuously over the head, and not in separate tufts, like the Bushmen. The nose is broad and somewhat flattened (but the last is by no means invariably the case), and the lips thick, from being turned outward more than they are in Europeans; but this, too, is not always very marked. The hair is black, and the eyes generally dark brown, sometimes hazel.

The colour of the skin varies very much in different tribes, and even in individuals of the same tribe. Sir Harry Johnston says: 'There are extremes met with in the individual members of a tribe, as well as a general tendency to be detected in one tribe or another towards greater average darkness or lightness of skin. As a rule, the negro of British Central. Africa is decidedly black, so far as any human skin is really black—the nearest approach to actual black being a deep, dull slaty-brown. I should say that the average skin-tint is . . . a dark chocolate.'

If I can trust my recollection of the Anyanja, they were many of them not quite so dark as this; but in the Blantyre district they are intermixed with the Yaos, who are described by the same writer as 'probably the lightest-tinted tribe' in the region under review. The soles of the feet and palms of the hands are always much lighter, and give a curious impression, as if the colour had been washed out.

Among these Anyanja you find, chiefly on the River, tall, broad-shouldered, finely built men, with well-developed muscles, though rather smoother and more rounded in outline than an athletic European. The Rev. H. Rowley, who saw them before the Yao invasion, describes the Hill Mang'anja as smaller and poorer in physique than the River people, and lays stress on their small jaws and weak mouths and chins. Their physical inferiority and want of union among themselves fully account for their subjugation. This writer also says: ' In stature, the Mang'anja were not a tall race, though you rarely met a little man.' But tall individuals are fairly common. The length of the arms is particularly noticeable. Measurements show that very often the distance between the finger-tips of the outstretched arms is considerably greater than the height of the individual, whereas, in a well-proportioned European, they are supposed to be equal.

The second type is that of the people usually, but erroneously called ' Angoni,' who live in the districts west of the Upper Shiré, and are really Anyanja con-quered by the Zulu Angoni and subject to their chiefs. These are small, active, wiry men, usually rather dark. They sometimes have good features and even, aquiline noses.

Here and there, among these last, you find yet a third kind, very tall men, over six feet, but painfully lean and slender, and perhaps a shade lighter in com-plexion than their neighbours. So far as it was possible to trace the history of these men, they seemed to come from a distance; but I will recur to this in a later chapter. I do not remember any women of this type, though one of the men in question had two daughters, slim, delicate-looking girls, who might have been like him when grown up. One of them, a really pretty creature, died suddenly—I fancy

of consumption—aged, most likely, about fifteen or
sixteen.

The description given by the writer already quoted
will still serve fairly well for a good many of the
Anyanja :—

'The forehead of the Mang'anja was high, narrow,
but not retreating; and now and then, among the
chiefs and men in authority, you found a breadth of
brain not inferior to that of the best European heads.
The nose, though decidedly African, was not always
unpleasantly flat or expansive; occasionally you saw
this feature as well formed as among the possessors of
the most approved nasal organs. The cheek-bones
were not high ; indeed, they rarely interfered with the
smooth contour of the face. The jaws were small
and not very prominent; the chin, however, was
insignificant and retreating. But the mouth was
their worst feature.'

This requires some deductions, and Mr. Rowley
goes on to qualify it in the case of the River people,
who, however, 'had less amiability of expression—
indeed, many of them looked fiercely vile.' Perhaps
time had mellowed them in this respect, for I cannot
say I observed any lack of amiability when I came on
the scene some thirty years later; and I must own
that I cannot form a very clear idea of a man's expression when he looks 'fiercely vile.' A cast of
countenance with which I am more familiar is that of
the 'Angoni' (=Anyanja).

The original home of the YAOS seems to be in the
Unango Mountains, between Lake Nyasa and the

Mozambique coast. They were driven thence by the encroachments of other tribes from the north, and forced into the Shiré Highlands, where they partially displaced the population, but in course of time settled down side by side with them. In 1893-4 the villages surrounding the mission station at Blantyre were reckoned, some as Yao and some as Nyanja; but a good deal of intermarriage had taken place, and many of the present generation are Yao by the mother's side, and Nyanja by the father's, or *vice versâ*. When this is the case, they usually speak both languages. Even in the villages west of the Shiré, where the people are supposed to be pure Nyanja, there were families whose mothers were Yaos, brought back in the Angoni raids of 1880-1890.

Perhaps the appearance of the Yaos cannot be better described than by the authority already quoted for the Anyanja. 'Compare an ordinary Mang'anja with an ordinary Ajawa man, and the latter was at once seen to be physically the superior: his face was broader; his frontal development more masculine; the organs of causality fuller; the perceptive faculties larger; the jaws not more prominent, but more massive; the chin large and well to the front; the mouth, though of full lip, shapely and expressive of strength of will; while the eyes . . . had a steadfastness and an intensity of expression. . . . Compared with the Mang'anja, the Ajawa head was large and round. . . . The Ajawa varied greatly in height. You saw men not more than five feet two or three, and you saw others five feet eight or ten.'

I should have said—but it is dangerous to make such statements without actual measurements—that a good proportion of them were six feet and over.

The Yaos of some of the Ndirande villages used to have a great reputation for strength and stature, and were much in request as machila-carriers. A gang of them took me from Blantyre to Matope—forty miles, though, it is true, most of the way is downhill—between 8 A.M. and sunset—say 6 P.M.; and I do not think I ever saw a finer set of men. They are usually, as Mr. Rowley describes them, of square and sturdy build, even in youth; but sometimes you see lithe and slender boys, graceful, and at the same time full of fire and vivacity, like a spirited horse. The Yao women, as a rule, are bigger and stouter than those of the Anyanja, and are said to be not so good-looking. Personally, when I try to recall individuals among both, I should find it hard to say that they were typically different—one finds Yao girls with slender figures, and small, neat features, as well as faces on a larger scale, which are by no means unattractive. The younger woman in the illustration is, apart from the *pelele*, by no means a favourable specimen.

The ANGURU, or ALOLO, are a tribe belonging to the Makua group who occupy the country inland from Mozambique. Some of them live in the Mlanje district. The Lomwe country, which is entirely inhabited by them (A-lomwe is either a synonym for Alolo, or the name of a tribe closely allied to them), is west of Lake Chilwa. Some Alolo were, about forty years ago, living at the back of Morambala. A correspondent tells me:

TWO YAO WOMEN

GROUP OF ANGURU : WOMEN WITH "PELELE"

To face p. 33

'Anguru are localised on the east side of Shirwa round the Luasi hills, and are a sort of mongrel lot, as these hills seem to have been a sort of junction of Yao, when they were driven from the north, Lomwe driven from the east, and Mang'anja, on the Shirwa shores.' The Anguru speak a dialect of Nyanja, the Alolo one of Makua, a language, as Father Torrend points out, resembling Sechwana in several important particulars, in which the intervening languages differ from both. The Lomwe country was for many years harassed by slavers, and its people were continually at war with one another—so much so that, in 1894, the villagers did not know the names of hills more than a day's journey from their own homes, and travellers could not get guides except to the next village ahead of them. Perhaps this state of things accounts for the comparatively poor physique of the Alolo.

The BATUMBUKA. These are a set of people considered by Sir H. H. Johnston as indigenous to the plateau west of Lake Nyasa, and including, besides the Batumbuka proper, the Wapoka, Wahenga, and Atonga. These last live along the western shore of the lake, to which they were driven by the conquering Angoni, under Mombera. Father Torrend, however, supposes that they are a branch of the Batonga on the Zambezi, whom he thinks 'the purest representatives of the original Bantu.' In that case, they have either disused or greatly changed their original language; that which they now speak being closely allied to Tumbuka, Henga, and Poka, which are virtually identical. The Atonga are well known at Blantyre, as they are (or were some

C

years ago) in the habit of coming down in gangs to work in the plantations, or otherwise. They are usually tall, strongly built men, with well-developed muscles, and (like the Alolo) very dark skins.

The AWA-NKONDE, or Nkonde people (this is said by some to mean 'people of the plain') live at the north end of Lake Nyasa—some of them in German territory. They include the Awakukwe, Awawiwa, and several others, whose names we need not enume- rate. They are very dark, usually tall, and sometimes described as extremely well shaped; but to judge by the photographs reproduced by Sir H. H. Johnston and Dr. Fülleborn, a good many of them would seem to have a tendency to bow-legs, and to be what is called 'in-kneed.' The legs are also, in some cases, of ex- cessive length in proportion to the rest of the body. M. Edouard Foà[1] says that the Awankonde are, on the whole, good-looking, and, both men and women, 'plump and well-liking,' in consequence, no doubt, of their diet, and the pleasant, easy life they lead—now that they are no longer raided by Arabs and others. They are, with the exception of the Angoni and Achewa, the only people in the Protectorate who keep cattle to any great extent; and they live chiefly on milk and bananas.

The ANGONI were originally a Zulu clan who came from the south, under Zwangendaba, about 1825, and incorporated with themselves large numbers of the tribes whom they conquered by the way, so that there are now few, if any, of unmixed descent remaining.

[1] *Du Zambèze au Congo Français*, p. 106.

The 'southern Angoni'—formerly known as 'Chekusi's people'—are mostly Anyanja ; but there were, in 1894, a few head-men and others, besides Chekusi's own family, who spoke Zulu, and some of the elders wore the head-ring, but of a different pattern from the Zulu *isigcoco* (which is a smooth, round ring), being more like a crown done in basket-work. The northern Angoni (Mombera's people) all speak Zulu, with considerable dialectic modifications, such as the gradual elimination of the clicks, and the substitution of *r* for *l.* But their speech is quite intelligible to Zulus from the south. As already stated, there is a great variety of types. The young warriors introduced to me under the name of 'Mandala's boys' (Mandala was the brother of Chekusi or Chatantumba, at that time chief of the southern Angoni) were big, swaggering, long-limbed fellows, somewhat vacant of face, and, I think, somewhat lighter in colour than the sturdy little men who went to work on the Blantyre plantations. But whether the difference between them was a matter of race, or merely of an easier life and a diet of beef, I would not venture to say ; for these warriors must have been, in part at least, recruited from the sons of the small, dark, hard-working Anyanja, who lived on scanty rations of maize and millet porridge in the Upper Shiré villages. These were always liable to have their growing lads sent for '*ku mdsi*'—*i.e.* to the chief's kraal in the hills— where they had to herd Chekusi's cattle, and, later on, entered what we may call the 'Life Guards.'

The history of the Angoni and their migrations will be considered in a later chapter.

The Makololo of the Shiré valley, though they cannot be enumerated as a separate tribe, have had no small influence on the affairs of the Shiré valley tribes, and must not therefore be passed over without notice. Their history will help to illustrate what I have already mentioned and shall have to come back to later on—the ceaseless drifting backwards and forwards, and consequent intermingling of the Bantu tribes, which has gone on, more or less, ever since Europeans knew anything about them, and may be compared with the movement which brought the Germanic peoples into the Roman world, and for which we seem to have no compendious designation equivalent to the German word *Völkerwanderung*. The original Makololo were a Basuto tribe, driven from their home by the onslaughts of the Matebele, about 1823. Under the name of 'Mantatees,'[1] they spread terror and desolation among the Griquas and Bechuana, and finally, under the leadership of Sebituane, made their way northward and settled in the Barotse valley on the Zambezi, where Livingstone visited them in 1851. They had even then begun to incorporate with themselves the Barotse and other darker tribes about them, and had introduced their language into the country, where it is still spoken, though the Makololo were expelled, after Sekeletu's death, by Sipopo, one of the former line of Barotse chiefs. Sekeletu, Sebituane's son, furnished Livingstone with an escort, when he left Linyanti for Loanda in 1853, and again when, after his return from the West coast, he started down the

[1] See Moffat's *Missionary Labours and Scenes in Southern Africa*.

Zambezi. These Makololo (most of whom, however, belonged to the subject tribes—Baloi and others) remained behind at Tete when Livingstone returned to England; and though, when he came out again in 1858, he offered to take them all back to Sekeletu's, some preferred to stay where they were. Some others, among whom was the well-known Ramakukane, came back with him from Sesheke, after he had taken the rest home in 1860. In course of time, having settled on the Shiré below the Cataracts, and married women of the country, they became powerful chiefs, and, though somewhat oppressive towards the Anyanja, they were a check on the Yao advance from the east. One of these chiefs, Mlauri, is still living, and as active as ever, in spite of age. Masea, whose village was on the west bank of the Shiré, two or three miles below Katunga's, died a few years ago. In 1893 he was still a very fine, vigorous old man, and his numerous family of sons and daughters (some of them educated at the Mission) are mostly noticeable for good looks and intelligence: they show their descent in the lighter complexion. Livingstone says that Sebituane was 'of an olive or coffee-and-milk' colour. As far as language and customs go, these descendants of the Makololo are now completely merged in the Anyanja.

As we have seen, the breaking-up and absorption of one tribe by another has gone on to such an extent that, though in some cases we might confidently pronounce a man to be a Yao or a Nyanja from his build and personal appearance generally, yet very often it would be quite impossible. A surer criterion—though even that is nowadays beginning to fail us—is that afforded by artificial deformations—such as the filing and chipping, or even removal, of the teeth, the boring of noses, lips, and ears for the insertion of ornaments, and the scarifying and tatuing of the skin. These arts seem to be resorted to all the world over by people who do not go in for much clothing—apparently on the principle that the human face and figure need some modification in order to differentiate them as such. If your teeth are not chipped, you might as well be a dog—such, in general, seems to be the native line of reasoning.

The African knows nothing of tatuing proper, and the introduction of colouring matter under the skin is hardly known. For the coloured designs of Polynesia is substituted the raised scar. The process is very rough and usually consists in making cuts which heal and leave 'proud flesh' (*keloid*) behind. Dr. Kerr Cross says : 'The tissues of the negro seem to have a tendency to take on a keloid growth. That is to say, the cicatricial tissue grows large. If a native gets a cut, it becomes like a tumour or a new growth. If he has been vaccinated, the mark rises up like a two-shilling piece. If he tatus (*i.e.* scars) himself, the surface becomes a series of little growths protruding above the general level of the skin.' But in case the natural tendency should not be enough, the operator sometimes assists nature by pinching the lips of the cut away from each other. Some tatu-marks (*mpini, konde*) are not raised much above the level of the skin ; they have a smooth surface and a

A Mnguru, showing Keloids down centre of Chest

To face p. 39

dark-blue colour, which blends well with the skin, and is produced by rubbing in charcoal or wood-ash, and sometimes gunpowder. Formerly the various scars always indicated the tribe to which a person belonged, and the children were marked with the mother's pattern; now the tribal marks are no longer strictly kept to. The distinctive Yao tatu (called *mapalamba*) was two rows of small cuts across the temples. Some have stars in dark blue on the chest and elsewhere. I have seen them on Yaos, but do not know if they are distinctive. The Nyanja women used to score long lines over shoulders, chest, and back. The Lomwe tribes have various patterns—one a crescent, turned downwards, just between the eyebrows, others a series of from three to six crescents in the same position. The Alolo have a mark on each side of the chest, consisting of a crescent turned up, and two short, vertical cuts below it. The Makua make a line of cuts above the eyes, deep enough to form 'little pouches' in which they keep snuff, as I hear from Mr. J. Reid. Some tribes add dots all over the forehead, and some, on the Zambezi, raise a line of small lumps down the middle of the forehead. I have seen Yao women whose chests and shoulders seemed to be covered with small marks like those left by ordinary vaccination; and some seem to have the whole body more or less covered. Besides marks intended for decoration, there are those caused by a favourite method of treatment for various kinds of indisposition, viz., to make a cut and rub in the juice of a herb, or some other form of 'medicine'; and I remember a poor girl, evidently suffering from a bad attack of influenza, who had just had a series of these cuts made all down the inside of her arm.

I was once present at a discussion between a number of young people (this kind of debate is called *makani*, and is a recognised fireside amusement) on the question whether 'it is better to make holes in one's lips, like the Yaos, or in one's ears, like the Angoni.' The *pelele*, which was referred to, was a Nyanja decoration, but is now seen more frequently amongst Yao women. The upper lip is bored and a bit of grass-stalk inserted into the hole, which at first is scarcely larger than would be made by a stout darning-needle. After this has been worn for some time—I have often seen girls of ten or twelve with it —a slightly thicker one is inserted, and that, in time, again exchanged for a thicker, till at last the hole is large enough to admit a small plug of ivory, say a quarter of an inch across. The plug becomes larger and larger, till a ring is substituted for it, which also grows in size, with the wearer's advance in years, till you see matrons wearing one like an ordinary napkin-ring. It seemed to me, however, that there was a tendency to stop short at the earlier stages, as I remember quite elderly women, with only a moderate plug. The Alolo women, not content with the *pelele*, wear a brass nail, two or three inches long, in the lower lip as well. Certainly, as far as personal pre-ference went, I was inclined to side with the Angoni in the *makani* above alluded to.

The favourite ear ornaments are a kind of conical

stud, ornamented in patterns with beads. They are quite small, and do not distend the lobe of the ear much. I think they are considered by natives to be a speciality of the Angoni. I have once or twice seen young warriors wearing in their ears ornaments about the length of one's finger, which may have been very diminutive tusks of the bush-pig (*nguluwe*), or perhaps the teeth of some other animal. Both sexes have the ears bored. I have seen girls who had only recently had it done, wearing a flower stuck in the hole.

A style of ornament for the ear which I have only met with once was that of a woman at Mlanje, from Matapwiri's (on the Portuguese border), who had her ears pierced with a series of holes in the *outer* edge of the cartilage, and loops of white beads strung through them. She probably belonged to the Alolo, or some other tribe of Makua. Some Yao and Makua women wear a stud (*chipini*) of lead or some other metal in the side of the nose.

As to the teeth, it was a standing wonder to me that the way they were treated did not ruin them entirely; but it does not seem as if chipped teeth decayed any more readily than whole ones. Naturally, as most travellers have reported, natives usually have splendid teeth; though Dr. Fülleborn, in his observations on tribes at the north end of Lake Nyasa, says he found a considerable percentage of people with decayed teeth. I have come across one or two cases of toothache myself, but should say that, on the whole, there is no need to revise the general opinion.

The Yaos chip the edge of the four upper front teeth into saw-like points. This is usually done to boys and girls at about fifteen or sixteen. I never saw the operation performed, but fancy that a mallet and chisel are the instruments used. They are brought up to face the prospect, I suppose, and seem to contemplate it with more equanimity than most of us do going to the dentist. The Mambwe (on the Nyasa Tanganyika plateau) have the two middle teeth of the lower jaw removed. One of them told M. Foà that they were knocked out with an axe, adding 'it is very quickly done!'

A triangular gap between the two upper front teeth is made by different tribes—the Anyika [1] of North-west Nyasa being one. I have a note of a man whose teeth had been chipped in this way, and whom I understand to have been a Yao ; but, as he had gone to Zanzibar early in life ('I do not know how—probably through slavery,' said my English-speaking informant), there may have been some irregularity about his teeth.

Some of the Makua tribes file each separate tooth to a point (as shown in the fourth example of our illustration) ; this is also done by the Basenga, and, I believe, other tribes near the Luangwa. The Batonga knock out the upper front teeth—or did so, in Livingstone's time. 'When questioned respecting the origin of this practice, the Batoka reply that their object is to be like oxen, and those who retain their teeth they

[1] Sir H. H. Johnston includes the Anyika among the Batumbuka, but Dr. Elmslie says that the latter 'have their teeth pointed.'

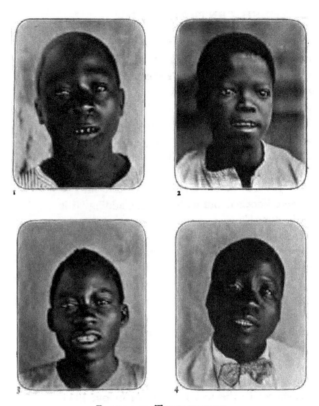

FASHIONS IN TOOTH-CHIPPING

1. Makua ; 2 and 4. Yao ; 3. Anyika and other North-end Tribes

To face p. 42

consider to resemble zebras.' As the Batonga venerate the ox and detest the zebra, we have here, what is absent elsewhere, some sort of a clue to a connection between this custom and the people's religious beliefs. Livingstone further points out that the knocking out of the teeth is of the nature of a solemn ceremony, without which no young people can be considered grown up.

Fashions in hairdressing, though not precisely of the same kind with the adornments just enumerated, may perhaps best be considered here. Most natives, I fancy, would look on a person who let his or her hair grow without doing anything to it (unless in mourning, or otherwise debarred from ordinary social intercourse) as little better than a wild beast. The usual thing among the Yaos and Anyanja is to shave the head from time to time for the sake of coolness and cleanliness, never letting the hair grow more than an inch or two in length. This is often clipped and shaved into all sorts of patterns. A favourite one for little girls is to have two bands shaved diagonally across the head, from the left temple to the back of the right ear. Sometimes a ridge or crest is left, running along the middle of the head, from front to back, and then clipped into points like a cock's comb; or some young men, while shaving the back of the head, leave the hair an inch or two long over the brow, like a coronet. The Angoni are very fond of the long pigtails called *minzu*; these are not plaited, but very neatly and tightly rolled round with twisted palm-fibre, fastened off at the ends. The most popular fashion used to be to have these arranged in a

line (like the crest already referred to), forming a
kind of lateral halo, if such a thing were possible. The
dandy with *minsu* nine or ten inches long is a proud
youth indeed. It is a quaint spectacle to see such an
one seated on the ground and a chum squatting beside
him, doing his hair. But the caprices of fashion are
endless. The illustration shows another style of coiffure worn by a Mngoni, who may have evolved it out of
his own inner consciousness, or borrowed it, directly or
indirectly, from the Bashukulumbwe of the Kafue. As
many Angoni have of late years travelled overland to
Salisbury and even farther south, to work in the mines
or otherwise, it is possible that the subject of the
picture may have seen his model for himself in the
course of his wanderings.

Referring back to the picture of the Mnguru already
given, we find that he wears his hair fairly long and
divided into strands, with beads tied to the ends of
them. Now and again we see a Yao woman (but I
think the fashion is not confined to any particular
tribe; it is not very extensively followed, comparative
wealth, leisure, and one or more skilled assistants being
necessary) with what looks like a wig of red beads.
This is made by stringing on every few hairs the beads
known as *chitalaka*, which are like red coral, and white
inside. How long it takes to complete the dressing of
a head in this way, I have no notion; but African
women possess an almost unlimited capacity for
passive endurance. A pretty variant of this is sometimes seen in little girls who have a few loops of
chitalaka strung to the hair on the top of the head,

2. WOMEN MAKING PORRIDGE IN AN (IMPORTED) IRON POT

The one on the left takes out a handful and moulds it into shape to add to the pile
on the basket (p. 136)

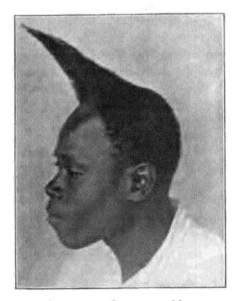

1. EXCEPTIONAL COIFFURE OF MNGONI

To face p. 44

THE PROGRESS OF CIVILIZATION !

adding a touch of bright colour and no suggestion of discomfort. Some of the Atonga shave the hair all round, leaving a patch on the top of the scalp, which they plait into small tails.

Dress, which is a comparatively simple matter, apart from the singlets, shirts, and other garments of European introduction, may be reserved for another chapter which deals with native life from the cradle to the grave.

·CHAPTER III

RELIGION AND MAGIC—I

Ancestor - worship.   Offerings.   Mulungu.   Mpambe.
Chitowe.   Evil spirits.   Spirits of the dead.   Dreams.
Morality.

IN 1894 swarms of locusts, for the first time in thirty
years, came down on the Shiré Highlands and consumed all the crops in the native gardens—even
attacking at last the white men's coffee-trees. Fresh
broods kept succeeding each other throughout the dry
season, and as the time for the rains drew near, the
villagers became anxious. What was the good of
sowing their maize if the *dsombe* were there, ready to
eat up the young shoots as soon as they appeared
above ground? Great discussions went on among the
elders in the *bwalo* as to the source of this visitation—
if one could only conjecture its reason, it might be
possible to find a remedy. Chesinka, an old head-
man on Mlanje mountain, had a dream, one night
in October, which, at any rate, suggested a solu-
tion. His old friend, Chipoka, dead some four years,
appeared to him, and told him that it was he himself
who had sent the locusts, as a hint to his people that
they were not treating him properly; it was a long
time since they had given him any beer, and he was
very thirsty in the spirit-world. So Chesinka sent

word to Chipoka's son, who at once took steps for repairing the omission.

Chipoka had been 'a person of importance in his day'; he was the principal chief on Mlanje in Livingstone's time, and, when he died in 1890, 'had, with the consent of all his sub-chiefs and subjects, transferred the sovereign rights of his country to the Queen, in order to pledge the British Government to the protection of the indigenous Nyanja people against Yao attacks.'[1] His son, of course, does not occupy anything like the same position; but the village, when I saw it, must have been in its old place—or very near it —on the bank of the Mloza, a clear stream coming down out of the heart of Mlanje, between the two peaks of Chinga and Manga. Chipoka's grave, with some huge bamboos growing on it, was within a short distance of the huts.

I had heard that a ceremony was to take place for the purpose of propitiating the old chief's spirit; and when I walked over, on the morning of October 29, I found a sort of subdued stir, the people very busy, but all looking extremely solemn. Young Chipoka— a man of about thirty—and some other men were seated under the eaves of a hut, while the women moved in and out of the huts with pots of beer, and other people were busied about a group of neat miniature huts, made of grass, about two feet high. The roofs of these huts, which had been finished separately, were not yet put on, and I could see that a couple of earthen jars were sunk in the ground inside each.

[1] Sir H. H. Johnston.

These jars were now filled with beer, and then the roof was lifted on. Chipoka, draped in his blue calico, came forward very courteously to greet me, and explained that the houses were 'for Mulungu.'

Now 'Mulungu' is the word which is generally translated 'God,' and it really does sometimes seem to denote a supreme Deity ; but here it clearly meant Chipoka's spirit. Mr. Duff Macdonald has made it clear that the 'gods' of the Yaos—or, at least, those most definitely thought of as such, are the spirits of the dead—of a man's father or grandfather, or the chief of his village,—sometimes of a great chief, who ruled over a large extent of country, like Kangomba of Sochi. When such an one lived long ago, people are apt to forget who he was when alive, and to think of him as a spirit only. Such spirits are often associated with particular hills, as is the case with Sochi and Ndirande, and might easily be mistaken by inquirers for genuine nature-powers.

I have more than once seen these little spirit-huts in villages, though I never on any other occasion received so straightforward an explanation of them. Once, the children who were with me objected to my approaching the hut, saying there was a *chirombo* there. *Chirombo* is a comprehensive word which may mean an insect, objectionable or otherwise, a lion, or other beast of prey, a mythical monster or bogy, or, simply, any animal or plant not good to eat. They may have meant the uncanny Something which was believed to have its abode there, or they may have been trying to keep out unauthorised intrusion by the fiction of a palpable *chirombo* with claws and teeth. Whether or not they consciously think of the dead as little shadowy figures, a few inches high[1] (like the representation of the soul as it issues from the body, on some Greek vases), such was evidently the thought that suggested the erection of these miniature dwellings.

Duff Macdonald says, ' The spirit of every deceased man and woman, with the solitary exception of wizards and witches, becomes an object of religious homage.' Of course, no one can worship all, and the chief of a village worships his immediate predecessor as the representative of all the people who have lived in the village in past times, and the whole line of his ancestors. In presenting his offering, he will say, '"Oh, father, I do not know all your relatives, you know them all, invite them to feast with you." The offering is not simply for himself, but for himself and all his relatives.' Sometimes a man approaches his deceased relatives on his own behalf; but, as a rule, it is the chief who prays and sacrifices on behalf of the village. As all the people living there are usually related to the chief, the deceased chief is the one to whom they would naturally pray; but any immigrants from elsewhere would probably pray to their own ancestors on matters connected with their own private concerns, while joining on public occasions in the recognised worship of the village god.

Naturally it is difficult for an outsider to gain any exact information as to religious practices, and, still more, religious beliefs. The Rev. Duff Macdonald,

---

[1] This idea was suggested to me some years ago by Miss J. E. Harrison.

D

whom we have just quoted, enjoyed almost unequalled advantages, as regards the Yaos—spending three years in their country at a time when it was still virtually untouched by European influences, and being able to acquire a sufficient knowledge of the language to obtain the people's own account of things at first hand. Great patience and tact, it is needless to say, are necessary for inquiries of this sort; and, even if one knows the language, it is not, as a rule, much use asking direct questions—unless of natives with whom you are fairly well acquainted. Of things which the stranger can see for himself in passing through the villages, the most noticeable are the little spirit-houses already mentioned, where sacrifices are presented from time to time. Sometimes these offerings are seen under trees, either in the village, or away from it—in fact, Mr. Macdonald says that the huts are erected, if there is no tree handy, close to the dead man's house. (The house itself, as we shall see, is usually either pulled down, or shut up and left to decay.) If the tree is quite outside the village, the site may have been shifted, as often happens; or perhaps the spirit may be one of the ' old gods of the land.' This is possibly the case with the tree in the illustration, which is on Ndirande mountain, a few miles from Blantyre, though I am not sure whether this particular tree is close to a village or not. Ndirande, like Sochi, has a spirit of its own; and I suppose this is the reason why the boy who was accompanying me in the ascent of Nambanga (an isolated peak or knob at the northern end of the mountain) showed a sudden reluctance to go on. I thought

Tree, with Offerings to Spirits

To face p. 50

he was tired, and told him to rest, and I would go on alone; but this seemed equally objectionable, and he was evidently making up his mind to go with me, as the lesser evil, when I decided to avoid the risk of inhumanity by turning back. As I could by no manner of means induce him to explain, I suspected the spirit might have something to do with the matter.

In Mr. Macdonald's time, the chiefs of the Blantyre and Zomba villages were all Yaos, and their canonised predecessors therefore belonged to the same tribe; but a certain amount of reverence was also paid to 'the old gods of the land'—*i.e.* the spirits of dead Nyanja chiefs who haunted the principal mountains, and were specially appealed to for rain. We have already alluded to Kangomba of Sochi. The Rev. H. Rowley, when at Magomero, in 1861, saw Kangomba in the flesh; he was then 'about forty years of age, had a frank, open countenance and a good head, and was altogether a very manly fellow.' Apparently he did not live to be old. Mr. Macdonald says: 'One tradition concerning him is this—When the Wayao were driving the Wanyasa[1] out of the country, Kangomba, a Wanyasa chief, saw that defence was hopeless, and entered a great cave on the mountain-side. Out of this cave he never returned; "he died unconquered in his own land." The Wayao made the old tribe retire before them, but the chief, Kangomba, kept his place, and the new comers are glad to invoke his aid to this day. Their supplication for rain takes the form *Ku Sochi, kwa Kangomba ula jijise*, "Oh, Kangomba of

---

[1] Yao form of the name Anyanja.

Sochi, send us rain!" The Wayao chief, Kapeni, often asks some of the Wanyasa tribe that can trace connection with Kangomba to help him in these offerings and supplications.'

The offerings usually consist of native beer and maize flour (*ufa*), sometimes also calico, as seen in the illustration. It is torn into strips lest it should be appropriated by some needy and unscrupulous passer-by, or perhaps because each offerer only feels it incumbent on him to present a mere shred as a symbolic gift, since spirits, properly speaking, have no use for calico. Mr. Macdonald quotes the native reasoning on the subject. Spirits intimate their desire for various things—in dreams, or by means of the oracle, and, if their request be at all reasonable, it is granted. But, 'if a spirit were to come, saying, " I want calico," his friends would "just say that he was mad," and would not give it. "Why should he want calico? What would he do with it? There was calico buried with him when he died, and he cannot need more again."' Food and tobacco, and even houses, are, it would appear, quite another matter.

Perhaps this opinion as to calico has been modified since the above was written; certainly I have seen at least one tree covered with strips of calico, and that within a mile or two of a mission station. That on the Ndirande tree is a special sacrifice for rain. Usually the stones at the foot of the tree support one or more pots of *moa* (native beer made of millet), and there is either a little basket of flour, or some is poured in a heap on the ground.

According to Mr. Macdonald, men would often sacrifice to their own particular ancestor, by putting down a
little flour inside the hut, at the head of their sleeping-
mat. Omens were drawn from the shape of this little
heap of flour—whether it fell so as to form a neat cone,
or otherwise. Beer, also, was made to furnish omens;
it was poured out on the ground, and if it sank in, the
god accepted the offering.

The same writer says that 'when a deceased smoker
wants tobacco, his worshippers put it on a plate and
set fire to it.' Matope, the chief of a village near
Blantyre, died in 1893. In the following year, the Rev.
J. A. Smith (now of Mlanje), happening to be at the
village, saw, as he told me, the head-men take out the
dead chief's snuff-box, fill it with snuff, and place his
stool in a certain spot, sprinkling snuff all round it.
'This is done from time to time' (I quote from my
diary) 'during the first year or two after a death—after
this time the spirit ceases to haunt the place.'

In the Upper Shiré district, I was not very successful
in gleaning information, but have a note that a girl told
me the 'Angoni' *a-pempera Mulungu* ('pray to God')
after the following fashion: ' The people here sometimes
sacrifice (*kwisula*) a goat; it is done by the head-man,
and the people all stand round *nda ! nda ! nda !* (*i.e.* in
a row or circle); they eat the meat afterwards.' Here
too, evidently, the head-man acts on behalf of the
village; and though it is not clear whether *Mulungu*
here means the spirit of a dead chief, or a Supreme
Deity, this is, for the moment, immaterial. I do not
know whether the word *kwisula* is Nyanja or not,

as I never heard it on any other occasion, and have hitherto been unable to trace it.

We have already seen that *Mulungu* is a name applied to the spirits of the dead—the *amadhlozi* or *amatongo* of the Zulus (we shall come back to these presently), and as local deities seem to be in many instances (perhaps in all, if we could trace them) identical with deceased chiefs, it looks as if the religion of the Bantu consisted, in the main, of ancestor-worship. However, other ideas, though dim and vague, seem to attach to the word *Mulungu*. Originally, perhaps, it meant no more than 'the great ancestor'—the Zulu *Unkulunkulu*. This name, literally 'the Great, Great One,' seems to have been used by the Zulus as if conveying the notion of a supreme being and creator; but some of them, on being questioned, stated that he was the first man, the common ancestor, at any rate, of themselves and those tribes whom they acknowledged as akin to them. No special worship, however, was offered to him, as he had lived so long ago that no family could now trace its descent to him; and worship is (as with the ancient Romans) a family, or at most a tribal matter. The word *um-lungu*, in Zulu, means 'a European'; it is used in no other sense, but seems originally to have been bestowed under the idea that white men were supernatural beings of some sort.

One might feel inclined to doubt the above etymology, which is Bleek's, since, in some languages, as in Nyanja, the word *Mulungu* and the adjective *-kulu* ('great') exist side by side. But against this we may set the possibility of the former being borrowed from other tribes. Mr. Rowley, writing of the time when the Yaos were only beginning to settle in the Shiré Highlands, says expressly that they used the name *Mulungu* where the Anyanja spoke of *Mpambe*. Speaking from my own observation, I should say that the former had quite displaced the latter throughout the Blantyre and Upper Shiré districts. Now in Yao, precisely, the word for 'great' is not *-kulu*, but *-kulungwa*.

However that may be, some Yaos, at any rate, think of *Mulungu* as 'the great spirit of all men, a spirit formed by adding all the departed spirits together.' This might almost seem too abstract a conception to be a genuine native view, but it was clearly stated to Mr. Macdonald, and is confirmed by Dr. Hetherwick, who has had many years' experience of the Yaos. This writer also states the view (which Mr. Macdonald hesitated to accept), that the form of the word, or rather its plural (which shows it to belong, not to the first, or 'personal' class, but to the second, including things without a separate life of their own, such as parts of the body, trees, etc.), points to *Mulungu* not being regarded as a person. Dr. Hetherwick was once trying to convey to an old head-man the idea of the personality of God. The old man, as soon as he began to grasp what was meant, talked of *Che Mulungu*, ' Mr. God !'

I have noted down some uses of the word I have come across, which I think could not possibly be set down to missionary influence. On two occasions, people told me that their dead friends or relatives had ' gone to Mulungu '; on another, a mother said that

'Mulungu had taken away' the little sick girl I was inquiring after. On hearing thunder, at the beginning of the rainy season, another woman remarked, '*Mulungu anena*'—'Mulungu is speaking.' This is very suggestive of the theory on the subject of earthquakes held, according to the Rev. A. G. MacAlpine, by the Atonga of Lake Nyasa, viz., 'that it was the voice of God calling to inquire if his people were all there. When the rumble of the earthquake was heard, they all shouted in answer, "*Ye, ye*," and some went to the flour mortars and beat on them with the pounding sticks.' Any person who failed thus to answer '*Adsum*' would be sure (it was believed) to die before long. The name used, in this case, was not *Mulungu*, but *Chiuta*.

We have mentioned the name *Mpambe* as used by the Anyanja. Livingstone, on his first visit to the Shiré Highlands, notes, 'They believe in the existence of a supreme being called Mpambe and also Morungo' (Mulungu). Mr. Rowley gives an interesting account of supplications addressed to Mpambe for rain. The principal part was taken by a woman—the chief's sister. She began by dropping *ufa* on the ground, slowly and carefully, till it formed a cone, and in doing this called out in a high-pitched voice, '*Imva Mpambe! Adza mvula*' ('Hear thou, O God, and send rain!'), and the assembled people responded, clapping their hands softly and intoning—they always intone their prayers—'*Imva Mpambe.*' The beer was then poured out as a libation, and the people, following the example of the woman, threw themselves on their backs and clapped their hands (a form of salutation to superiors), and, finally, danced round the chief where he sat on the ground. The ceremony concluded with a rain-charm; but as this is rather magic than religion (the previous proceedings, as being distinctly an appeal to unseen and superior powers, come under the latter head), it will be more convenient to return to it later on. In this very neighbourhood, I heard, one sultry afternoon in September 1894, weird, shrill cries, which I was told were 'the people shouting for rain' on Mpingwe—one of the mountains between Blantyre and Magomero. Distant peals of thunder had been heard before the crying began, and the rain came before morning.

It is worth noting that, here, Mpambe is thought of as sending rain, while, in some parts, as on Nyasa, the word means 'thunder.' The connection between rain and thunder is obvious, especially where, as is the case in these countries, the latter always heralds the breaking-up of the dry season. Sometimes the word is said to mean 'lightning'—which comes to much the same thing as far as the idea is concerned.

This certainly looks like a personification of nature-powers, which seems more probable than the suggestion that *mpambe* only came to mean thunder or lightning because these were the work of the being to whom the name was originally applied.

It is worth noticing that in Yao the rainbow is called *Mulungu*, or *ukunje wa Mulungu* ('the bow of Mulungu') and an earthquake *chilungu*, which is the same word with another prefix.

Chiuta (which is treated by the Rev. D. C. Scott as synonymous with *Mulungu* and *Mpambe*) is perhaps

derived from the Nyanja word *uta*, 'a bow,' and connected with the rainbow (called in this language *uta
wa Lesi*). *Lesi*, or *Lesa*, meaning 'lightning' in the
Kotakota dialect, is another synonym.[1] I have never
heard it used except in the above compound. *Chiuta*
is the word used by the Atonga, and, according to the
Rev. A. G. MacAlpine, 'is very difficult to derive with
certainty, but whatever its root may be, it now denotes
one who inspires wonder and awe.' If, however (as is
quite possible), the name was borrowed by the Atonga
from the Anyanja, this may be a secondary meaning
imported into it.

We shall see, later on, that a distinction seems to be
made between deaths 'by the act of Mpambe,' and_
from other causes.

Before leaving this part of the subject, we may note
that, according to the Yao belief, Mulungu 'arranges
the spirits of the dead in rows or tiers,' and some
mysterious beings called 'the people of Mulungu'
figure in their fragmentary legends of creation.

Besides the above, the Yaos seem to have had
special deities of their own, connected with the
country whence they came, and, therefore, probably,
ancient chiefs of theirs, as 'the old gods of the
country' were of the Anyanja. Such was Mtanga,
supposed to dwell on Mount Mangoche, lying midway
between Lake Chiuta and the Shiré, and the old home
of the Mangoche tribe. It was believed that the voice
of Mtanga could still be heard on Mangoche. Some

---

[1] It has been derived from a word meaning 'to nourish,' but the above
seems more probable.

said (twenty or thirty years ago) that 'Mtanga was never a man,' and the name is only 'another word for Mulungu.' However, both meanings would seem to have been lost sight of in more recent times, since, in Dr. Hetherwick's Yao vocabulary we only find '*Mtanga*, a hobgoblin.' This definition would also suit Chitowe (or *Siluwi*), who is enumerated along with Mtanga by Dr. Macdonald, but figures in fairy tales as a kind of monstrous being, with only one arm, one leg, one eye, etc., the rest of his body being made of wax. 'He is associated with famine. . . . He is invoked by the women, on the day of initiating their fields . . . when the new crop has begun to grow.' Chitowe may become a child or a young woman. In this disguise he visits villages and tells whether the coming year will bring food or famine. He receives their hospitality, but throws the food over his shoulder without eating it. Chitowe is a child or subject of Mtanga, and some speak of several Chitowe who are messengers of Mtanga. The Nyanja bogy, Chiruwi (the word is translated in Scott's *Dictionary*, 'a mysterious thing'), is probably the same as Chitowe ; he is constructed as above described, and, in addition, carries an axe. He is in the habit of meeting travellers and wrestling with them in lonely places ; if the traveller falls, 'he returns no more to his village —he dies.' If, on the contrary, he throws Chiruwi, he says, 'I will kill you, Chiruwi,' and Chiruwi entreats for his life, promising to show the man 'lots of medicines.' Then the ·man lets him go, 'and Chiruwi goes on before and says this tree is for such a disease, and that tree is for such a disease'—in short, gives him a lecture on *materia medica*, which proves exceedingly useful.

Mbona of Tyolo seems to have been one of these local deities. Mr. Rowley says that he was supposed to be the supreme ruler of the Anyanja, superior to the Rundo, or Paramount Chief, who consulted him in all special emergencies. This was done through the medium of Mbona's wife—a woman chosen for the purpose, who lived in a solitary hut on Tyolo Mountain—or elsewhere, for 'he was thought to be ubiquitous,' and huts on other mountains were consecrated to his service. 'He was spoken of as having a visible presence, but no one could say they had actually seen him or heard him. . . . If the Rundo wished for Bona's advice, he or his deputies would proceed to the top of the mountain, with horn-blowing and shouting, to make the bride of Bona know of his approach. She then retires to the seclusion of her hut, hears without seeing those who come to her, seeks and finds Bona in sleep, receives from him, in this condition, that which he wishes her to declare, and when she awakes she declares to the expectant people the message Bona has given her to deliver.' As Mbona's wife was thus condemned to solitude for the rest of her days, the position was naturally not much coveted, and the Rundo usually had women kidnapped to fill it. Mr. Macdonald, some twenty years later, merely refers to this spirit in passing, as a 'local deity.' The word appears now to be used as a common noun, in the following senses: (1) 'A wonder,' (2) 'something

desirable', (3) 'one who looks after people or things'
—as the overseer at the *namwali* ceremonies, which
will be referred to later on, and (4) 'a witness.' It may
be connected with the verb *bona*, meaning 'to look at'
(in Nyanja, *ona* is 'to see'); and possibly (3) is or was
used as the name of the spirit. I cannot help won-
dering whether a story I once heard, of an old woman
living on Morambala, who kept a number of spirits
shut up in her house, has any reference to this tradition.
I once, at Blantyre, questioned some Chikundas from
the River about this old woman, and they said that
they had heard of her, and that her name was *Mbonda*.
I knew nothing about Mbona at the time, and perhaps
misheard *Mbonda* instead of it; the sounds are not
unlike, if both *o*'s are pronounced open. The application of the spirit's name to the woman is just the
sort of confusion that might arise when a tradition is falling into oblivion. About the same time
(in 1894) I heard of another old woman living in
a cave on Malabvi—a mountain a few miles east of
Blantyre. No European had been able to acquire the
land in the immediate neighbourhood, as the people
refused to sell it during her lifetime. It has since
occurred to me that she might have been one of
'Mbona's wives.'

I do not think that, as a rule, the Bantu have much
notion of anything that can be called a devil, or,
indeed, of evil spirits as such; the spirits of the dead
seem to be thought of as beneficent or hostile, according to their dispositions when alive, or the behaviour of
the survivors. Dr. Hetherwick says, 'While there is

no trace of a devil in the Mang'anja faith, they have the *siwanda*, who are . . . the *misimu* of men and women, but who work only ill. They are always feared. Their nature is that of the other *misimu*, but they have only the wish to do harm.' The Wankonde, however, according to Dr. Kerr Cross, 'firmly believe in a spirit of evil '—Mbasi.

'In one place Mbasi is a person, an old man, who exercises extraordinary power. He only speaks at night, and to the head-men of the tribe, and during the interview every other voice must be silent and every light extinguished. In Wundale the people believe in such a person as having the power to make lions, and being able to send them off as messengers of evil . . . against whom he chooses. His house is surrounded with long grass, in which he keeps his lions as other men keep dogs.'

Coming back to the spirits of the dead, we find that the Yaos use the word *lisoka* to express that part of a man which survives when he dies; when it is an object of worship, it is called *mulungu*. These spirits, as we have already seen, are frequently prayed to, and may give evidence of their existence in three ways—by answering the prayers addressed to them, in dreams, and through the prophetess. There are also various means of divination (such as that of the flour already mentioned) and omens, which may be consulted and interpreted by professional diviners.

Every village has its 'prayer-tree,' under which the sacrifices are offered. It stands (usually) in the *bwalo*, the open space which Mr. Macdonald calls the 'forum,' and is, sometimes, at any rate, a wild fig-tree.[1] The Wankonde offer prayers—at least their priests (*waputi*) do—in the sacred groves where the dead are buried. The nearest approach to a temple among the Anyanja is a small hut called *kachisi*, which is sometimes built near the house of the village chief, if not actually under his eaves—sometimes in the bush, at a short distance from the village. 'The chief utters the prayers in the house himself, alone, while the people answer by chanted accompaniments and clapping of hands at the door.' The same sort of ritual was observed in the prayers for rain described by Mr. Rowley. The shower which fell on that occasion was, of course, accepted as an answer to the people's supplications.

The natives say, 'A man complains, and the spirits can hear him, but they can have no intercourse with man except in dreams, and in the silent care which they can exercise, having power to lead men, and to watch over them with favour, or when a man is going into danger to turn him back.' If more explicit communication is needed, they inspire some person, and make him rave (*bwebweta*); his words are not directly intelligible, but some one is found to interpret them ; 'one man is laid hold of by the spirits that he may tell all people and they may hear.' The person thus inspired may be a man or a woman—among the Yaos perhaps more frequently the latter.

The dead *may* manifest themselves in the shape of

---

[1] This is the principal tree used for making bark-cloth. Livingstone says, 'It is a sacred tree all over Africa and India'; and I learn from M. Auguste Chevalier that it is found in every village of Senegal and French Guinea, and looked on as 'a fetich tree.'

animals; but this does not happen so often as among
the Zulus, who quite expect their deceased relatives to
come back, like Cadmus and Harmonia, as 'bright and
aged snakes,' and are very glad to see them when they
do. The Yao theory seems to be that none of the
departed will do this, unless they mean to be nasty.
'If a dead man wants to frighten his wife, he may
persist in coming as a serpent. The only remedy for
this is to kill the serpent'—which no Zulu in his
senses would dream of doing. However, the accidental
killing of 'a serpent belonging to a spirit' seems to
demand some sort of apology. 'A great hunter
generally takes the form of a lion or a leopard; and
all witches seem to like the form of a hyena.' But
witches often turn into hyenas without dying first—
which belongs to another part of the subject. The
Makanga, in the angle between the Shiré and Zambezi, refrain from killing lions, believing that the
spirits of dead chiefs enter into them.

There seems to be some difference of opinion with
regard to the degree to which the spirits will make
communications in dreams. An old Nyanja chief said
to Livingstone, 'Sometimes the dead do come back,
and appear to us in dreams; but they never speak nor
tell us where they have gone, nor how they fare.' On
the other hand, as we have seen, communications in
dreams are expected as a regular thing. The Anyanja and Makololo (says Mr. Macdonald) were
inclined to lay more stress on dreams than on the
oracle of the *ufa* cone. They argued that, if you put
the flour down carefully enough, it will always assume

the proper pyramidal shape, and if you cover it with an upturned pot overnight (the usual practice), it will keep it—unless the rats overturn the pot. Perhaps this was due to the rationalising influence of the Makololo, who had been longer in contact with white men, and (like other natives in like case) were always burning to assert the superiority which this gave them.

If the dreams are not sufficiently explicit, we must fall back on the prophet or prophetess. Macdonald's account tallies with the description of the woman set apart for the service of Mbona, except that he speaks of one living in a village with her family, who may arouse the neighbours with her shrieks in the dead of night. The people assemble to hear the message delivered by the spirits, and then return to bed ; 'or there may be a great meeting in the morning, when the prophetess appears, her head encircled with Indian hemp, and her arms cut as if for new tatus.'

But the *Kubwebweta* inspiration may come on any one, at any time, or in any place. Thus, one of a party of carriers on a journey suddenly finds himself 'possessed,' and his companions listen to his ravings with the greatest reverence. These utterances of possessed people always require some one to interpret them, and 'an old woman or other skilled person' is usually found. Macdonald says nothing of this, in the case of the prophetess, but if, as is probably the case, she is more or less of a professional,[1] she will

---

[1] Like the Zulu *isanusi*, who is a person of nervous, hysterical temperament to begin with, and goes through a course of training calculated to develop any ' psychic' gifts he or she may possess.

E

have the necessary skill herself. The messages are
not, as a rule, of a very recondite character—either
the deceased chief wishes to help his people by warning them of war, or telling them where game may be
found; or he feels himself neglected (like old Chipoka),
and demands such and such offerings. Namzuruwa, an
ancient chief of the district below the Murchison
Cataracts, occasionally inspires people in this way.

The dead sometimes appear in visible form, as a
native told the Rev. D. C. Scott: 'People sometimes
see those who have died and are dead walking outside
in the gardens.'[1] I have never had the luck to hear
a ghost story at first hand myself—the 'night fears' of
the small boys whom I found objecting to go out after
dark were connected, not with ghosts, but with *wisards*,
of whom more presently.

There are haunted places in the Bush, where spirits
are supposed to be heard, but not seen. M. Junod
was told, over and over again, in the Delagoa Bay
country, of people who had heard the drumming and
singing of the spirits. These haunted spots were the
burial-places of the chiefs, and no doubt this is so in
other cases. The Anyanja have a curious account of
'the spirits' hill,' where people who go, carrying pots
on their heads, have them lifted off by the baboons,
and hear a sound, 'as of people answering.' They also
speak of the 'spirit-drums'—the small ones sounding

[1] 'They have the firmest belief possible in ghosts, and will tell long
circumstantial stories about the "spooks" they have seen—prosaic stories
usually connected with daylight, as where a woman declares that while
winnowing or pounding corn in the noontide, she looked out in the courtyard and saw the spirit of So-and-So passing along, looking exactly
as though he were alive.'—Sir H. H. Johnston, *British Central
Africa*, p. 449.

piye ! piye ! and the big one *pi ! pi !* as though a dance
were going on, and so far as one can gather, these
spirits seem to be thought of as in sight like ordinary
men and women—not the little εἴδωλα who dwell in
the spirit-houses.

The notion of a connection between religion and
morality comes comparatively late in human development ; but we can perhaps see traces of it in the idea
of the *chirope*. This means that, when a man has
killed another man, he will either be ill, or be seized
by a sort of murderous madness till he has performed
some expiatory ceremony. The accounts I have
before me are somewhat different, but are not,
perhaps, inconsistent with one another. Among the
Yaos, in Macdonald's time, it seems to have been a
condition that the victim should not be an enemy
(towards whom no obligations were recognised), or
even a person of the same tribe, whose kinsfolk could
take up the feud and demand compensation. But, if a
Yao killed his own slave (or, apparently, his child, his
younger brother, or any one under his charge), he
feared that he 'would pine away, lose his eyesight,
and die miserably, unless he went to the chief, paid
him a certain fee, and said, "Give me a charm, for I
have slain a man."' The Angoni, like the Zulus, apply
the notion to killing a man in battle, and think that,
unless they gash the bodies of the slain, so as to let
out the air from the intestines, and prevent the corpse
from swelling, they will be attacked by a mysterious
disease which causes their own bodies to swell up.
(This precise symptom is not given in the accounts
before us, but is believed in by the Zulus, and probably

by the Angoni.)   The Angoni afterwards dance a war-
dance 'to throw off the *chirope*.'   The word appears to
be connected with *mlopa*, 'blood,' used particularly of
blood shed in killing—as of animals in hunting—and
the idea is that the spirit of the slain enters the body
of the slayer.   This is even the case with animals;
and hence it is the custom for the hunter to cut off
a small piece of the meat as soon as he has shot any
animal, throw it on the fire, and eat it, 'because of the
spirit of the beast that enters into one if one does not.'

The Angoni and various other tribes west of the
Lake have a belief that there is a distinct relation
between smallpox and morality; that, if the disease
attacks a village where the moral tone is good, all
the patients will recover; whereas, in a place given,
as the native statement puts it, 'to adultery and other
sins,' every one who sickens, young or old, will die.
The locality, and various other circumstances, make
it unlikely that this is an imported notion.

It is generally believed that the Eastern Bantu
have no 'idols' properly so called; and their charms,
to which we shall come back later, do not usually
take the form of human figures.   But the Tonga
chiefs used to carry about with them little wooden
images called *angosa*—representing men, women, or
animals.   Sometimes they were only sticks with a
little head carved at one end.   The Rev. A. G. Mac-
Alpine, who seems puzzled what to make of them,
does not state whether any are now in existence.
'Long ago they used to be owned by chiefs only, and
were lodged in the house of the head-wife. . . . They

were not displayed except on special occasions. In the talking of important cases, they are said to have been brought out and planted in the ground at some little distance from the chief, and when he went on a journey they might be carried along with him, both of which uses would suggest their being an emblem of authority. . . . Often people came asking to see them, when they would be brought out covered up and not exposed till some gift had been made.' We find that the Achewa have articles described as ' fetiches' and consisting ' of a few short pieces of wood the size of one's forefinger, bound together with a scrap of calico into the figure of a child's doll. Inside the calico is concealed a tiny box made of the handle of a gourd-cup, . . . [and] supposed to contain the spirit of some dead ancestor.' Spirits wandering homeless in the bush are apt to annoy the living in various ways, till captured by a 'doctor' and confined in one of these receptacles.

The Yao children play with dolls bearing about as much resemblance to the human figure as a ninepin, but evidently intended to represent it. If games are survivals of religious ceremonies, they may originally have been *teraphim*, or fetiches of some sort. The ' ugly images' found by Livingstone near Lake Mweru, in 'huts built for them,' which were used in rain-making and cases of illness, seem to have been somewhat different from the *angoza* of the Atonga.[1]

[1] 'Among the tribes in the neighbourhood of Tanganyika . . . a carved image of a human being . . . is set up in or near the village, and thus becomes the village idol to which all prayers and sacrifices are directed.'—*Life and Work in British Central Africa*, June-July 1900.

CHAPTER IV

RELIGION AND MAGIC—II

Creation. Origin of death. Lake Nyasa. Rain-
making. Charms. Witchcraft. Lycanthropy, Divination. Food tabus. Dances.

SO far as we can get at the notions of the Bantu about
creation, they do not seem to have thought that this
world ever had a beginning. All the stories one has
met with assume it as already existing, and explain
how this or that feature—mountains, rivers, lakes,
animals, men—was introduced into it. The Yaos tell
that Mtanga pinched up the surface of the earth into
mountains, Chitowi—who had failed in performing the
operation himself—having called him in for the purpose. He then dug channels for rivers, and brought
down rain to fill them. The Yaos, being mountaineers,
assumed that a plain would be unfit for human habita-
tion : Mtanga, on first viewing their country, remarked,
'This country is bad because it is without a hill.'
There are also legends of the introduction of the sun,
moon, and stars, and of the origin of clouds, wind, and
rain ; but all these presuppose the existence of people
on the earth.

Mankind is held to have originated at Kapirimtiya,
a hill—or as some say, an island in a lake, far to the
west of Nyasa. Here it is believed that there is a rock

covered with marks like the footprints of men and animals, and that, when men were first created, the island was a piece of soft mud, and Mulungu sent them across it, so as to leave their footmarks there, before they were dispersed over the world. One native account says that 'they came from heaven and fell down below upon the earth'; another, that they came out of a hole in the rock, which was afterwards closed by 'the people of Mulungu,' and is now 'in a desert place towards the north.'

In the Bemba country, the natives speak of two such places; and one of them was seen in 1902 by a European, who describes it in a letter to *Life and Work* as 'a conglomerate rock showing what the natives call footprints of a man, a child, a zebra or horse, and a dog.' The Bemba people say that these footprints were made by Mulungu (or, as they call him, Luchereng'anga) 'and the people and animals he brought to occupy the country.' Offerings of beads, calico, and beer are placed on this rock. The writer thought the marks certainly looked like footprints, but were merely hollows where the rain had washed out the softer parts of the rock. The old head-man of the place, naturally enough, would not hear of this explanation, and maintained that the marks had once been much plainer, but were now partly washed away by the rains.

This account agrees well enough with the vague indications given by the Blantyre people as to the direction of Kapirimtiya. It seems to show that the Yaos and Bemba had some common centre, though the latter also say (which is confirmed by other testimony) that they came from the west in comparatively recent times.

The story of the Chameleon is found among so many of the Bantu as to suggest that they derived it from a common source. Whether it came from the Hottentot legend of the Moon and the Hare—or from the story out of which that was developed, I do not feel competent to discuss. The Yaos, the Anyanja, and the Atonga all possess it in slightly differing versions. I shall give the last-named.

'*Chiuta* deputed the Chameleon and the Lizard (or Frog, as it is variously given) to take to men the message, the one of life and the other of death. The Chameleon was to tell men that they would die, but that they would return again, while the Lizard was bid tell them that when they died, they would die for good. The Chameleon had the start, but in its slow, hesitating pace was soon outrun by the swift Lizard, which darted in among men with its tale that dying they should end their existence. A good while after, the Chameleon came lazily along and announced that, though men should die, they would return to life again ; but he was met by the angry and sorrowful reply that they had already heard that they must die without returning, and that they had accepted the message first delivered.'

This is exactly like the Zulu story, where the people say, 'Oh! we have taken hold of the word of the Lizard, when it said, "People shall die." We never heard that word of yours, Chameleon—people *will* die!' Consequently, Zulus, Yaos, Anyanja, Atonga, and, I suppose, most Bantu, detest the poor Chame-

leon, and consider him an unlucky beast. The
Anyanja never pass one without putting snuff into its
mouth, 'that it may die,' and any one who knows what
a value they set on this commodity, and what minute
quantities they seem, as a rule, to carry about with
them, will allow that this is, indeed, carrying enmity
very far. However, the Lake Anyanja seem to take
a different view of the matter from the Blantyre people.
They hold that their ancestors were grateful for the
Chameleon's message, though it came too late—perhaps they reflected that it was not his fault: he was
not built for fast travelling;—and they give him
tobacco as a reward; so that chameleons who die by
nicotine poisoning are the victims of ill-judged kindness, not of revenge. It is worth noticing that the
creature's name in the Lake dialect—*gulumpambe* or
gwilampambe—seems to mean 'seize the lightning' (or
'Mpambe'). Possibly there is some still recoverable
tradition at the back of this.

The Yaos have another very curious tale, in which
the Chameleon is directly concerned in the introduction of Man into the world. At first Man was not
—only Mulungu and the beasts. Apparently the
Chameleon has been forced by changed circumstances
to alter his mode of living, for, in those days he used
to set traps for fish in the river—wicker arrangements
on the principle of the lobster-pot—as natives do now.
One morning, on visiting his trap, he found two
unknown beings in it—no other than the first man and
woman, who had somehow blundered into it during
the night. (I have seen a *mono* big enough to contain
one person, with his knees drawn up, but the size of the

First Parents is not stated.) He consulted Mulungu as to what he should do with them, and was told, ' Place them here, they will grow.' They did grow, and developed various activities—among others that of making fire by twirling a hard stick on a bit of soft wood (*kupeka moto*), as is done to this day. But in the end they set the grass alight, and thus drove Mulungu from his abode on this earth. The Chameleon escaped by climbing a tree ; but ' Mulungu was on the ground, and he said, " I cannot climb a tree." Then Mulungu set off and went to call the Spider. The Spider went on high and returned again and said, " I have gone on high nicely," and he said, " You now, Mulungu, go on high." Mulungu then went with the spider on high. And he said, " When they die, let them come on high here." And behold, men on dying go on high in order to be slaves of God, the reason being that they ate his people here below.'

That is, as soon as they had found out the use of fire, they began to kill and cook buffaloes and other animals. No hint is given here as to where or how these human beings originated. Mulungu evidently knows nothing about them (while the animals, with which they have been interfering, are ' his people '), and makes the Chameleon responsible for them, just as a chief at the present day would hold any man who introduced strangers into a village responsible for their conduct. Two other points are noteworthy—the region into which Mulungu makes his escape is ' above '; and the Spider, who helps him, is a conspicuous figure in West African folk-lore and mythology. This is the only

instance except one where I have met with him in an
Eastern Bantu story; but we have numerous examples
in Duala, and one at least from the Congo.

This tale seems to be a very crude form of the myth
in which a divine being is driven from earth by the
wickedness of mankind—like Astræa and the Kintu
of the Baganda. The curious, and, to us, inconsistent
limitations of his power are just what one may expect
to find in stories of this kind.

Perhaps we might include among legends of creation
a story told at the mysteries (to which we shall recur
later on) to account for the origin of Lake Nyasa.

'In old days the Lake was small as a brook. Then
there came a man out of the west with a silver
sceptre.' (The story is 'taken down from native lips';
I do not know what is the original wording in this
place; but we may suppose that the Lake people
knew silver through the coast traders even before they
were acquainted with Europeans. In any case, the
'silver sceptre' need not prove the story to be a recent
invention; one constantly finds touches of 'actuality'
introduced by the tellers of these tales.) 'He married.
and brought his wife to return with him to his country.
She consented, and her brother said, "Yes, and I will
go too." But his brother-in-law said, "I will not have
you go too." Then he wept bitterly for his sister,
when he saw her cross the lake, and he grew very
angry, and he took his stick and struck the water, till
it swelled up and covered all things and became a
flood. Then the woman and her brother died, both of
them together, and the corpse of the woman went to

the north, and that of her brother to the south. When a cloud weeps in the south, the sister rests quietly in the north, and when a cloud appears and weeps in the north, the brother rests quietly in the south.'

In another chapter we shall find a legend of a river struck with a staff with the opposite purpose, viz., to make a passage through it. It is possible that these may be echoes of the Biblical stories heard from the missionaries, though, as a matter of fact, I do not think this is the case.

In the last chapter I spoke of magic as distinguished from religion. By the latter I mean appeals to—or attempts to propitiate—some unseen, superior powers, whether these be thought of as ancestral spirits, nature-powers, or what we generally understand by a Deity. Magic, on the other hand, consists in performing certain actions which will, in some occult way, have such an effect on natural forces as to produce the result desired ; that is to say (to put it roughly), it enables man to control nature on his own account. I must confess, however, that I do not always see where the line should be drawn, and have included several matters in this chapter without attempting to decide how they should be classified. Usually people attempt to do magic on the principle that like produces like—as when water is poured out on the ground in the hope of bringing rain.

It will be remembered that, when we spoke in the last chapter of Chigunda's people calling on Mpambe for rain, it was said that the ceremony concluded with 'a rain-charm.' This is described as follows:—'The dance ceased, a large jar of water was brought and placed before the chief; first M'budzi (his sister) washed her hands, arms, and face; then water was poured over her by another woman; then all the women rushed forward with calabashes in their hand, and dipping them into the jar, threw the water into the air with loud cries and wild gesticulations.'

This, however, might be taken as prayer and not magic, if we are to understand the water to be thrown into the air as a sign that water is wanted. Sometimes people smear themselves with mud and charcoal to show that they want washing. If the rain still does not come, they go and wash themselves in the rivers and streams.

In 1893 the rains were unusually late. In the West Shiré district we only had one or two showers up to December 12—by which time the crops should have been in the ground in the ordinary course of things; and though that day and the next were wet, the weather cleared again—except for delusive thunder and lightning which led to nothing. After about a week of this, I happened to go to a village, and found all the women busy cleaning out the well whence they obtained their usual water-supply. It was a large hole, three or four feet across, and perhaps ten or twelve feet deep, and pegs had been driven into one side, by which even the white-haired old grandmother of the party ascended and descended with the greatest agility. They had already dug out a large heap of mud, and seemed serious and preoccupied, and none of the men were to be seen—in fact, the huts appeared to be deserted. But it never struck me that they were doing anything else but digging out their well because the water had come to an end.

Some years later, when I read M. Junod's *Les Baronga*, a passage in it forcibly recalled this scene, and showed that it had a meaning which had never occurred to me at the time. The Ronga women, it appears, have a solemn rite of clearing out the wells in time of drought. For this, they lay aside all their usual garments, clothing themselves only with grass or leaves, and start for the well, with special songs and dances. I did not notice anything special about the costume of the women at Pembereka's, nor did I hear any singing, but probably that would accompany the dance, which would have taken place before they actually got to work. As the well was quite close to the huts, there would be no marching in procession— two or three of the women may have come from other kraals, but there were so few in all that the ceremony must have taken place on a very small scale. Not knowing of the Ronga usage, I could not ascertain whether or not the Anyanja women carried it out on the following points: (1) Before starting for the well, they go in a body to the house of *a woman who has had twins*, and pour water over her out of their calabash dippers; (2) When they have finished cleaning out the well, they go and pour water on the graves in the sacred grove.

It will be remembered that the ceremony at Chigunda's was conducted (though in the presence of the chief and all his people) by women only. I did not hear of any case of twins among these people during the time of our stay, and do not know how they are looked on. I have been told that the Yaos, when twins are born, kill one, but this is an unsupported statement (made by a native, however), which I have not been able to test. It seems clear that the Atonga and other tribes by the lakeside consider them unlucky, and act on that belief in varying degrees.

We do not find a special class of rain-doctors apart from the ordinary sorcerer, diviner, or 'witch-doctor.' Public ceremonies are conducted—or at least presided over—by the chief, though no doubt the 'doctor' is frequently consulted. M. Junod, in the account above referred to, says that the chief gives orders for the women to go out and clean the wells, after having ascertained, through lots cast by the principal diviners, that such a step is necessary.

There is no bar, however, to the exercise of special powers by individuals who possess them. Sir Harry Johnston speaks of an old rain-maker named Mwaka Sungula, at the north end of Lake Nyasa. His power extended to wind as well as rain. He was once resorted to by the native crew of the *Domira* when she stuck on a sandbank, and, as the wind changed during the night following his incantations, he had a triumphant success.

There are charms, as might be expected, not only for bringing rain, but for keeping it away. When travelling from the Upper Shiré district to Blantyre towards the close of the rainy season, I found that one of the carriers was provided with *mankwala a mvula* (rain-medicine) to ensure fair weather during the

journey. I inspected this talisman, and found it to
consist of two sticks, about a foot long, firmly lashed
together with strips of bark, and, inserted between
them, a piece of charred wood, and perhaps some
other things which I could not clearly make out. He
had paid the local practitioner a goat for it. He kept
it in his hand on the march, and, from time to time,
pointed it towards the quarter from which rain might
be expected. It is a fact that none fell till we were
within a few miles of the Mission; and Chipanga
might have argued that the power of the charm was
here neutralised by the more powerful influence of the
white men.

This brings us to the subject of *mankwala*, variously
translated 'medicine,' or 'charms,' and including what
we understand by both terms. I have never been able
to ascertain the etymology of the Nyanja word *mankwala* (a plural without a singular); in Yao, *mtela*, 'a
tree or plant,' is, like the Zulu *umuti*, used with this
meaning. Native doctors, both men and women, often
have a very good knowledge of medicinal herbs, but
it is the other kind of 'medicine' with which we have
to do just now.

This may be divided, roughly, into offensive and
defensive. You enter the little courtyard and see
growing in the space between the huts, a cherished
bush of cayenne peppers, to which is tied a protective
apparatus consisting of a small wooden hoop with a
goat's or ram's horn filled with heaven knows what
messes, fastened into it. Or a string is hung at the
door of a house, which is supposed to turn into a

snake if any one enters to steal.   Or a bamboo is set
up close to the garden, with a horn on the top of it;
or a string is run round the crops, or you may see
ashes laid beside the path which passes by them; or,
again, the medicine may be buried.   Snail-shells and
bundles of leaves may be used in this way.   Those
who attempt to steal in spite of these contrivances will
either die on the spot or be taken ill afterwards.

The word *winda*, which means to protect a garden
(or anything else) in this way, is also used of women
letting their hair grow while their husbands are on a
journey, lest any ill should befall the travellers.   They
are also supposed (among the Yaos at any rate) to
refrain from washing their faces or anointing their
heads till the absent ones return.

It would be impossible to enumerate all the different varieties of 'medicine.'   I believe there is some
preventive of every ill likely to befall mankind, and
those who understand such things can do a profit-
able business.   The Shiré people venture recklessly
into the water if they are provided with 'crocodile
medicine'; and there are medicines against lions,
leopards, and, I suppose, every variety of dangerous
wild beast, not to mention the 'gun medicine,'
which enables the hunter to shoot straight, and
which, perhaps, ought to be classed in the 'offensive' category, but that it is free from sinister
associations.   Most European sportsmen, if at all
successful, have been importuned for this, and it used
to be firmly believed that the late Mr. Monteith
Fotheringham, who was a very good shot, wore a

F

belt charged with exceedingly powerful 'medicines' next his skin. There are also 'medicines' to make a man bullet-proof, like Chibisa, the Nyanja chief, who was brought down at last by a sand-bullet, as Dundee was with a silver one at Killiecrankie. Some natives once assured me that Chikumbu, a Yao chief, who at one time gave the Administration some trouble, was invulnerable by shot or steel; the only thing that could kill him—since he had not been fortified against it by the proper medicine—was a sharp splinter of bamboo. This reminds one of Balder and the mistletoe. The East African Wadoe have a legend about a magician who could be killed by one thing only—the stalk of a gourd. But as the gourd-stalk was 'a forbidden thing' to him, this suggests the subject of *miiko* or tabu-prohibitions, which we must take up presently.

Various seeds, nuts, claws of animals, and other things are worn round the neck as 'medicine' of this kind. Sometimes it takes the shape of wedge-shaped wooden tablets, or bits of stick about an inch long, which are also seen strung on the band which people wear round the head as a remedy for headache—a kind of combination of 'natural' and 'supernatural' means, as the string is supposed to give relief by pressure.

As for 'offensive' medicine, there are various kinds. Some are 'buried against people'—usually in the form of horns—by the witch (*mfiti*) who wishes to do the said people a mischief. I have no doubt that horns are really sometimes buried with such intent; but it more frequently happens that they are *un*buried by the witch-detective who has probably the best of reasons for

knowing where to find them. Then there is a very im-
moral kind of medicine which, like the Hand of Glory,
enables thieves to steal without detection, by throwing
the owners of the stolen property into a deep sleep,
or even (adding insult to injury) forces them to answer,
unconsciously, any questions as to the whereabouts
of their wealth. There are several kinds of this
charm, but I do not know the composition of any;
though, in some parts of East Africa, a plant with the
botanical name of *Steganotaenia* is supposed to possess
these marvellous properties. There is also a charm by
means of which thieves can make themselves invisible;
but as it might also enable honest men to escape from
their enemies, it ought perhaps to have been enumerated
in the first category. One kind, at least, of this medicine
is the drug *strophanthus* (obtained from a plant locally
called *kombe*), and with this the chief Msamara poisoned
himself in 1892, imagining that it would enable him
to walk unseen out of prison at Fort Johnston. He
had previously taken off all his clothes, reasoning
that the drug would not make them invisible.

I remember being told that native burglars (I understand that such exist, but cannot say I have come
across them personally, and do not believe that they
are common, except in the coast towns), when setting
out for their night's work, strip and oil themselves all
over. This, I understood at the time, was to make it
difficult for any one to get a grip of them, if caught;
but it has since occurred to me that it was also part
of the process for rendering themselves invisible—the
medicine being applied externally as an unguent.

Secret theft is looked on with horror, as probably connected with witchcraft. Natives are so ready to share everything they have with their neighbours, that a person who stealthily takes what he might have for the asking lays himself open to suspicion of yet darker dealings. It is the Bewitcher, the *Mfiti*, who is the great terror of native life.

Witchcraft is not, so far as I can make out, thought of as a system of compelling the unseen powers (whether dead ancestors or nature-spirits) to work one's will. The *mfiti*, however, employs certain animals as messengers — the owl, and the jackal, whose bark summons him to midnight orgies; but I do not know that he intrusts these creatures, as Zulu sorcerers are said to do the baboon and the wild cat, with 'sendings' to injure an enemy. Besides be-witching, as aforesaid, by means of 'medicines,' the things one most frequently hears of his doing are turning himself into a hyena, leopard, or other animal, and digging up graves to eat the flesh of corpses. But I am not sure that the latter ever happens without the former, it being usually for this purpose that the hyena shape is supposed to be assumed. So much of the funeral ceremonies is con-nected with this belief that we shall have to treat it more fully when we come to them.

Witchcraft and cannibalism are synonymous. 'Why did So-and-So have to drink *mwavi*?' '*Chifukwa wodiera antu*—because he was an eater of men.' This need not imply that he actually has eaten any one, only that he has caused (or tried to cause) some one's death with the intention of eating the corpse.

It is the reverse of the vampire superstition, where the corpse will not stay dead, but gets up and feeds on the living; and as there was a recognised remedy for this evil in the Middle Ages, so there are various ways of preventing witches from getting at the graves, as we shall see in due course. It has been said that cannibalism of this sort is actually prevalent among the Anyanja; but the statements on this subject require to be carefully sifted. The Yaos were thirty years ago in the habit of using certain parts of their slain enemies as a charm for producing strength and courage; they reduced them to ashes and mixed them with gruel, which had to be eaten in a particular way. Ordinary cannibalism may have been practised in times of scarcity. But the Europeans who were in the Shiré during the terrible famine of 1862-3, heard of no such cases, though nine-tenths of the Anyanja population perished, many committing suicide in despair. There *may*, of course, be some foundation in fact for this very widespread belief, but it is quite capable of flourishing on little or none.[1]

Certain medicines (called *mphiyu* by the Atonga) have the power of turning those who take them into some animal—each kind, leopard, hyena, crocodile, or what not, having its own particular medicine. The Atonga belief presents some interesting features.

'The living man might inform his friends that he had medicine to change him into a crocodile, and if after his death a crocodile made its appearance in a pool where crocodiles had not often been seen before, it was of course believed to be their friend come back.

[1] See note at end of chapter.

If these animals took to killing people, a representation would very probably be made to the relatives of the dead to go and attend to their spirit, and have it appeased. That a man-eating lion or other beast of prey was a real *msuka* (one risen from the dead under another form) people could easily tell, when the corpses were left uneaten : a real lion, it was thought, would be sure to devour its victim. If this killing went on after complaint had been made to the supposed relatives of the *msuka*, the issue would probably be a *mlandu* with these on account of their alleged carelessness of the rites due to their dead. People who were known to have eaten *mphiyu* were not mourned for in the ordinary way with loud wailing and outcry. They were silently wept for by their relatives, the only sound of mourning that might be heard being the mimic pounding in the empty grain-mortar into which pieces of rubber were thrown from time to time to still further deaden the sound. When after a time they heard lions or leopards roaring in the bush, the villagers said, " There's Karakatu (*i.e.* one risen), he's mourning for himself."'

Not only do the natives firmly believe that their neighbours can thus on occasion transform themselves, but occasionally a man is found to be convinced that he can do so himself and has actually done it. Du Chaillu mentions a case like this in West Africa, and Sir H. H. Johnston has recorded another. A number of murders had taken place near Chiromo in 1891 or 1892, and were ultimately

traced to an old man who had been in the habit of
lurking in the long grass beside the path to the
river, till some person passed by alone, when he would
leap out and stab him, afterwards mutilating the body.
He admitted these crimes himself.

'He could not help it (he said), as he had a
strong feeling at times that he was changed into a
lion and was impelled, as a lion, to kill and muti-
late. As according to our view of the law he was not
a sane person, he was sentenced to be detained
"during the chief's pleasure," and this "were-lion" has
been most usefully employed for years in perfect con-
tentment keeping the roads of Chiromo in good repair.'

An Englishman who had lived for some time in
the Makanga country told me that these people
credit the were-hyena with a human wife, who lives
in a village and performs the ordinary work of a
native woman by day, but by night opens the door
of the goat-kraal to admit her husband, and then
goes away into the bush with him to join in the
feast. A goat was carried off one night from the
village near which the narrator lived, and the people
showed him, in the morning, the hyena's tracks, and,
running parallel with them, the print of bare human
feet. It was in vain to point out that some one might
have attempted to pursue the hyena and rescue his
prey, or, at any rate, have run out to see what had
happened—they were positive that the footprints were
those of the hyena's wife. Rats, too, may be wizards
in animal shape, which is a reason for their nibbling
the toes of sleepers.

Watching the grass-fires one night towards the end
of the dry season, I remember seeing a strange, sudden
blaze on Nyambadwe Hill; the flames rushing to an
enormous height—whether from some change of wind,
or because they had caught a large dead tree, I do not
know. I happened to speak of this next day to an old
man (a good-for-nothing old man he was, by the bye,
though that is nothing to the present purpose), and
he said that he had looked out of his hut and seen it
too, remarking, cryptically, that it was due to *afiti*.
He went on to tell me that he sometimes heard them
passing by at night—they flew over the tree-tops with
a great whirring of wings. In fact, it appeared that
they could do 'most anything.' The boys, who dared
not go out at night for fear of *afiti*, asserted that they
carried a light which you could see afar off, but put it
out when you came near them, and that they could
make themselves large and small instantaneously.
Some held that it was good to pluck up heart and
address them; others, that if you spoke to them, you
would become dumb like Mœris, when the wolf saw
him first. I did not at the time understand the
precise connection between the witches and the fire;
but it appears that the grave itself becomes luminous
when they gather there. 'When a fire is seen on a
distant hill, where no fire can be accounted for'—that
is the place of their assembly. They call the dead
man by his childish name (which none ever uses after
he has once passed through the mysteries), and he
cannot choose but come out of the grave—then they
tear him limb from limb and eat him. When you

consider that people believe this, not as a piece of
curious folk-lore, but as a solid conviction forming
part of everyday life, it is hardly surprising that they
think no treatment too bad for the witches—if they
can be caught.

This may be done in various ways—most, if not all
of which, we must remember, are used for the detection of other things besides witches. There is the
Mabisalila or Mavumbula, the woman who dances
herself into a state of frenzy, and reveals the name of
the guilty person. She comes to stay at the village
which has requisitioned her services, and so gains
time to glean all the gossip of the place before pro-
nouncing her opinion, and also to bury the horns
during her nightly prowls, ostensibly undertaken for
the purpose of spying on the Witches' Sabbath, and
seeing who leaves the village to attend it. She is able
to make her investigations quite undisturbed, as no
one likes to venture out after dark during her stay,
lest he should meet her and be fixed on as the culprit.
When her preparations are complete, the people are
called together by the sound of the great drum.
Then she begins to dance, working up herself and the
spectators to a furious pitch of excitement, rushes
round, smells their hands to see if she can detect any
traces of strange food eaten at the unholy banquet,
and at last calls on the guilty person by the name she
pretends to have heard him addressed by at the grave.
When no one answers, she says 'So-and-So is known
in the village by such and such a name,' and then
leads the way to his house, where the horns are

dug up. The enraged people usually lynch the accused on the spot.

The ordeal of the mwavi is resorted to when people are suspected either of witchcraft or of some other crime, such as theft; and as it is a regular form of judicial procedure, it is perhaps best to consider it more fully under that heading. Here I need only say that the poison is administered to the suspected person; if he dies, his guilt is established; if he recovers, he is *ipso facto* acquitted. In some districts the poison used does not cause death, but the guilt or innocence of the accused is decided according to the different symptoms produced.

Under the heading of 'oracles' we may include a great many different processes of divination, some partaking of a judicial character, such as the following, of which a very curious description is given by an eye-witness, the Rev. H. Rowley. If there was no cheating, it seems to have been a case of what is known as 'motor automatism.'

'Some corn had been stolen from the garden of one of Chigunda's people. The owner complained to the chief, who employed the services of a celebrated medicine-man living near. The people assembled round a large fig-tree, and the magician . . . first of all produced two sticks, about four feet long, and about the thickness of an ordinary broom-handle; these, after certain mysterious manipulations and utterings of unintelligible gibberish, he delivered, with much solemnity, to four young men, two being appointed to each stick. Then from his goat-skin bag he brought

forth a zebra-tail, which he gave to another young
man, and after that a calabash filled with peas, which
he delivered to a boy.   The medicine-man rolled himself about in hideous fashion and chanted an unearthly
incantation ; then came the man with the zebra-tail,
followed by the boy with the calabash, moving, first of
all, slowly round the men with the sticks, but presently
quickening their pace and shaking the tail and the
calabash over the 'heads of the stick-holders. . . . Ere
long the spell worked.   The men with the sticks were
subject to spasmodic twitchings of the arms and legs.
These increased rapidly, until they were nearly in
convulsions ; they foamed at the mouth ; their eyes
seemed starting from their heads. . . . According to
the Mang'anja notion, it was the sticks that were
possessed primarily, the men through them. . . . The
men seemed scarcely able to hold the sticks, which
took a rotary motion at first and whirled the holders
round and round like mad things.   Then headlong
they dashed off into the bush, through stubborn
grass and thorny shrub, over every obstacle—nothing
stopped them ; their bodies were torn and bleeding.
Round to the gaping assembly again they came, went
through a few more rotary motions, and then, rushing
along the path at a killing pace, halted not until they
fell down, panting and exhausted, in the hut of one of
Chigunda's slave-wives.   The woman happened to be
at home, and the sticks were rolled to her very feet.'
She, however, vehemently asserted her innocence, and
offered to take mwavi to prove it, which she did by
proxy, the poison being administered to a fowl.   The

second oracle reversed the decision of the first, and the defendant was acquitted; but, curiously enough, no one's faith seems to have been shaken by the contradiction between two infallible ordeals.

The Rev. Duff Macdonald alludes to this kind of divination, but very briefly; it seems to be more Nyanja than Yao. He says that the sorcerer ' occasionally makes men lay hold of a stick which, after a time, begins to move as if endowed with life, and ultimately carries them off bodily and with great speed to the house of the thief.'

I have never heard of this oracle of the sticks in the Blantyre or Upper Shiré district. Of course, it by no means follows that it is not used; but from various indications I fancy that the witch-detective, the *Mabisalila*, whose operations have already been described, has been more popular since the time of the Yao settlement. The 'sticks' are still in vogue on the Lake. The Rev. H. B. Barnes, of the Universities' Mission, was told of a man at Ngofi who possessed this charm, and 'had bought it with much money at the coast. . . . It was described to me as consisting of two short pieces of wood, with a large feather behind the second. The master of the charm sets it on the ground near the place whence the disappearance has taken place, and keeps his hand on the feather, following it as it moves off on the track. It is also used when war is threatening, in order to ascertain the safest direction in which to flee.'[1]

There are various methods of divination besides

[1] MS. communication.

those already referred to. The sorcerer puts bits of
stick and pebbles into a gourd, shakes them up, and
throws them out, deducing his answer to the questions
put from their position as they lie on the ground. I
am sorry to say I never saw this done, and cannot
discover from any of the native accounts before me
whether there is a system of interpretation which
allows one to get an answer out of almost any possible
combination of the ' pieces '—as among the Delagoa
Bay people; but it is probable that the diviner follows
some such rules. Neither the ' divining tablets ' of the
Mashona, nor the knuckle-bones of sheep and goats
seem to be used—their place is taken by small pieces
of wood (*mpinjiri*), sometimes neatly cut into shape,
and the claws of the tortoise, which are divided into
four pieces—the front or tip of the claw being halved
to make a ' male ' and a ' female ' piece (which are
marked on the under side), and in like manner the
back. One way of consulting this oracle is to spread
all the pieces on a dry skin and then knock it from
underneath, and catch in the hand the piece (if any)
which jumps off; if the same piece comes twice
running, it is a conclusive proof that the person whom
the diviner thought of, when he made the inquiry, is
the correct one. Another way is to put the lots into a
jar, cover it up, and leave it for a time; if they still
keep their relative positions when next looked at, the
omens for the journey or other undertaking inquired
about are favourable. Mr. Macdonald found that the
Yao professional diviners were usually very intelligent
men, who gave sensible advice according to their own

lights, and invested it with a certain impressiveness by
means of the 'lot,' thinking people would care nothing
about it, or perhaps take offence, unless they could
attribute it to a supernatural source.

Many men consult the oracle on their own account,
especially on a journey, either by means of the flour-
pyramid, as already described, or by sticking a knife
into the ground and leaning two small sticks against
it, or laying two sticks on the ground, and a third across
them. If they fall down, or are disturbed from their
position, the omen is unfavourable. There are many
other omens which would cause a party to turn back,
unless very much set on an expedition—such as one
of them striking his foot against a stump (a common
accident, to judge by the number of ulcerated toes one
sees), or certain creatures crossing the path—some kinds
of snakes, the chameleon, etc.—the partridge's cry, and
so on. The evil-smelling *mdzodzo* and *mtumbatumba*
ants, on the other hand, are supposed (perhaps by the
rule of contraries) to be of good augury.

There is a certain system of abstinence from different
kinds of food which is probably connected originally
with totemism; but either no one has succeeded in
getting at the matter except in a very fragmentary
way, or else the natives of the present day have forgotten
the reasons for the practice, and it only survives in
a number of apparently casual and isolated usages.
Certain people will not eat some particular kind of
meat, either 'because it makes one ill, or because of
some religious scruple or vow, or because one's mother
has for no apparent reason decreed in one's infancy

that a certain food is to be tabu to one.' It might
be more correct to reduce these three alternative reasons
to one, because, as a matter of fact, people who have
been forbidden some food in their infancy usually
become ill if they eat it ; and it is no stretch of language to say that they are transgressing 'a religious
scruple' in doing so. Further inquiry is needed before
we can decide whether or not there is a reason behind
these prohibitions; quite possibly, as already stated, the
people have forgotten that there ever was one, and have
no notion of any relationship supposed to exist between
them and the forbidden animal or plant, such as the
Bechwana clans recognise in the case of the lion, the
crocodile, etc. The Rev. D. C. Scott says: 'Each
tribe or family has its particular abstinence from certain
foods.' The Achikunda, so my boatmen told me on
the Zambezi, don't eat hippo; the Apodzo do, as
might be expected, they being a tribe who get their
living by hunting that animal. This really resolves
itself into 'Apodzo and not Apodzo,' because the
Achikunda are not really a tribe, but a mixed multitude of slaves brought into the country by the Portuguese; and a good many different tribes look on the
hippopotamus as sacred. Some of the boys at Blantyre
mission-school 'did not eat hippo'—but on what exact
tribal or family grounds, I never made out. The practical result was that some other food had to be provided
for them, when one of the teachers arrived from the
River with a supply of this meat sufficient for the whole
school. The Machinga are looked down on by some
other tribes because they eat fish, which the Angoni,

e.g., never touch. Rats are forbidden to women, and to those who offer sacrifice; they are considered 'uncanny,' for very comprehensible reasons, though this does not prevent their being a very popular article of diet with those not so restricted. Doctors or others who have to treat a patient by scarifying, or, as the natives say, 'cutting medicine in,' must not eat elephant. 'In other cases the individual himself objects to certain meats as being bad for him, specially producing heat and spots all over. . . . God, they say, made men with these necessities in them; people can't make mistakes in what abstinence is essential for them.' On the whole, the various regulations one can find look like scattered parts of a system no longer understood. Doctors, as on the Congo, prescribe abstinence from various things when their patients are recovering from illness. The animals most generally avoided are those which we should class as unclean feeders, such as crocodiles, hyenas, vultures, etc.; because they are *afiti*—feeding on the dead.

Folk-stories frequently refer to such prohibitions. Thus, in one, when a girl is married, her mother tells the bridegroom that she must never be asked to pound anything but castor-oil beans. His mother, determined to overcome this fancied laziness, insists on the young wife's helping to pound the maize; she does so, and is immediately turned to water.

Various 'dances on several occasions,' which are important items in native life, ought, perhaps, to be mentioned in this place, since they undoubtedly are religious ceremonies; but they can be considered more

fully in the course of the following chapters. The same
may be said of the *unyago* or *chinamwali* 'mysteries';
but one or two points in connection with the latter
may be just touched on here. The *sinyao* dances held
in the villages of the Anyanja on these occasions perhaps embody some tradition, though what it is, no one,
so far as I know, has yet made out. Figures are
traced by scattering flour on the smooth ground of
the *bwalo*, representing animals, usually the leopard,
the crocodile, and, strangely enough, the whale. What
the word *namgumi*, which is thus translated in Dr.
Scott's dictionary, really means, or is derived from, it
would be interesting to know—though reports of such
an animal may have been received from the coast
people. Never having seen the *sinyao*, as these figures
are called, I can form no opinion as to what the
namgumi is intended to represent. The word is
common to Nyanja and Yao; perhaps adopted by
the former from the latter, in which it means 'a large
fish, the picture of which is drawn on the ground by
the head-instructor on the day of sending the boys
back to their homes.' But some light may be thrown
on the matter by the fact that Mr. Lindsay (of the
Limbi, Blantyre), passing through the bush where one
of these ceremonies had been held, saw a huge clay
model (he thought about forty feet long) of some
creature which the English-speaking native with him
told him was 'a whale,' but which was more like one
of the extinct saurians of the Oolitic period. He was
certain it was like no living creature he knew of. One
observer describes circles filled with geometrical patterns

traced on the ground, but makes no mention of the animals, except from hearsay. Besides the drawing of these figures, dances are performed by men got up as various animals. This is done by means of real heads carefully preserved and mounted on sticks, while the bodies are represented by calico stretched over wooden hoops. One such figure—say that of an elephant or buffalo—requires several men to move it, of course hidden by the draperies. Other performers wear masks of plaited grass, and are weird figures supposed to represent the spirits of the dead. These dances are held by moonlight; and the explanation generally given is that they are intended to frighten and impress the young people who have that day come of age. What ideas are embodied may be a matter of conjecture, but, for the present at least, nothing certain can be said on the subject.

Note.—Since the above chapter was written, I have learned from a correspondent in Nyasaland that there are secret societies among the Yaos, which practise cannibalism, and that the practice has been spreading of late years. In the absence of further particulars, it is impossible to determine how much of this was ceremonial in origin and how much due to a depraved taste in certain individuals which may have originated in a time of famine. See also Sir H. H. Johnston, *British Central Africa*, pp. 446, 447.

CHAPTER V

NATIVE LIFE—I. CHILDHOOD AND YOUTH

Villages. Huts. Birth. Naming. Dress. Childhood's
rights. Games. Plastic art-work. Daily life.

I CANNOT begin this chapter better than by describing
one of the villages I know best—those of the Anyanja
in the Upper Shiré district.

This district lies between the Kirk Mountains on
the west and the Zomba range on the east, and the
part I am thinking of is a fertile plain, slightly undu-
lating in parts and crossed by two good-sized streams,
which slopes down from the western mountains to the
river. As you look from the hill on which our house
stood, you see a wide level—green during the rains,
yellow when the grass is dry, with patches of bush
here and there and one grove of great trees plainly in
sight—the *nkalango*, where the dead are buried. Here
and there, dotted about the plain, are little groups of
huts, several of which, taken together, may be held to
constitute a village. Each group, as a rule, contains
one family (*i.e.* husband and wife or wives with their
children), and is enclosed in a stout fence of grass and
reeds, woven as closely as matting, and tall enough to
keep any ordinary wild beast from leaping over. There
is a door to this enclosure, but, not being on hinges, it is

usually invisible in the daytime, as the people take it down, and, as often as not, lay it on some short posts fixed in the ground, and use it as a table, on which they can spread out grain or other things to dry. At night the door is fastened by cross-bars, and perhaps thorn-bushes are stuck in at the sides to give additional security.

Inside the enclosure stand the round huts, with their conical thatched roofs—three, four, or more, according to the number of the family. Between them are the corn-bins, called *nkokwe*—in a small enclosure only one, or perhaps two. In the picture, which is that of a Yao village near Domasi, several of these *nkokwe* are to be seen—one with the top off—but they do not look as neat as one often sees them. They are like huge round baskets, woven of split bamboo, seven or eight feet high, without top or bottom, raised from the ground on a low platform roughly floored with small logs, and covered with a conical roof like those of the huts, but not fastened down, so that it can be tilted up by means of a stick, or taken off altogether when corn is wanted. They are reached by a primitive ladder made of two poles, and cross-pieces lashed between them with bark.

This Yao village is in several ways different from the one I am describing. It is larger, and, being in a more settled district, not enclosed in a fence, though some of the huts may have a semicircular one before the door, to screen it from the wind. The houses, too, are many of them square, a fashion introduced, in some places by Europeans, in others by coast people.

The huts in the enclosure have their doors facing inward; there may be a tree (probably the 'prayer-tree') in the middle of the vacant space; in any case, you will see the mortars, in which the women pound the grain, perhaps a reed mat, with flour drying on it, or millet waiting to be husked, and one or more little fires, with their three stones for supporting the cooking-pot. Perhaps there will be also a pigeon-house, like a neatly plaited basket, with a pointed roof, raised on a post, and another post close by, supporting half an old water-jar, which has come to grief, but can still be used as a bath and drinking-place for the pigeons. The fowl-house, if any, is somewhere between, and rather behind the huts, and perhaps there is also a house for the goats, but some people prefer to have their stock sleeping in the hut with them, for security's sake. I remember calling at Sambamlopa's one day, and finding his mother engaged in plastering three or four stalls for the goats against the circular wall of the hut, just leaving room for some of the family to sleep between them and the central fire-place.

Sometimes there is a single enclosure, standing by itself; sometimes several are grouped very closely together, the entrances being reached by narrow, winding paths between the stockades, which, I suppose, are intended to puzzle the enemy, in case of a night attack. Two old men, brothers, Pembereka and Kaboa, had their enclosures side by side, and the sacred tree in the narrow space of ground between the two. A little way off, on one side of the path, was the well mentioned in the last chapter, which I saw the women clearing out; and near this, too, some trees had been left standing.

Entering Pembereka's stockade, one day in early spring, we found a certain bustle and excitement pervading the place, the cause of which was soon apparent, when we saw the head-wife, old Anapiri (the same whom I found conducting the rain-ceremony a fortnight later), seated on a mat, with a new-born baby on her knees. It was a queer little yellow thing; they always start in life very light-coloured, but grow darker before long. They also seem, to me, at least, to have more hair than European babies, though they are not allowed to retain it. The mother on this occasion was not visible—she was a younger wife of Pembereka's; she was in one of the huts, which she would not leave for some days—perhaps eight or nine, perhaps less. The baby is supposed to stay with her, till formally 'brought out into the world'; but it may be that Anapiri had been giving it its first bath and oiling. The eldest child of a family is called the 'child of the washing,' or 'of oil'—not that the others are not bathed and oiled, but this is a ceremonial washing (with 'medicine') and anointing. (Both children and grown-ups require plenty of oil to keep their skins from cracking and chapping; they neither look nor feel well without it.)

A Yao woman used—sometimes, at any rate, if not always—to go out into the bush a few days before the birth of a child. One or two women would go with her, to put up a little grass shelter and look after her, till they could bring back mother and baby to the village, where, in the case of a first child, they were met with great joy, the grandmother coming out to welcome them and singing, 'I have got a grandchild, let me rejoice.' The mother would then go into the special house set apart for her—no one being allowed to enter it except the older women—and stay there for three or six days. If the baby dies during this interval, no mourning is held for it; it has not been formally introduced into the world, and its spirit is not supposed to count, or require propitiating. Perhaps they think it has not really attained to a separate existence of its own.

When the time of seclusion is over, the old women shave the mother's head and also the baby's, and they are brought out and rejoiced over. The baby is now named by one of the women. I am not sure, however, that the name is always given quite so soon. A Nyanja woman once seemed very much amused when I asked her baby's name, and said, 'It has no name— it's only an infant.' She was going about with it on her back, so that it must have been more than a few days old if the custom of seclusion had been observed. But perhaps she only thought it unlucky to tell me the name, being a stranger.

Children are sometimes called after their father, or other relations, and frequently a person who is no relation 'may make "friendship" with the babe and give it his own name, or the name of his brother or sister.' Very often, too, the name is determined by some circumstance connected with the place or time of

birth. The father may have been making a canoe
(*ngalawa*), and finished it on the day of the child's
birth, so he will name it Ngalawa accordingly. I knew
a small boy called Chipululu, 'the wilderness,' because,
as his mother explained, 'he was born at the time of
the hunger, when the people had to go into the bush
to gather food.' The baby at Pembereka's was named
Donna,[1] in honour of ourselves, as we happened to
visit the family on the day when he arrived. His
being a boy is nothing to the purpose—there is no
such thing as grammatical gender in the Bantu languages, and no one thinks (in Nyanja, at any rate) of
making any difference between the names given to
girls and boys. In fact, one occasionally finds the
same name borne by both. Most names have some
obvious meaning—'Leaves,' 'Affliction,' 'Wind on the
Water,' 'It goes,' 'We shall see it when we die,' 'I have
been a Fool,' 'Ends of Grass,' 'The Day of Beer,' are
a few specimens. But there are others not so easy to
make out, and if you ask, people will tell you 'they are
just names—nothing more.' Probably, unless they are
found to be borrowed from another language, these
will be old words, obsolete except as proper names.
Sometimes, too, a compound, used as a name, is so
contracted that its separate parts are scarcely recognisable.

Mothers, when seated, hold their babies in their arms
and on their knees, just as they do in other countries.

---

[1] Popularly current as the feminine of *msungu* ('white man'); it has
spread up the Shiré from the Portuguese settlements. People not
acquainted with the word address you as *mai* ('mother'), or *mfumu*
('chief'—common gender).

A MAKUA FAMILY

WOMEN ON LIKOMA ISLAND

To face p. 105

But when walking about, they carry them on their backs, supported by a piece of cloth knotted in front, the two upper corners passing under the arms and over the breast, the lower round the waist; or, in some parts, by a goat-skin, with strings tied to the four legs. The babies develop a most marvellous power of holding on. One sees them sometimes spread out like the letter X; sometimes, when the cloth is quite firmly fixed, and allows of a comfortable attitude, seated in 'the bight' of it, with their feet appearing round the mother's waist in front. I do not remember seeing babies seated astride the hip (as in India), but no doubt it is sometimes done, as shown in the group of Likoma Island women in the photograph.

Babies are not dressed, but the mothers wash and oil them carefully, and hang a string of beads round their necks or waists, and a charm or two to keep them from sickness or accident. In some parts they shave their heads on both sides, leaving a little band in the middle, running from the forehead to the nape of the neck. Of course, in cold weather, they are wrapped in anything that comes handy, and the skin or cloth fastening them to the mother's back keeps them as warm as clothing would do. When not being carried about, they are laid to sleep on a mat. They are not weaned till two or three years old—sometimes later; in tribes where cattle are not kept, it is somewhat difficult to get suitable food for them, but a kind of thin porridge or gruel is made. The Anyanja, though many of them keep goats, never drink milk.

As soon as the children can walk, or even crawl,

they are left to play about among the huts while the mothers are busy, cooking or pounding grain. They are left in charge of the grandmother, and perhaps one of the elder children, when the women have to go away to the gardens. They are allowed to do pretty much as they like, so long as they keep out of the fire, or refrain from climbing up any of the many tempting places whence a fall might be dangerous— the fence, or the *nkokwe* ladder, or what not. If there is any one to keep an eye on them, they will be snatched back in the first case, and fetched down in the second, and slapped in both, to emphasise the lesson that 'we don't want to have a mourning for you because you died by accident'—that being a wholly wilful and gratuitous proceeding. One sometimes sees scars of bad burns that must have been caused by a tumble into the fire; but, on the whole, these infants learn to take care of themselves after a fashion at a wonderfully early age. It is when the mothers have begun to put them into European garments that fatal accidents are apt to occur; the child stands at what would be quite a safe distance from the fire but for the little shirt or frock, and the calico is ablaze before any one is aware.

Children wear nothing much for the first few years, unless they feel cold, and are supplied with a skin, or a piece of cloth, to wrap themselves in. The little boy in the illustration has a pretty complete toilet. This family, like the group above them, were photographed at Likoma, but the mother is a Makua and wears the *chipini*—the leaden ornament like a drawing-pin stuck through a hole in the side of the nose—which is in fashion among the coast women and some of the Yaos.

Very little Angoni boys have a mat of beads, three or four inches square, worked for them by their mother or elder sister, and wear it like an apron. Sometimes also they have a 'sporran,' made from the skin of some small animal, such as a field-rat. In most homes now there is enough calico to give each of the children a piece to wrap round the waist, as they grow bigger. The only difference between the dress of the boys and girls, as a rule, is that the latter put theirs on a little higher up. The stuff used is the cheap 'unbleached,' which can be got in this country for about twopence a yard. Babies are washed very carefully; older children are left to do much as they please in the matter of cleanliness; but they love bathing, when the means are accessible, and near a lake or river all know how to swim.

Small children's heads are shaved, from time to time, in the interests of cleanliness, by their mothers; older boys and girls do it for each other. I saw a woman performing this service for her little girl who was squatting on the ground before her; she first greased the hair with some mixture which she took out of a small earthen pot, and which had the consistency of soft soap, and then scraped from the nape of the neck forward and upward, with a little spatula-shaped iron razor, held firmly in the right hand. Having finished the hair, she went on to shave the eyebrows, but I do not think this is always done.

The strings of beads which the very little girls wear round their waists disappear from view when they grow older and wear a cloth ; but they are kept on all the same, and added to from time to time, till, when they are grown up, they may have several thick rolls. These, of course, are not worn for ornament, but it is considered the safest and handiest way of storing property, and a woman thus carries her private fortune about with her.

Children and young people often stick flowers in their hair, or into the perforation of the ear, and girls at Likoma weave wreaths or crowns out of the *namteke* blossoms, a small kind of sunflower.

As soon as children are able to eat solid food, they fare much the same as their elders, though there are two or three kinds of sweet, thick gruel, besides that already mentioned, which are made specially for the younger ones, and also sometimes for sick people. It is sweetened—not with sugar, but with malt (that is, sprouting maize or millet), or the juice of a kind of millet, which is almost as sweet as sugar-cane. The stalks of this *msale*—and also sugar-cane, where that is to be had—are constantly being chewed, both by children and grown-up people. The results are visible on every native path as little bundles of tousled white fibrous matter—and the new comer is apt to wonder what they are.

There is a game which mothers sometimes play with children supposed to be too old for special infant diet ; they tickle the child's back with a stalk of grass, and, if he starts, accuse him of having ' eaten the baby's gruel'—which would be more attractive than the ordinary *nsima*.

It can readily be inferred that the young are not overburdened in the way of education. Some training there must be—some elementary inculcation of modesty and manners, to judge by results: but the deference shown to very small children—especially boys; the girls begin to make themselves useful at an early age, and are duly kept in their places—is somewhat ludicrous, and one would expect it to be disastrous, only that the effects do not seem to answer such expectation. When a six-foot Ntumbi native informed me that his son (a precocious youth of perhaps eight, and extremely minute for that age) had failed to attend school because he had gone 'to a beer-drinking at So-and-So's,' and I expressed some not unnatural surprise, not unmingled with reprobation, the father replied, 'If he has made up his mind to go, who can hinder him?' '*Akana mwini*—his lordship refuses,' was the answer given by the female relatives of another youthful truant to the teacher of the Blantyre mission-school.

I was still new to the country when I went out for a walk at Blantyre with one Limwichi—aged, I suppose, ten, and with something of a reputation for *chipongwe* (the best translation is 'cheek')—to carry my butter-fly-net. We met a big Yao, meditatively walking along and eating a piece of *chinangwa* (cassava root) as he went. Whether Limwichi was previously acquainted with this gentleman or not, I don't know; but he walked coolly up to him and asked (with what degree of politeness my proficiency in the language did not enable me to judge) for a share in this delicacy. I half expected to see Limwichi's ears boxed, instead of which the man broke off a piece of his *chinangwa* and handed it to him. I fear he did not say ' Thank you.' (Some hold that natives never do—perhaps not understanding that ' *Chabwino* '—' It is good '—conveys the same thing.)

Limwichi, I am sorry to say, had been to school— not long enough, let us say, to have his manners (though these were not precisely ferocious) softened by learning; but nothing could be gentler and prettier than the ways of the unschooled Ntumbi village children who, having got over their first shyness at the unwonted white faces which made babies shriek and dogs bark from end to end of the kraals, followed one along the narrow native paths—somewhat embarrassing in their desire to walk alongside, where the nature of the ground made it difficult, and to hold one's hands, half a dozen at once—but not really forward or troublesome. I never, with fair opportunities to have come across that sort of thing if it had been at all common, saw a child struck or otherwise ill-treated. On the whole, I think, if native parents fail in their duty, it is through being too easy-going.

I cannot understand the statement sometimes made, that native children do not know how to play, are without toys and games, and have rather a melancholy time of it altogether. The traveller who speaks of their portentous and unnatural solemnity has, of course, only observed them under the inspiring influ-

ence of his own immediate neighbourhood. It is
curious to contrast the pathetic appeals on this score
to the compassion of English children which one sometimes reads with the experience of the missionaries
at Magomero. 'Indeed it was a question with us at
one time what it was we could teach these children of
ours in the way of amusement. At last, Scudamore
and Waller thought to surprise them with a kite. The
kite was made, the children assembled to see it ascend,
but it was lop-sided and heavy, would not go up, went
down, and the children made merry thereat. Said
Waller, "You have never seen anything like this before,
have you?" Said a little urchin in reply, "Oh yes!
we have, though. We have seen them, but ours were
different to yours. Ours went up, yours go down."'

These children had been hunted away from their
homes, some of them had lost their parents, they had
all suffered more or less from hunger and some of them
from illness, so that a certain amount of depression
would have been excusable; but the spirit in which
they entered into the kindly meant effort to amuse
them is thoroughly characteristic. But for that casual
question, their instructors would never have learned
that they knew how to make kites which would go up.
Miss Woodward tells me that she has seen the Likoma
children playing with kites, but I have never seen one
myself, and cannot describe their exact construction.

There are two kinds of tops, the wooden one (*nguli*),
which is kept up by beating, like our whipping-top,
with a lash of three strands of bark tied to a bit of
stick. The other, the *nsikwa*, is made of a round

piece of gourd-shell, with a spindle of cane through
the middle of it.

' The game is played by two parties sitting opposite
to each other, with a bare space of hard ground between them, and spinning the tops across the empty
space with as much force as a twirl. between the
finger and thumb is capable of, at little pieces of
maize-cob set up before their adversaries.' Any
number can play, one top and one piece of maize-cob
being allowed to each, and the game is to knock over
all the pieces on the opposite side before those on
one's own side are overthrown. The player whose
piece is knocked over catches his adversary's top and
fires it back at him.

Maize-cobs (*sikonyo*) are also used in the game of
ponyana sikonyo, or throwing these missiles at each
other ; and in that of *tamangitsana* (literally ' making
run,' in which one side pretend to be Angoni, and
carry shields). There is a very popular game called
chiwewe, which is a somewhat original exercise with
a skipping-rope. One player squats down and whirls
the cord, weighted at one end, round his head, so
as to describe round himself a circle of two or three
yards in diameter, while the others jump over it ;
the one who fails to clear it has to take his place in
the middle.

Children build little houses of grass, and otherwise
imitate the proceedings of grown-up people ; the boys
make themselves little bows, with arrows of grass-
stalks (sometimes these are tipped with sharp bits of
bamboo and strong enough to kill small birds with),

1. " Mchombwa " or " Msuo "   2. Nyanja Ball-game

To face p. 113

and girls grind soft stones to powder, pretending they
are *ufa*, and carry maize-cobs on their backs for babies.
The little Yao girls have a kind of wooden doll called
a *mwali* ('girl'): there is no attempt at representing
the human figure; in fact, the thing is more like a
ninepin than anything else, except that both ends are
rounded, so that it will not stand up, and one of them,
by way of suggesting the head, is covered with small
scarlet seeds, fitted on like a wig.

Cat's cradle is played, though I am not certain how,
and there is a variety of guessing games, called 'tricks'
(*zinyao*), such as *chagwa*, which is something like 'hunt-
the-slipper'; and another where 'three arrows or three
sticks are set, and one guesses which is chosen—if
he guess wrongly, his companions laugh and beat him
in fun with the sticks.'

An elementary kind of swing is sometimes extem-
porised by means of a convenient creeper hanging
from the branch of a large tree; but I think I have
also seen one made with a rope.

There is a genuine native ball-game (*mpira*) played
with an india-rubber ball, in which the players stand
in a circle, and, after every catch, clap their hands
rhythmically and leap into the air. This, being done
with great regularity, has a very pleasing effect. In
one account I have seen, an umpire is described as
calling out 'Hock! hock!' after every good catch.
This is an impossible word in either Yao or Nyanja;
one conjectures it may be meant for *yaka*, 'catch.'
The well-known game of 'mankala,' which seems to be
played all the way down from Abyssinia to Mashona-

H

land, and to be of Arab origin, is here called *mchombwa*
and *mswo*. The Abyssinians play it on a board, but
this is not at all necessary; the four rows of holes can
be made on any bit of smooth ground, and one often
sees them in the *bwalo* of a Nyanja village, where the
men sit smoking and gossiping and weaving baskets.
It has been said that no European has ever succeeded
in mastering this game; and I must own that I have
always failed to follow the explanations obligingly
given by the players, but Dr. Scott's description
seems fairly clear.   Premising that there are two
players, each provided with a handful of pebbles or
seeds, and six (or nine) holes in each row, it is as
follows: ' The game consists in distributing one's men
along the rows of holes on one's own side, and again
moving them up one hole at a time, until those in
any one hole surpass in number those in the enemy's
hole opposite, when the latter are appropriated and
placed out of the game; the game is won when one
is able to appropriate the last remaining one on his
opponent's side.'

Chuchu is a kind of combination of this game and
' hunt-the-slipper.'   A spiral is drawn on the ground,
and holes made in it; three stones are chosen and two
put into the holes. ' The people are divided into two
bodies, and the stone belonging to each party is
moved up according to the skill of that party in
guessing who has the other stone—this third stone is
put in the hands of one by a person who goes all
round and pretends to give the stone to each.'   A
somewhat similar game is played with ten holes and

nine stones, and the boy who goes away (or hides his face) has to guess whether there is a stone in any particular hole at the moment he is asked, or not.

Some of the above, especially the *mchombwa*, are also played by adults, who enter into them with great zest. On the coast, and in the Portuguese settlements, they also play at cards, though the game, or that form of it which has now spread to the Shiré Highlands, is said to be 'unintelligible to Europeans.' They call the court-cards after local celebrities, such as Sir Harry Johnston ('Jonsen') and the late Mr John Buchanan ('Makanani'). Speaking of games adopted from Europeans—though it does not strictly belong to our subject — I cannot forbear quoting the following description from Mr. H. L. Duff's *Nyasaland under the Foreign Office* :—

'The football played at Kota Kota has scarcely more in common with Association than with Rugby or any other known rules. Indeed, the distinguishing peculiarity of the game would seem to be its gay immunity from any rules or restrictions whatever. No limit is apparently set to the extent of the ground, to the period of time to be covered, or to the number of those who participate in the game. The spectators may and do join in when and where they please, and continue to play as long as they can stand or see. The ball, once fairly committed to the mêlée, disappears for good. So, of course, does any man who has the misfortune to tumble down in a scrimmage. The goal-posts are rickety superfluities, a mere concession to appearances, heeded by nobody and nearly

always prostrated at the first rush. The same
abundant energy and the same lack of restraint are
noticeable wherever these Central African natives
take to any European game, and they take to European games of the rougher sort very readily indeed.
I have seen them at Blantyre clubbing one another on
the head, under pretence of playing hockey, just as
they rend one another to pieces at Kota Kota under
pretence of playing football. It is, however, only fair
to add that they show great activity, enthusiasm, and
pluck; nor is there much reason to doubt that they
might develop into really sound players, if they could
only be induced to adopt a coherent system and a
somewhat more chastened style.'

Games are very often played by moonlight; some
of these come rather under the heading of dances, and
vice versâ. In fact, the words *sewera*, 'to play,' and
bvina, 'to dance,' are used interchangeably; on one
occasion, when the drums boomed all night long from
Chona's kraal, and the dancing was still going on at
8 A.M., we were told that 'it was the Angoni playing.'
As the drums are an essential feature of the dance,
this moonlight diversion becomes trying for the hearer
in the vicinity of European settlements, where empty
tins can be got hold of and made to do duty in the
orchestra. The boarders at the Blantyre girls' school
used to let off their superfluous gaiety by drumming
on the zinc baths used in the laundry, and this was
permitted, within limits, lest worse should befall.

One of these moonlight games, at Likoma, consists
in the players joining hands in a ring and dancing

round and round, singing the words *Zunguli, zunguli,
bwata* ('Go round, go round, crouch!') over and over
again. Every time the word *bwata* comes, the whole
ring drops into a squatting position. In another, 'a
ring of boys dance round one boy crouching in the
middle with a cap or something on his head, and each
one of the ring has in turn to dance round the boy in
the middle, keeping his back to him, not losing his hold
of his companions on either hand, and not displacing
the object on the boy's head.' One refrain sung with
this game is: '*Katuli, katuli, eee katuli*—don't tread
on the boy who has it, don't tread on him!'—I have
not been able to find out the meaning of *katuli* (*e-e-e*
is just the repeated vowel sound, very common in
songs, of which the refrain is often nothing more than
i, i, i or *o, a, o*), it probably has none, as now used, and
belongs to the same category as ' *Tit, tat, toe* ' and the
like. Words sung in games are often more or less of
this kind, though sometimes quite intelligible, like
Nkondo lelo ijija — 'War comes to-day,' which
belongs to a game something like 'Fox and Geese.'
'Two captains, each with a long tail of followers,
holding tight one behind the other, face one another,
singing this song, and each seeks to swoop upon the
last man in his opponent's tail and make a prisoner
of him, without his own tail being broken.' Wrestling
is practised (at least by the Yaos), and a kind of single-
stick.

One sometimes comes on a little group of children
quietly busy and happy on the bank of a stream
and finds that they are engaged in modelling figures

out of clay. One does not see this art carried into
adult life; and as there is no attempt to make the
results permanent by burning them, they are not often
met with. I suppose it was an unusually successful
group I once saw, set up on the ant-heap just outside
Ndabankazi's kraal; it was, I think, meant to represent a European (there could be no mistake about
that, for he had a hat on) riding on an ox. I was so
struck with this work of art that I offered to buy it if it
could be baked, and understood that the offer had
been agreed to—but nothing came of it.

It has been remarked that what knowledge they have
seems to come to these African children instinctively
—for no one ever sees them taught, or chastised for
not knowing! Certainly one wonders how they learn
some things which the smallest children do quite easily.
Twisting string, for instance, out of bark, or the fibre
of the *bwasi*, the *sonkwe* hibiscus, and other plants, is a
thing which requires a certain knack, yet you see the
whole population at it, when they have the materials
handy, and nothing else to do—from the old grandmother sitting on the ground to have a chat with you,
to the little boy or girl whose attention is found to
be wandering in school. I imagine they must always
have bunches of fibrous stuff secreted somehow about
their persons. The process begins with rubbing a
bit of it against one's leg with the open hand—further
than that, I cannot tell exactly what is done, or how they
manage to twist two strands round each other without
making the whole thing curl up, as it does when I
try it.

Having got a sufficient supply of string, the next thing is to make string bags—which is done by making a row of loops for the bottom of the bag, and working round and round, putting the end of the string through each loop to make a fresh row. Usually the end is fastened to a hen's feather to make it go through easily. It is a kind of netting without the knot, and is often quite tastefully done in string of two colours.

But the realities of life begin to make themselves felt. Girls get real babies tied to their backs instead of dolls, as soon as they are big enough to carry them. I have no doubt that this injures their growth less than dragging them about in their arms; and anyhow they are usually very cheerful about it. Then they have to fetch water, and, as soon as they are able, to help their mothers in pounding corn and hoeing in the gardens. The boys have an easier time—at ten, or so, perhaps earlier, they are set to herding the goats, and will start for the *dambo* in the early morning, as soon as the kraal gate is opened, with their sticks, and, during the rainy season, an old worn-out shield to shelter under in case of a shower. They take a bit of cold porridge with them, done up in a leaf, or some roasted maize cobs, unless they are near enough to run home for the family meal a little before noon. Sometimes they make a fire in the *dambo*, and roast their maize themselves—or any small game they may have taken. They shoot small birds with arrows, or knock them down with sticks; they set various kinds of traps in the grass, and, if they can find the burrows (which are fairly common), they dig out field-mice (*mbewa*), which are considered a rare delicacy, and roast them as shown in the illustration.

The various kinds of traps will be described more fully under the heading of Hunting and Fishing.

When not cooking, eating, or keeping their charges from straying, they will find plenty of diversion to help them through the day. They build little houses in trees, putting up a platform of sticks and a grass shelter over it; they dig out mole-crickets (*lololo*), guided by the sound of their chirping, or they make models, as aforesaid, if they find a patch of moist clay, or an ant-heap and water in happy conjunction. In fact, whenever, in walking through bush or dambo, you come across any phenomenon obviously due to human agency—such, for instance, as hats made out of leaves pinned together with thorns or bits of grass—yet without visible author or apparent object, you may be sure your escort will attribute it to the *abusa*—herd-boys. When I asked the meaning of a number of tufts of grass knotted together in the middle of a piece of meadow, the children cheerfully said that the *abusa* had done it in order to trip people up. I think, however, that they need not be credited with this, as it is more probable that some one had been marking out a plot for hoeing next rainy season; and besides, natives are not in the habit of walking off the path.

They divert themselves also with music, of a sort, making flutes and whistles out of hollow reeds, or joints of bamboo—it is surprising what sweet sounds they get out of a very simple bamboo flute. There was a boy, Bvalani, who used to play on his flute all

1. Boys Digging out Field-mice   2. Caught!
3. Roasting the "Meat," Spitted on a Stick   4. Eating

Note the flat basket of porridge, for which the roast mice are the "relish"

the way up the hill, as he came to school. He further distinguished himself by wearing a charming little coronet, plaited out of pale green palm-leaves, into which he had stuck two or three blossoms of the crimson 'Turk's cap' lily. Sometimes they fasten several lengths of reed together to make a kind of Pan-pipes. The only times they are likely to get into serious trouble are when they let the goats get into the gardens—or when (being set to watch the fields when the crops are ripening) they fail to drive off the baboons.

Then, as the sun gets low, they drive their respective flocks home, put them up for the night, and join the family at the evening meal—or, if that is over, the mothers are sure to have put aside something for them. And then come the evening games, on moon-light nights—or the sitting round the fire, telling stories and asking riddles. This is the appropriate hour for such amusements. A little Yao boy told Mr. Macdonald that 'the old people' said that 'if boys recited riddles at midday, horns would grow on their foreheads.' This *might* be intended as a pre-caution against their attention being absorbed by this pastime when they ought to be herding.

The girls sometimes join the games and dances, but they also have their own amusements apart; and the boys, as they grow older, stand on their dignity and 'keep themselves to themselves.' They have their own dormitory (*gowero*) when too big to sleep in their mothers' huts with the babies; and in some villages, they have an open shed reserved for their use, where they make a fire in the evenings, and sit round it, telling tales and roasting sweet potatoes till a late hour. When they are older, and after they have attended the dances in the bush and been recognised as men, they are admitted to the bachelors' house, the *bwalo*, till they marry and set up an establishment of their own. In a village like Ntumbi, of small, scattered kraals, the grown-up men of each family will most likely have a small hut to themselves, as there will not be a regular *bwalo*, in this sense—which is not quite the same as when the word is used to mean the 'village green' or 'forum.'

Like most other boys, they quarrel occasionally, and fight sometimes, with fists, sticks, and anything else— scratching and biting not barred. But on the whole they are not particularly combative, unless under exceptional provocation, and their affectionate com- radeship is a very pleasing trait. A boy will never eat alone; and special treats, such as biscuits, are often subdivided into very minute portions to make them go round. The boy in the illustration is performing a service for his friend which is only too frequently needed of late years, since the non-indigenous pest, the jigger (*matekenya*), was introduced by Arab caravans at the North End, and gradually found its way south to the Zambezi. Unless the insect's egg-sac can be extracted (usually from under the toe-nail) before the eggs are hatched, a very bad sore is the result.

With the 'mysteries,' childhood ends, and a new phase of life begins, which will be dealt with in the next chapter.

1. Boy Extracting Jigger from a Companion's Foot
2. Herd-boys Cooking their Mid-day Meal

To face p

CHAPTER VI

NATIVE LIFE—II

Initiation.   Marriage.   Division of labour.   Meals.
Food.   Hut-building.   The *bwalo*.   Affection.

ALL Bantu tribes regard the passage from childhood
to adult life as a solemn event to be marked by more
or less elaborate ceremonies.   These vary in different
places, and some may have disused them altogether,
either through European influence, or because they
have been so harassed by enemies and driven from
place to place as to have lost many of their old
usages.   But it is safe to speak of the custom, in
one form or another, as universal among them.   Indeed, it exists, or has existed, all over the world ; and
the rejoicings over the 'coming of age' of the heir
to an estate, or the pleasant little excitement of a
girl 'coming out' at her first ball, represent it to
this day among ourselves.   These things, with us,
are mainly a matter of sentiment—that is to say,
they are not supposed to exercise any mysterious
influence on the future life of the boy or girl—to
ensure good luck or avert disaster.   But among the
people whom, for want of a better word, we call 'savages'
—it is an unsatisfactory name for various reasons
which I am not concerned to discuss here—they are

the outcome of a feeling that life is surrounded by
unknown and incalculable forces which must in some
way be propitiated and made harmless. Besides this,
there is the desire to give their children such instruction as may give them some help through the difficulties that lie before them. In fact, in many tribes,
the only systematic teaching of any sort is that given
at the ' mysteries.'

Every year, during the dry season, and before the
grass is burnt, if arrangements have been made to
hold one of these ceremonies, the Yaos send people
out into the bush, to clear a space of ground and
build some huts and booths for the *unyago*. The
boys who have reached the age of sixteen or there-
abouts go there, carrying their sleeping-mats with them,
and stay, under the charge of one or more elderly
men, for perhaps two months. They are armed with
sticks, to be thrown at any person who may intrude ;
for no one but the boys and their instructors is
permitted to be present. Various dances are said to
take place, the opening one lasting three days, and
the boys are given advice about the conduct of life,
and instructed in the traditions of the tribe. The
story of the origin of Lake Nyasa, mentioned in
Chapter IV., is one said to be told at the mysteries.

But as no European has ever been present at
these celebrations, and as those natives who might be
willing to tell Europeans about them have never
been initiated themselves, it is very difficult to say
anything with certainty on this head. The booths
are, as a rule, destroyed when the *unyago* is over,

with all other traces of what has gone on—the clay figure of a lizard seen by Mr. Lindsay in the bush was quite an exceptional case. The sticks above mentioned, with others used in the dances, are burnt or broken up; though some are 'put together at a cross-road'—doubtless as a charm of some sort. I once saw a short club of dark wood, with a carved head, said to have been used at one of these dances, which was sufficiently remarkable. It was polished with handling, as if it had seen service for many years, and the head at the top had a head-dress very like that on Egyptian mummy-cases, and a curiously long and narrow face with features which I should not like to call un-African, because I have occasionally seen natives with similar ones, but which was rather the type of the Wahima[1] than that of the average Bantu. For a wonder this stick had been offered for sale to the lady who showed it to me, by a boy who brought it to the house and either could not or would not—certainly he did not—give any account of how he came by it. He called it *tsanchima*, which is the name given to the maskers or mummers taking part in the dance already referred to in Chapter IV.

The principal person at these Yao mysteries is a man called 'the rattler of the tails' (tails of wild cats and other animals are a great item in witch-doctors' outfits, and believed to be possessed of all sorts of occult virtues), who communicates to the initiated

[1] The Wahima or Wahuma, the nomadic pastoral race believed to be akin to the Abyssinians, whose blood predominates in the royal houses of Uganda and Unyoro.

all information about the customs of the tribe, and
delivers moral lectures, as for instance, on unselfish-
ness. A man who refuses to share his food with
another is laughed at as 'uninitiated' (*mwisichana*).
Before they go home, all the boys are given new
names ; and henceforth it is a deadly insult to address
one by his childish appellation. When they go home,
they are promoted to sleep *m'bwalo*, with the other
unmarried men, and continue to do so till they marry
and set up a house or houses of their own.

The girls' *unyago* lasts a month. They go out to
the bush with their instructresses, the head-woman
(who gets a fee in calico for each candidate) being
called 'the cook of the mysteries.' They are instructed in house-building, making pots, cooking, and
other duties of married life, and put through a
regular drill in these and other things, such as
pounding corn, carrying water, etc., which they
have probably done often enough before. They
also go (symbolically, of course) through the whole
round of agricultural operations, pretending to sow
the grain, then hoeing, weeding, and reaping. The
old women give them advice as to housekeeping and
the duties of married life, and warn them of the
penalties which await them if unfaithful to their
husbands. They are anointed with oil, mixed with
certain 'medicines,' their heads are shaved, and they
are dressed in bark-cloth, which is now almost disused in everyday life. Towards the close of the
ceremony, the roof of a house—or a skeleton model
of one—is put over the heads of, say, ten at a time,

and they have to carry it about. This is supposed
to be symbolical of their position as pillars of the
home. They are not allowed to leave the scene of
the mysteries till everything is over; and, as in the case
of the boys, no one not taking part is permitted to
approach ; while sticks are laid in a peculiar way on
the path leading to the place, to show that it is
barred. Some friends of mine once met the band
of girls leaving for home, 'all freshly anointed and
dripping with oil,' and soon came to the deserted
encampment, with grass sheds built round three sides
of a square, and divided into small compartments in
which the girls had been sleeping. In the middle of
the square were traces of pots having been made, and
ufa pounded.

The whole proceeding is called 'being danced.'
The Yaos 'dance' girls very young—mere children of
seven or eight sometimes—and, from what I have
seen, I should say, personally, that they were not
improved by the process. But the Yao practice cannot be regarded as typical, as there is reason to
believe that it has been modified by the influence of
the coast people.

The Anyanja do not 'dance' boys at all, and the
ceremonies for the girls only last, in some parts, for
one day, and the candidates are all of full age. The
old women who are their teachers go outside the
village with them into the grass which has been left
unburnt, and there they remain all day, coming back
after dark to the *sinyao* dances in the *bwalo*, which
have already been referred to. Figures of animals are

drawn on the smooth ground with ashes or flour, and the people dance round them.[1] The men also go out into the bush to disguise themselves, as already described, in grotesque masks of wood and cloth, with grass, horns and skins of wild beasts, and, returning, lead the girls out one by one and dance with them in the centre of the ring. When it is over, the women carefully see the girls home. They too have their names changed, and their former ones are not supposed to be pronounced, unless they fall into disgrace. There is, too, a strange belief that when witches are at their cannibal orgies, they call the dead out of the grave by his or her childish name, and this call cannot be ignored.

On the Lake the course of instruction lasts for several days; and the girls wear caps made of beads, with other ornaments of the same. There is also a preliminary course for children, who wear ornaments made of reeds cut into strips and strung together. A curious feature in this course is a procession round the village, out at one gate in the stockade and in at the other, headed by a woman carrying a basket (*mnkungwa*), which contains 'certain mysteries.'

Marriage is the next step in life, at least for the girls—though even in their case it does not always follow immediately. Young men may have to wait for some years, owing to lack of means or for other reasons. In the country under the Angoni chiefs they are called on, as we have seen, to 'serve their time,' herding the chief's cattle, and later, perhaps, going to war.

[1] See Chapter IV.

This is something like the Zulu system, and probably a relic of it. I have not been able to discover anything similar in the case of the Yaos or the Anyanja, perhaps because their government is less centralised, and all chiefs and head-men would have their work done by their own slaves, who are always on the spot. But the young men without, as yet, any family ties of their own, may join some caravan going to the coast, or (in the times when elephants were more abundant and there was no European administration to interfere) put in the time hunting or slave-raiding, or go to work for the white men, or, finally, stay about the villages, and have a good time at beer-drinkings and dances for a year or two.

There are several different forms of marriage, and there is no theoretical limit to the number of wives any man may have; but there is a difference between the status of free and slave wives. The rules as to who may or may not marry each other will be considered in another chapter.

Neither Yaos nor Anyanja, in the Shiré Highlands, at least, buy their wives (unless, of course, in the case of a slave woman); but this term, by the bye, is a very misleading one. The price paid by the Zulus (under the name of *lobola*) and others cannot properly be called purchase, being rather in the nature of a settlement or a guarantee that the suitor is able to support a wife; it is held by her family in trust for her and her children.

It is very common for girls to be betrothed in infancy, or even (conditionally) before birth—the

I

suitor (or his parents) giving a present which has to be returned if she refuses to ratify the engagement when of age; he also clothes her during the period of waiting—which, as may be supposed, does not involve any ruinous outlay. The acceptance of a calico waist-cloth, and the girl's wearing it, make the transaction a binding one. She is sent to him after the *unyago*, or, sometimes, even before, in which case she has a special charm given her on that occasion.

I remember hearing of a case where such an arrangement had a tragic end. A Yao girl, promised by her parents in the way above described to an elderly man, refused to marry him when the time came, as she preferred a young man named Tambala, a teacher in the Blantyre school. Whether the proper steps for dissolving the engagement had been taken or not, I do not know; in any case the old man refused to give up his claim; and, a day or two before the marriage was fixed to take place, Tambala was found dead in the gardens near his village—shot by the disappointed suitor. But the Anyanja, at any rate, seem to regard the question as quite an open one, which may be settled by arrangement. A native statement on the subject is as follows: 'If the girl, when she is grown up, refuses, her father takes money (*i.e.* cloth or beads) and gives it to that man, because, he says, you have clothed my child.' Nyanja girls, too, are very often not betrothed in this way. It should also be remembered that the marriages thus agreed on beforehand by parents are often between boys and girls of suitable ages, and turn out quite happily.

When a man takes a fancy to a girl whom he finds to be disengaged, he first of all comes to an understanding with her, then goes to her village and tells her family—all the relations, including the grandparents, the elder brother, and, above all, the maternal uncle, are consulted, as well as the parents—and, if they have no objection, he then goes to his own people. Having obtained their consent, 'he returns to build the house, and when it is nearly completed he calls his own people to meet his bride's people on a certain day. The bride's people cook native porridge, which is eaten with a fowl, and the marriage is finally ratified. Unless this porridge and fowl are eaten by the parents of both parties to the marriage, it is neither legal nor binding, hence this meal may be regarded as their ceremony of marriage.' This is stated to be 'the normal and legal form of marriage among both Yaos and Anyasa.' Though not mentioned in this account, it appears that a present is usually, if not always, made to the girl's uncle.

In the Western Upper Shiré district, they have some sort of a dance at the wedding; but my only authority is a girl who did not give a very detailed account—only saying that the bride and bridegroom stand by, while 'the people dance before them.' The Wankonde marriage ceremonies show distinct traces of marriage by capture. It sometimes happens that women are actually 'stolen' and carried off as wives; but this is an illegal act, not a recognised form of marriage.

Other authorities represent the young man as going

first to his own 'surety' (who may be his father, his
uncle, or his elder brother), and getting his consent
before approaching the girl's relations.   It will be
noticed that he goes and builds a house at the bride's
home.   This is the universal custom, where the
marriage of free women is concerned, with both
Anyanja and Yaos.   It is connected with the fact (to
which we shall return later on) that children belong
to the mother's kin, not the father's.   One of the new
husband's first duties is to hoe a garden for his mother-
in-law, though he is bound by the rules of propriety
to avoid her to a certain extent.   He must not eat in
her presence nor see her eat, and there are various
other restrictions, all of which come to an end when
he has brought her the first grandchild, with a present.
The same rules apply also to the father-in-law, and to
the maternal uncles of both; while the wife has to
observe them with regard to her husband's parents,
and *their* uncles.   The important position which the
mother's brother holds in the family will be referred to
again later.

In practice, the number of wives varies from one to,
in the case of a chief, perhaps twenty.   The Makololo
and Angoni chiefs used to delight in showing their
consequence by huge harems of over a hundred women,
and the latter, at least, were in the habit of demanding
additional wives, from time to time, from their Anyanja
subjects, making them send up a selection of their
daughters, as they sent their sons to herd the chief's
cattle.   But this custom was not followed by the
indigenous tribes.   Mr. Macdonald says that, ordinarily,

it is a man's ambition to have five—one free wife, and
three or four slaves, who might at that time (some
thirty years ago) be bought for two buckskins apiece
in the Angoni country. A number of the Anyanja I
knew on the other side of the Shiré had two, some,
I think, only one. If a man has more than one free
wife, he spends his time between their different villages,
since each of them will remain at her home. His
slave wives are brought to his village, or rather to
that of his chief wife, where he settled on his marriage.
They are supposed to be under her orders and do
most of the work; she is sometimes a stern and even
cruel taskmistress, but often they get on very amicably
together. She usually calls them her 'younger
sisters.'

If a man has a second free wife, it is, as a rule, because
he has inherited her from his elder brother according
to Bantu custom. He also inherits the wives of his
maternal uncle, if the latter has no younger brother
living at the time of his death.

Wives may be captured in a raid, in which case
there are no particular formalities about the marriage.
Some of my Anyanja friends at Ntumbi had Yao
wives who must have been obtained in this way, but
appeared to have settled down quite happily.

'Another way'—to complete the enumeration—is
when a young man's master or guardian (for he may,
even if free, be under the tutelage of a real or nominal
elder brother) provides him with a wife.

We have spoken of the 'sureties' or 'sponsors,' who
take part in arranging a marriage. They, especially

the wife's, are of great importance in married life.
They are usually the maternal uncles or elder brothers
of the parties, and the woman's represents her in all
transactions of any moment.

The feast (if it can be so called) mentioned above as
constituting the marriage ceremony is sometimes (or
used to be) celebrated in a more elaborate form.   In
this case, it was the *entering the house*, as soon as it
was finished, which was held to constitute the act of
marriage.   The woman would bring with her pots,
baskets, a sleeping-mat, and some flour to cook the
first meal with.   The man would contribute an axe
and a hoe to the common outfit.   One of his wife's first
duties is to plaster the house he has built, though this
will not always be needed.   The meeting at which
what we may call the marriage-contract is drawn up,
takes place some time later; perhaps not till the first
produce of their new garden is ready.   The wife's
surety is said to ' come to settle her' in her home.

She prepares two pots of beer for her husband's
surety or sureties and two for her own.   The former
contribute a cock to the banquet, the latter a laying
hen.   Both then lay down certain rules for the behaviour
of the young couple, warning the wife against unfaith-
fulness, and binding both to resort to the diviner in
case of illness or other trouble.

The division of labour between husband and wife
varies a good deal according to local circumstances.
Where the husband goes away with trading caravans,
or on hunting expeditions, or works on a plantation,
or as a *tenga-tenga* man (carrier), or where he is liable

WOMEN POUNDING MAIZE IN YAO VILLAGE

Note the cooking-stones and pots in the foreground ; also the square house (cf. p. 144)

To face p. 135

to be summoned away for weeks at a time (as he was under the Angoni and Makololo) to work for the chief, the field-work, of course, falls on the wife.

This we shall describe more fully when treating of Agriculture. She also has to go to the bush to cut firewood, and to the stream or well for water; to plaster the floor and walls of the house with mud (which looks like grey stucco when dry); to fetch in supplies of food from the gardens, to pound and husk the grain, and to do the cooking. I have only once seen a man pounding at a mortar; this was a Ngoni who lived temporarily in one of the Blantyre villages, while working on a plantation, and, no doubt, he was lending a hand with the pounding by way of payment for his board.

When the husband is at home, he helps in the gardens, cuts grass for thatching, executes repairs generally on huts and fences, makes the grain mortar (cut with an adze out of a tree-trunk), spins and weaves (where this is still done), sews his wife's calico, and makes mats and baskets. On the Lake and River many are engaged all day in fishing, and some in making canoes; the fishing by hand-nets or traps is also done by women. Sometimes he accompanies his wife to the Bush for firewood, and has been much reprobated for carrying nothing but his weapons while she is heavily loaded. But this leaves out of account the ever-present possibility of attack by raiders or wild animals—of course now rapidly becoming a matter of tradition. Still, no longer ago than 1894, I saw men patrolling the gardens with spear and shield, while their wives gathered the millet—in very real danger of being carried off by the Machinga.

The wife, as time goes on, is helped by the junior wives, and in due course by her daughters, sometimes also by slaves, men and women. The pounding of the grain is about the heaviest work; the maize is first husked, then the grain is stripped off the cobs with the fingers, and put into the mortar for the first rough pounding. It is then taken out and winnowed by being shaken in a flat basket, and after being separated from the bran (which is given to goats, fowls, and pigeons, or used to make coarse porridge in time of scarcity), pounded over again, sifting out the coarser particles after each pounding, till at last it is fine and white like flour. Millet is usually, when brought in from the garden, spread out on mats to dry in the sun, and then beaten with thin sticks to separate it from the husk. It is pounded with a little water, the bran sifted out, the meal washed and partly dried, and finally ground fine between two stones.

Porridge is made by stirring the maize or millet flour (usually the former) into boiling water, and is ready in a few minutes, once the water has been brought to the boil, which, with a large jar and a small fire, is apt to be a work of time. The pot is supported over the fire on three stones. Maize porridge (*nsima*) is, if well made of good flour, about the colour of a suet dumpling; if inferior, it is more or less greyish. It is very stodgy, trying to a European digestion, and exceedingly sticky to the touch. Natives will eat surprising quantities of it; but they

TWO MEN EATING

Note the small earthen pot with the *ndiwo*

feel it a privation to be obliged to take it without salt,
or some kind of 'relish' (*ndiwo*). This may be beans,
or ground-nuts, or green vegetables of some sort,
such as the leaves of the manioc ; or, more rarely, a
fowl, or a bit of goat's flesh. Whatever it is, it is
put on to boil in a small pot beside the large one,
after the latter has been on for some time. Occasionally roasted rats, such as the boys bring in from the
fields, are eaten as *ndiwo*, or winged white ants—a
great delicacy—or dried locusts. Some tribes consider
dried (and very high) fish a choice kind of *ndiwo*—
others will not touch fish in any shape.

In the spring and early summer, when the old maize
is finished and the new is not yet ripe, pumpkins,
gourds, and cucumbers of various kinds are a great
stand-by, and are eaten boiled. Sweet potatoes are
most frequently roasted in the ashes, and manioc-root
is eaten either boiled or raw.

In the planting and weeding seasons, people set out
for the gardens before daylight, and return before noon,
resting during the hottest hours of the day. There
are only two formal meals in the day—one about noon
or somewhat earlier, the other about sunset. Mothers
put away some of the cold porridge overnight, to give
the children in the morning, and boys are always
roasting sweet potatoes in the ashes at odd times.
Any one who feels hungry between meals can usually
find something to nibble at ; perhaps a roasted maize-
cob, or a piece of raw chinangwa (manioc-root). Men
on a journey often make 'pop-corn' over an improvised fire, roasting the grains (nowadays) on a shovel

usually made by fixing the lid of a tin box into a cleft
stick. Beer (*moa*) is made of maize or millet—more
frequently of the latter. The process is as follows :—

First a gruel is made by stirring flour with cold
water and then pouring boiling water into it. This is
allowed to stand till evening and then malt is added.
This has been previously prepared by leaving some
grain in water till it sprouts, letting it dry in the
sun and then pounding it. The mixture is left to
stand overnight and then is a sweet, non-intoxicating
beverage called *nyombe* or *mtibi*. This is often drunk
without further preparation ; but if it is desired to
make real beer, it is kept another day and then boiled
for two hours, then poured off and left standing for
two or three days more. It is now called *mlusu*, is
highly intoxicating, and is not drunk unless in very
small quantities. More malt is added, and on the
next day more gruel is made, as at the beginning—
perhaps twenty, thirty or more pots—according to the
number of guests expected, and the *mlusu* stirred into
it, till all the pots are of the same strength. The beer
is ready for use on the following day, after being
strained. There are two kinds of strainers; one
shaped like a bag, is made of palm-fibre; the other a
flat basket of split bamboo. These large brewings
are undertaken for funeral-feasts, hoeing-matches, or
'bees,' and on various other occasions; beer is also
made for dances, or to celebrate the return of travellers, and sometimes, on the conclusion of a lawsuit,
the loser pays the other party in beer. A Yao folk-
tale relates how, after hearing both sides in a certain

GANG OF ANGONI AT MANDALA

Note the sleeping-mats rolled up with the other luggage, and the man on the right roasting maize over the fire

To face p. 138

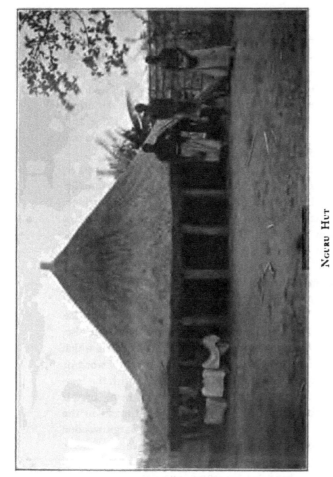

NGURU HUT

This is fairly typical for the whole of B.C.A., though the posts are unusually thick

To face p 141

case, the judges decided, 'You must just pay each other'—and the resulting conviviality must have lasted for at least a week. Moa does not, as a rule, keep more than three or four days; but the one family would begin their brewing three days after the other. On the last day of a 'beer-drinking,' porridge and perhaps fowls are cooked; but such solid food is not expected on the other days.

In a small village, the men and boys all eat together, in the *Bwalo*. The women of the several families take it in turns to prepare the food. The porridge, when not eaten out of the pot, is ladled out into a wooden platter or a flat basket, which is set down on the mat on which the men are sitting, with the *ndiwo* in a pot or bowl beside it; and they squat round and eat from the dish with their fingers, which they are careful to wash before and after. The women and little girls eat by themselves either in a different place or later; the mother, or hostess, helps every one else, putting their portions by hand into their plates, which may be small flat baskets, or shallow bowls of wood or earthenware. A mouthful is scraped off with the forefinger, rolled into the palm and eaten; being first, if the *ndiwo* is boiled fowl or the like, dipped in the gravy. No spoons are used except the large wooden ladles, often neatly carved, which serve to remove the porridge from the pot. On the Lake, shells are sometimes used for the same purpose. Salt is put into the food when cooking, if it is to be had at all; it is greatly valued because rather scarce, especially in the western part of the Upper Shiré district, where

men, women, and children suffered from an insufficiently nutritious diet and consequent poorness of
blood. One result of this was a great craving for
salt; they gladly accepted a few spoonfuls as payment
for work or provisions brought for sale; another was
the formation of a virulent ulcer every time a person
stubbed a toe or barked a shin. The need for salt is
not the same among people who, like the Zulus, have
plenty of fresh meat and milk. Language affords a
curious corroboration of this: there is no native Zulu
word for salt—they call it *usaoti*, from the Dutch *sout*.
There are genuine Bantu words for it in Yao,
Nyanja, and all the neighbouring languages. The
method of making salt will be described in treating
of Industries.

I do not know of any other condiment, strictly so
called, used by natives, except Chile peppers, which
are common on the River and near the Portuguese
settlements, but rare up-country. They are called
sabola, which is the Portuguese *cebola*, ' an onion.'
The word is used in its proper sense as well, and
probably, to the native mind, conveys the idea of
' flavouring ' simply.

The only sort of bread known to the natives of this
part of Africa is a kind of roll called *mkate*, made of
maize-flour, bananas, and honey. I have neither
seen nor eaten it, but it appears to be either baked
by being put on the fire, in a pot without water, or
rolled in leaves and dried in the sun.

Food, cooked or uncooked, is stored within the hut
in baskets or bags of various kinds, but maize, and

also millet, beans and ground-nuts, are kept in the *nkokwe* already described. It can only be the un-husked millet that is so kept; I have never, myself, seen anything but maize come out of a *nkokwe*. Some of the Middle Zambezi people tie up grain in bundles of grass, plaster them over with clay, and keep them on low sand islands in the river. The Badema, near Kebrabasa Falls, who in Livingstone's day were much harassed by their enemies, used to make cylindrical bins out of the bitter bark of a certain tree, which mice and monkeys will not touch, to put their grain in, and bury them in the ground. The Anyanja have large narrow-necked baskets, which they hang up to the rafters of the hut, and use for storing grain, beans half-cooked, manioc-leaves, and other things, and beans are also put into bags. The seed corn is left in the ear, and hung up, or laid on the stage over the fireplace, where the smoke keeps the insects from it, or sometimes sealed up with clay in earthen jars.

In building a house, the first thing is to drive in the posts, which are, so to speak, its skeleton. They are set in a circle about a yard apart, and forked at the top to support a circle of split bamboo which forms the top of the wall; then the interstices are filled with grass and bound with circles of bamboo perhaps a foot apart. A space is left for the doorway, and sometimes small shuttered loopholes,[1] about four feet from the ground—more for the purpose of letting the inmates see what is going on outside than of admitting light.

---

[1] I am not sure that these are usual, except where they are likely to be needed for shooting.

Most huts have only one door, but at times and in places where raiding is habitual, they are constructed with two—to facilitate escape from enemies.

A strong central pole is planted to support the roof, which is made separately, like a huge basket, and afterwards hoisted into position. A number of sharpened bamboos are stuck, at an angle of about 45, into a bunch of grass, which is to form the point of the roof, and is sometimes plaited into fanciful shapes, or covered with an inverted pot, to finish up the construction and prevent the rain from running into the ends of the straws. The radiating spokes are united by concentric hoops made of twisted grass placed at regular intervals, and tied at the crossings with bark soaked in water, which of course tightens as it dries.

The roof is always made to project at least three feet beyond the walls, and its edges are supported by posts. The space under the eaves makes quite a small verandah, and is banked up with clay to the height of a foot so as to form a step or low platform running round the house. The walls are not more than four feet high, perhaps less; the centre of the hut may be twelve feet. Small huts have a diameter equal to their height, or even less, and require no support inside ; larger ones are wider than they are high, and the roof is supported by a strong central post, and extra ones, if necessary, in proportion to the increased diameter. The walls are plastered with clay at the beginning of the cold (and dry) season ; this plaster (at any rate in the lower-lying districts) is either removed during the summer, or not renewed when it drops away of itself. It is always done by the women, who also do the floor of the hut in the same way as the verandah, and mould it into a circular ridge about two feet in diameter for the central fireplace. Sometimes one or more oblong platforms are made for sleeping-places; but many people simply spread their mats on the floor, and some make regular bedsteads (or, as it has been described, a 'family sleeping-shelf') by fixing stout sticks in the ground and spreading a mat on top of them. Whatever the sleeping arrangements, people lie with their feet to the fire, which is fed at night with one or more logs laid end on to the fireplace, and kindled at the inner end, so that whoever happens to wake in the night can, without any trouble, put on fuel by merely pushing the outer. The fire is not much used for cooking except in wet or windy weather; and in fact the hut is mainly a place for sleeping and storing things in. The fireplace is generally surrounded by four posts supporting a stage or shelf (*nsanja*), which serves all the purposes of a storeroom and larder. Strips of meat and fish are hung on it to dry; provisions, cooked and uncooked, are placed there in pots and baskets, and the seed corn is kept there in the smoke, where the weevils and other insects will not attack it.

Other things—spears, bows and arrows, the spindle and weaving-stick, bags of beans, the gourds for drawing water, etc.—are hung from the rafters or stuck in the thatch. Cloth and beads are stored away in baskets. Besides the articles already men-

tioned, a few cooking-pots, a carved wooden pillow
or two, a few skins, perhaps one or two small logs
to sit on, or even a stool made out of the root of
a tree, and a jar of water with a gourd dipper to
drink it from, will about complete the inventory of
the furniture.

Some of the people on Mlanje ornament the plastering of their houses with figures of animals in black,
white, and red, but I have not seen any of these. A
hut I saw at Ntumbi had the walls plaited in a neat
sort of basket-pattern and daubed inside with black
mud in a way that suggested an attempt at orna-
mentation; one of the circular rafters, too, was neatly
decorated with small white feathers, stuck on at
regular intervals.

The smoke is left to find its way out through the
thatch; consequently the inside of the roof, with the
nsanja and everything on it, is black and shiny, and any
article which has come out of a native hut may be
known at once by a peculiar smell, compounded of
wood-smoke and castor-oil.

Square houses, which are often built not only by
people at missions but by Yaos who brought the
notion from the coast, are much less typical, and from
a practical point of view less satisfactory; they are
always stuffy and frowsy, in a way the round huts
are not. The latter seem to ventilate fairly well
through the thatch, and the smoke, which might be
expected to make the atmosphere quite impossible,
is avoided if you do as the natives do and sit on the
floor. The square house, too, has corners in which

rubbish can accumulate, and though it has something by way of windows, they neither admit air enough to sweeten, nor light enough to see, the interior. Besides, a new and well-made hut has an artistic completeness of its own, and pleases the eye, as a lop-sided, straggling *nyumba ya gome* can never do.

Each wife has her own hut, where her children sleep with her—the boys till they are old enough to go to the *gowero*, or dormitory, the girls till they leave for homes of their own. The father of the family has sometimes his own separate hut, sometimes he lives in the others, turn about, or in the head-wife's house (*kuka*), which is the proper centre of the home. Frequently, however, his mother is the real head of the family and occupies the *kuka*, though she may also have a house of her own apart.

In a large village, the *bwalo* or ' forum ' may be the space round which all the huts are grouped ; in other cases it is a place by itself outside all the enclosures. The sacred fig-tree which marks it is often apparently a very old one ; so that, no doubt, the site is a more or less permanent one, round which the shifting kraals group themselves in various rearrangements. I have a sketch of the great fig-tree at Chona's which stood between the village and the maize-gardens. Various articles were hanging on this tree—gourd-dippers and a mouse-trap—but whether as votive offerings, or as a mere matter of convenience, I never made out.

The blacksmith's forge stood on one side of this *bwalo*, and very often mats were spread at the foot of the tree for men to sit in the shade. Here one sees

K

the rows of holes for the *mchombwa* game scooped
in the ground; here, too, dances are held, whether
ceremonial or merely for amusement, and cases are
tried, or in native idiom 'the *mlandu* talked.' The
ground is swept every day by a man whose business it
is to look after it, and who is called 'the master of the
bwalo.' He also receives strangers (the etiquette is for
them to go and sit down in the *bwalo* as soon as they
arrive), and informs the village chief that they have
come. He used to receive as his perquisite the heads
of all goats killed in the village. Sometimes there
is a shed in the middle of the *bwalo*, known as the
'strangers' house,' where they eat and sleep during
their stay; the villages west of Lake Nyasa have
structures exactly like band-stands for this purpose.

Natives are sometimes thought not to have much
family affection, because they are not as a rule very
demonstrative in words, but this is a mistake. I
remember the touching distress of an old man who
thought his wife had been carried off by the Machinga
and would have to drudge at pounding corn for
strangers in her old age. Fortunately she turned up
safe and sound, along with some other women who
had been hiding in the bush. A woman who lived
about twelve miles from Blantyre, hearing that her son,
a boarder at the Mission, was ill, walked in and carried
him home on her back—a big lad of thirteen or four-
teen. 'The boy is the light of the mother's eye.
When he goes off on a journey she awaits his return
anxiously; sometimes, it may be, making a vow not

to shave her head till he returns; on his return she
goes through a wild dance of joy, often casting white
ash or flour over herself and making a shrill noise,
lululuta. She clasps her child round the body, sometimes round the neck, herself kneeling; she sees nothing
of onlookers . . . then she must be poor indeed if she
cannot cook porridge enough for him and a friend or
two.' The elasticity which makes those carried into
slavery—especially young people—forget their troubles
is sometimes thought to be a proof of callousness; but
the eagerness with which they will seize any chance of
returning home after years of separation, or follow up
any clue to a lost relation, is sufficient disproof. There
is a pathetic belief in some parts that slaves going to
the coast find a plant in the hills, which they eat 'to
make them forget the friends of their youth,' lest
their grief should be too great. It loses its efficacy as
soon as anything happens to remind them of home,
or they get a chance of returning. The often-made
assertion that parents will sell their children into
slavery has very little foundation, as far as Anyanja
and Yaos are concerned. This only happens in very
exceptional cases: in the extremity of famine (and
even then it is condemned by public opinion), or to
redeem an important member of the clan, as in the
following instance: 'An old fellow at Msumba was
seized by the Angoni together with his younger brother,
and the joy of the little community was taken away;
they had no one to speak for them "in the gate."
Better a few go into captivity than the head of the
clan be disgraced.' A woman and a boy were sent up

as ransom, and, it appears, went willingly. 'Another time a son by a slave woman was paid for the ransom of his father; it was managed by the clan, and the father was not asked.'

One sometimes hears that, though mothers are very fond of their children, the fathers care little about them, and indeed cannot be expected to, because they have so many. This, again, is untrue, and the alleged reason will not hold, as—except chiefs like Mombera and Ramakukane—few men have more than they can easily keep count of. The impression has gained ground partly because, as already remarked, the native parent is not particularly demonstrative, and partly because it is not easy for travellers, even if observant and sympathetic persons, to arrive at the details of intimate family matters like this. Nearly every one who writes on the subject comes across some unmistakable instance of affection, and immediately records it as a remarkable exception. The fathers of my acquaintance were certainly not indifferent to their children.

The position of women, too, has been greatly misconceived. I cannot do better than quote the words of a competent observer at a time when native manners could have been very slightly, if at all, modified by European influence. The Rev. H. Rowley, whose experience was gained in 1861, says: 'The position of the woman with the Manganja and Ajawa was in no way inferior to that of the man. . . . Men and women worked together in the fields, and the special occupations of the women were thought to be no more degrading than the specialities of our women are to our own women at home. The men seemed to have much kindly affection for the women; such a thing as ill-usage on the part of a man to his wife I did not once hear of. Frequently the position of the woman seemed superior to that of the man; in their religious observances, for instance, the principal performer was generally a woman.'

Some of the native folk-tales give interesting glimpses of everyday experience, and especially of the relations between man and wife. They show the native husband, not as a savage monster, but a very ordinary human being, sometimes selfish, sometimes greedy, very sensitive to ridicule, so that he will make any concessions to his wife rather than be laughed at by the neighbours; and yet again solving the difficulties of domestic life with shrewd good sense. A Nyanja story of 'A Man and his Wives' brings out this last characteristic :—

'Once upon a time a man married two wives. And he hoed two rice - patches, and made a boundary between them, and assigned one to each. Both women sowed rice, and when it was time to keep off the birds, one of the women took her water-jar and placed it on the boundary as a drinking-place (for the use of those watching the crops?). And her companion planted some pumpkin-seeds near the other woman's water-jar. And a shoot of the pumpkin plant grew over the rim of the jar, and so a pumpkin got inside the jar and grew big, and they could not get it out again, for the jar was too narrow at the mouth. So one day the woman who owned the water-jar said to the owner of the pumpkin, "I say, I want my jar to take to the village. Go and take out your pumpkin." The other woman went and tried to break it up inside the jar, saying, "Let me get it out in bits." But the owner forbade her, saying, "Don't do that." So she said, "Well, shall I cook it inside the jar?" But she refused. "No, no, I won't have you making my jar all grimy!" So the other said, "Well, take the pumpkin and the jar too." But she refused again, "Not I! do you think I am hungry and want your pumpkin?" So there was a quarrel about it between these two women.

'Now, what was the husband to do to make peace between his wives? He wanted to break the jar and throw away the pumpkin. But the wife who owned the jar said, "If you want to break my jar, let me go too. I shall go home and stay there and have nothing to do with you." The husband said, "Woman, you are a bad lot." She answered, "Am I really a bad lot? Yet I am only vexed about my jar, and want nothing else beside."

'Now, just see the husband's clever trick. He feigned sickness, and in the evening pretended he was very ill indeed. Both his wives slept in the same house that night because their husband was seriously ill. And they tried to cook dainty dishes. "Let us see if we can cook for a sick man." But he would not eat at all, enduring his hunger till the morning.

'In the morning his mother arrived, and began to cry bitterly because her son was sick; and she asked,

" My son, would you like us to cook you some food ? "
He said, " I want no other sort of food, but if there is
a pumpkin I do want you to get it and buy salt and
cook it, and I think I may eat it to-day." Those two
women were there on the spot, and one of them, the
owner of the jar, took the head of the man and laid it
in her lap, and the owner of the pumpkin took his feet
and laid them in her lap. And the first, when she
heard that the man wanted a pumpkin, said to the
other woman, " Go at once and break the jar, and bring
the pumpkin, and let us cook it, so that our husband
may eat." She ran and got the pumpkin, and cooked
it, and gave it him to eat, and he got well of his
sickness. And so the trouble ended.'

A Yao story tells how a man and his wife contrived,
each in the absence of the other, to secure for themselves, in order to eat it alone (a flagrant breach of
good manners), a leg of the partridge that was being
cooked for the family. Both having retired to eat the
morsel into the dark interior of the hut, they came into
violent collision and broke their plates. 'She said,
" Eating a relish alone ! I was only tasting it ! " He
said, " And I was tasting it too ! " The man took goods
and gave the woman, saying, " Do not bring disgrace
on me ! " The woman brewed beer and gave the man,
and the matter ended.'

Something like this is the tale of ' The Man with
the Bran-Porridge.' A man who had told his wife
that he never ate bran-porridge went to the coast with
a caravan, sold his ivory to advantage and had a red
fez given him into the bargain. The party reached

their home and were met with the usual rejoicings;
and the man, wearing his new fez, sat down to wait
while his wife prepared him a meal. This was, as
usual, a long business; the woman first pounded the
maize, then put the bran on a plate, and took the grain
down to the stream to wash it before the second
pounding. The husband, growing more and more
hungry as he waited, forgot his scruples or his fastidi-
ousness, took the bran, poured it into his fez, poured
some water on it, stirred it up and began to eat it.
While he was doing so he saw his wife coming, and
put the fez half full of bran and water on his head to
hide what he had been doing. His wife, however, was
too quick for him and asked, 'What is that on your
head that you are hiding?' He said, 'Medicine that I
prepared for the journey.'

Whether she believed this or not is not recorded,
but in any case, the fib availed him little, for very soon
the bran-porridge began to trickle down his face. He
said, 'Oh! my wife, hunger, hunger! Some hunger
eats weeds of the field, some hunger eats what is bad.
My wife, do not tell people that I was seen with bran-
porridge on my head, and I will pay you with goods.'
So he paid her with goods. But she must have been
provided with a dangerous weapon in the event of
future quarrels.

The first of these stories makes mention of a separation. This, in fact, sometimes takes place—perhaps for
some quite trivial cause. An unfaithful wife is divorced
(or, if a slave, sold), and goes back to her uncle or other
guardian. If a Yao woman's children all die, her

husband may leave her; among the Wankonde, public opinion is said to decree that it is best in such a case to kill himself. Sometimes a wife demands a divorce because her husband does not sew her calico properly (which may mean that she is going to be neglected for a younger rival), or the husband because the wife is lazy about hoeing.

'When they separate, the wife takes away the few domestic utensils which she brought with her, none of which are used by the man.' She does not return the cloth given her from time to time, because she is considered to have rendered an equivalent service by cooking his porridge. 'In all separations, except for serious causes, the one party gives the other a token, which may be cloth, arrow-heads, beads, or such current money. The one that begins the strife and is the cause of the separation, pays the other.' On the Lake, the ceremony of divorce is accomplished by the man breaking a reed before witnesses on both sides and declaring that he renounces his wife. The woman is not free till this is done.

CHAPTER VII

FUNERAL RITES

Wailing and mourning. The grave. Inheritance. The
cause of death. Ordeal.

I HAVE already mentioned the *Nkalango* thickets or
groves, where the Anyanja bury their dead. I have
entered several of these, but saw no signs of recent use
—or anything to indicate the nature of the place
beyond a few broken pots—except in one case. This
was at Blantyre; it lay at some distance from the
main road, and, so far as I could see, no path led to it.
Seeing it in the distance one day, when I was out by
myself, and could discover nobody in sight whose
feelings might be hurt, I determined to visit it. I
only reached it after a struggle through burnt grass
(it was in September) which blacked me all over, and
a scramble across the dried-up bed of a stream. There
may have been a more convenient access, but I doubt
it, and fancy that a path would be cleared when
wanted. It is not the native custom to visit the graves
of dead friends, though, as we have seen, this does not
imply that they are forgotten; on the contrary, communications from them are expected and even hoped
for. But it is not at the grave they are sought; that
is an uncanny place, haunted by other presences than

that of the departed; and persons found there, or seen going thither, might expose themselves to serious suspicions.

The first thing I saw gave me something of a shock. It was an object wrapped in a reed mat, and slung from a pole, supported between two trees, the cords supporting it passed under the shoulders and knees, so that the latter were slightly flexed by the weight of the body, and allowed one just to perceive a human shape through the rigid outline of the *bango* mat. Looking round, I saw a number of graves—some fairly recent—but no other interment like the above. The mounds were not like ours, but nearly as broad as long, and looked more like rough garden-beds than anything else. On them were laid broken sifting-baskets, handles of hoes (or axes), and pots, these last with a hole in the bottom of each. Pots of all sorts and sizes were scattered all over the grove, some of them seemingly very old. There was nothing else to mark the older graves, which were now level with the surrounding soil. I noticed two or three shallow pits near the mounds; these were not half-completed graves (for the digging is not begun till the corpse is actually on the spot), but traps to catch the wizards, in case they should arrive with the views indicated in a former chapter.

There are two possible explanations of what I saw, neither of which I succeeded in obtaining at the time. One is that people dying of smallpox (and perhaps other infectious diseases) are not buried in the earth, but the corpse is 'hung up to let the disease fly away

with the wind, instead of keeping it about the place.'
The intention is thus excellent from a sanitary point
of view, if the result is unfortunately rather wide of
the mark. As it happened that the disease had just
about that time been brought down from the Lake by
some Atonga, and several people in the Blantyre
neighbourhood had died of it, this was probably the
reason in the above case. (*See note at end of chapter.*)

Some clans of the Atonga appear to have been in
the habit of burying their dead in trees, placing the
corpses in their mats on convenient forked branches;
and, as there were a good many Atonga temporarily
in the district, it is just possible that the man so buried
may have belonged to one of the clans in question;
though the grove was commonly known as 'the
Chipeta burying-ground,' and used, I believe, by
members of that tribe only—or at least by dwellers
in the villages called by their name. The Anyanja
and Yaos bury with the legs bent; the Atonga,
apparently, lay the body stretched at full length.

As soon as any one is known to be dead, the wail is
raised by the women about the hut. Sometimes
(among the Atonga) some of the nearest friends, when
the end is seen to be at hand, come out of the hut and
cry silently till told that all is over.

The 'first mourning' takes place inside the hut,
where the wife or mother holds up the dead in her
arms, or the body is laid across the knees of the
mourners as they sit on the ground. The wailing is
kept up till the 'undertakers' (*adsukulu,* or *awilo*)
enter to prepare the corpse for burial, when every one

else leaves the hut. These may or not be relatives—more usually they are not—but are thenceforth considered as connected with the family by a special tie. They close the eyes (a dead man who has no friends to do this for him is said 'to lie with glaring eyes'—*kutusuka maso*), wash the corpse, swathe it in calico, and lay it on a mat, which is then rolled round it and tied up with bark-string. When they have finished they wash their hands in 'medicine-water,' because they handled a corpse.

All this time 'the mourning at the door' is going on. It lasts two, three, or sometimes five days; in the case of a chief who is buried inside his hut, perhaps for weeks. In the hot climate of the Tonga country the burial is the same day, if the death takes place in the morning; but if not, it is felt to be more decent to wait till next day, so as to avoid all appearance of hurrying things over.

The spaces between the verandah-posts are filled in, so as to make small rooms, in which the family sleep till the mourning is over—sometimes on leaves spread on the ground instead of the usual mats. The women keep up the 'keening,' seated on the ground, or walk about, calling on the dead, ' Alas! alas! (*mai ine*), my father! Ah! Pembereka!'—or whatever the name may be. They put earth, ashes or flour, on their heads, tie bands of plaited grass or palm-fibre round their heads and arms (these are worn till they drop off), and let their hair grow; all ornaments are laid aside, and old, soiled clothes put on.

The death is reported to the village chief, while the

preparations for burial are begun, and at the same time messengers are sent to relatives at a distance, each of whom carries a present—perhaps a fowl or a hoe; the acceptance of this means that no suspicions of foul play are entertained. With the Atonga, a payment (sometimes quite a large one) is made, on their arrival, to those relations who come to the funeral; after they have received it, they go to view the body, and give permission for burial. If they do not consider the amount sufficient, the undertakers will not close the door of the hut (a sign that the preparations are complete) till more has been given.

During the mourning at the door, the drums are kept going day and night, to keep the witches from the body. The lamentations go on, interspersed with praises of the dead man—his greatness, his kindness, and generosity. 'That man gave us to eat,' they will say; 'we ate at his hands, he killed his fattest; were it riches, he was always giving; his mourning has gone forth far and wide; we feasted at his hands.' Guns are fired, where available, at frequent intervals, to let people at a distance know that there is mourning at the village.

When all is ready for the burial, the 'undertakers' fasten the body in its mat shroud to a long bamboo pole, and so carry it between them on their shoulders. The nearest relative does not as a rule go to the funeral, nor any one under age—i.e. who has not yet been to the mysteries; but there is a large following of other people. The men carry hoes and baskets for lifting out the earth; the women, who walk in the rear, carry the funeral offerings of porridge and beer. The site of the grave is marked out by the principal man present, and the body is laid aside under a tree while the digging goes on. When the grave is deep enough, stakes are driven in all round the sides, and two forked poles planted in the bottom, to receive the ends of the carrying-pole when the body is lowered into the grave, so that it is suspended without touching the ground. The space is covered in with cross bars on top before filling in the earth. These precautions are intended to prevent witches from getting at the dead, but are by no means universally observed. The Anyanja 'cover with a little earth, then tread it down, then pour in much and cover it up fully'; and the Atonga, after filling in the grave, break the pole in the middle, and plant one-half at the head, and the other at the foot.

The deceased's personal possessions are put into the grave with him before the earth is filled in. Ivory and beads, if buried with their late owner, are first ground to powder between stones, to make them useless to witches and perhaps to more prosaic resurrectionists, if any such can be found to brave the terrors of the place and the risks of prosecution. When all is finished, the women lay the offerings on the grave, also the deceased's water-jar, in which a hole is made, and gourd drinking-cup, which is broken. The 'undertakers' sometimes eat the offerings, but no one else touches them; it is believed that any one doing so would be seized with madness.

We have already seen that some Atonga clans suspend the corpse instead of burying it; others bury

in the usual way, except in the case of persons of high
rank, where they lay the body on the ground and erect
a fence round it, covering in the top with heavy logs.

Young children of a few days old are not formally
mourned for, and are buried by the women only.
People who die of the *mwavi* ordeal are not buried
at all; they are looked on as accursed and their bodies
thrown away into the bush to be eaten by hyenas.
This is also sometimes done with slaves. Men killed
in battle, if their friends can get possession of the
body at all, are not taken home, but buried on the
war-path.

Slaves used to be sacrificed at the death of a Yao
chief, but only in certain clans (the Abanda, Amilansi,
and perhaps others); ten for an important chief, or
fewer for one of less standing. The master's death
was kept secret for a time, till the required number
had been secured in slave-sticks. They were killed at
the grave-side and thrown in before the body was
lowered. Sometimes they were buried alive, and this
was done till recently by the Atonga, who, if one slave
was buried with a chief, made him lie in the grave,
clasping the dead man in his arms. If there were
several, they sat in the grave facing each other, and
the corpse was laid across their knees. If any of them
sneezed after taking his place in the grave, his life was
spared, as it was believed that the spirit thus signified
his refusal of that particular victim. Mr George Pirie
says of the Babemba, that the people so sacrificed died
willingly; and indeed slaves are often sufficiently
attached to their masters to make such devotion

possible. The funeral ceremonies of the Atonga include some interesting details not mentioned above; some of them may be Yao and Nyanja also, but I cannot find any record of them. I quote the account of the Rev. A. C. MacAlpine :—

'In taking the body out of the hut, exit was not made by the door, for by that the living only passed out, and they must not slight the dead by treating him as if he were still alive. So they broke down the back wall of the hut opposite the door, and through the hole so made passed out with the body. The children of the village had meanwhile been told to hide out of the way, although the children of the deceased were brought up to the bier and lifted over it by the *asukuru*.[1] Before they bore the corpse away, they swung it to and fro outside the hut, where it had passed out, chanting the while, "We are leaving to-day ; we follow our fellows." In front of the procession walked a man blowing a reed whistle, while other mourners followed the bier carrying weapons, utensils, trinkets, and offerings to be buried in the grave or laid on the top. Last of all went a woman with a hoe and a basket, into which she dropped various roots growing beside the path which the funeral had followed, and which she had dug up with the hoe. These were hurriedly prepared by her as a charm with which to purify the party on their return from the graves to the village.

'On arrival at the graveyard, the people begun to shout and clap their hands to warn the spirits supposed

---

[1] This is the same as the Nyanja word *adsukulu*.

to be about.' After the grave was dug and the body lowered into it, the chief undertaker (called *chimbwi*, or hyena, because he is not afraid to approach the dead), 'descended into the grave and untied the fastenings round the dead, exposing the face for a few minutes ; whatever had been brought to be buried along with the dead was arranged about the corpse according to custom, and finally arranging the grave-clothes and re-covering the face, the *chimbwi* climbed out again. The nearest relatives, one on each side of the grave, kneeling down and doing homage to the dead, pushed the first earth into the grave, using their elbows to do so. After a little, the whole company assisted in filling up the grave. . . . Prayers to the dead, conducted by the *chimbwi*, with responses from the other mourners, completed the obsequies at the grave, all the company having paid respect to the dead by falling from a sitting position on to their backs, clapping their hands.'

On their return from the grave, the whole party wash in 'medicine-water.' Sometimes, on the way back, they gather the leaves of a particular shrub, and prepare it for themselves ; but sometimes special men are called in from a distance to make the medicine. Atonga mourners go to bathe in a running stream before entering the village; after this, the *chimbwi* fetches a torch of grass pulled from the roof of the dead man's hut, lights it at the fire in the same hut, jumps over it himself, and then holds it a few inches from the ground for the whole party to jump over, one by one. As they do so, the woman who has gathered the roots rubs them on back and breast of each person; and they are then sufficiently purified to come home.

The Babemba seem to make some attempt at mummifying the corpses of their chiefs, by rubbing the body all over with boiled maize, repeating the process till the whole skin becomes dry and shrivelled.

The following is an account, by an eye-witness, of the funeral of the Angoni chief, Mombera, who died in 1891 :—

'Men were there from all parts of the tribe, sitting in the cattle-kraal—an immense enclosure open to the sky. Before the grave was dug, one of his brothers jumped up, and placing his hands behind his head, advanced towards the place of burial, mourning all the time and performing a sort of waltzing movement. All the men at the same moment jumped to their feet and stood mourning. After this subsided, the digging of the grave was proceeded with. It was not finished till next day. Meanwhile, companies of people were coming and going, and on entering the village, stood mourning and crying at the top of their voice, "*Baba be! Baba be!*" [1] Before the body was brought out, there was a curious procession of his wives on their hands and knees to the grave, decorated with great bunches of feathers that only the chief is allowed to wear. Soon after, the body was brought in, rolled in cloth, and deposited in the grave in a sitting posture with his face to the east. This was the signal for all jumping up, and closing round the grave in a big circle, and there mourning and rending the air with

[1] *Baba* = 'father.'

cries. Only men were allowed in the kraal at this
time. (The Zulus never allow women in the cattle-
kraal at any time.) They stood with their shields over
their heads, crying out. Afterwards the young men
came marching in in companies and stood mourning
for a little, then retired. Meanwhile they were
depositing in the grave along with him an immense
amount of calico, dresses, etc. — I dare say the
accumulation of years; cooking-pots, drinking-vessels,
mats, and pipes also went in. During this time, the
women were mourning in their own style and causing
a fearful din. They appeared as if bereft of their
senses, catching one another, and going through some
queer movements.'

Among the Anyanja of the Lake (at Likoma and
on the east side), the place of the sacred grove is taken
by something like a mausoleum. A small house is
built over the grave (instead of the grave being dug
within the house occupied when living), or it is
planted round with a hedge of euphorbia; these
fashions may perhaps have been borrowed from the
coast men. I have seen the grave of a Yao chief near
Domasi, covered with what looked like a flat slab
of concrete, but was probably an earthen mound
smoothly plastered over with mud. It was enclosed
in a high reed fence. The idea of this, too, was probably imported.

The subject of offerings to the spirit, which are
sometimes made at the grave, has been discussed in
a former chapter. As there stated, they are more
usually presented elsewhere, unless the deceased has

been buried inside his own house. But, though avoided by the relations, the grave is held sacred, and lawsuits may arise out of its desecration. One of the worst acts of sacrilege that can be committed—in fact, an act amounting to social suicide—is 'to break a pot at the grave of some family not your own . . . the offender's life is forfeited, and he lives only as the slave of the grave-owners till redeemed.'

The next step after the burial is to destroy the house occupied by the deceased. It is burned or pulled down, and the foundation dug over. The thatch and other things are carried away and burned at the cross-roads, and what is not burned is buried ; the site is swept all over, and fresh earth spread on it. Children are warned not to play there. 'A pot is put down to receive offerings of beer, and when any special offering is given to the deceased, it is usually presented here. If this place become too public (as when children play near and send dust into the pot), the pot will be removed and placed under a tree at a little distance from the village.'

If the man is buried in his own house, as is some-times done with chiefs, it is not taken down, but shut up and left to decay. A large part of the dead man's stock of calico is draped over the roof, and offerings are presented under the verandah. A local head-man named Matope died near Blantyre in 1893, and the white roof of his hut was a landmark visible for miles throughout the following year. In such cases, a hole is first dug in the floor, then a niche is made in the side of the hole. The position of this niche is carefully concealed from all except those immediately concerned, and no two graves of this kind have it in the same place.

On the day when the house is taken down, the mourners, in some cases, have their heads shaved, and some of the hair is buried on the site of the house. This is only where there are *two* shavings ; where there is only one, the hair is allowed to grow till the end of the mourning. It is thought that the hair which the deceased has seen must not remain after he is buried, or at any rate after the subsequent ceremonies are finished.

The mourning may last for two or even three months longer. Its duration is decided by the most influential relative. The survivors do not wash or oil themselves; in some cases they are forbidden to eat warm food, to use salt, or to drink beer. Yet beer is sometimes brewed during this period, to be drunk at the mourning dances which take place from time to time. The Atonga keep a fire burning all this time in front of the dead man's house (which seemingly they do not destroy), called the 'forbidden fire,' because it may not be used for any ordinary purposes. It has been kindled by the chief undertaker from the fire within the deceased's house, with a wisp of grass out of the roof—like the torch already mentioned. If a fire is wanted for cooking, a light must be fetched from one of the houses of the living. When the mourning is over, the first thing done is to brew a large quantity of beer, and, when that is ready, to kill fowls and cook porridge—in fact, to hold the funeral feast, which in other parts of the world takes place immediately after the burial. This is intended to convey that sorrow is not to last for ever; but the dead is not forgotten—on the contrary, he is especially remembered, and his spirit is supposed to share in the festivities. Regular drinking-songs are sung in chorus. The undertakers attend and superintend the shaving of the mourners' heads, taking off a little piece of hair in front and one behind for each person, and leaving the rest to be done by others. The hair is buried on the site of the house; the Atonga burn it in a fresh fire made by rubbing two sticks,[1] and the 'forbidden fire' is put out.

On the day of this shaving, what corresponds to the proving of the will is done—the deceased's affairs are settled, and his property, if any, handed over to his successor. With the succession to the chieftainship we shall deal in another chapter. A man's next heir is his eldest surviving brother, or failing brothers, his sister's son. We have already said that the dead man's wife or wives are inherited by his successors; but this requires some qualification. What really happens, among one section at least of the Anyanja, is this:—'The relations, after a decent interval' (it is the rule that, during the period of mourning, nothing must be said about the disposal of the property or re-marriage of the widows), 'take a corn-stalk, break it

---

[1] This is not usually done except on ceremonial occasions, or in case of great need, when fire can be procured in no other way. A fire is kept up through the night, and there are sure to be at least some embers in the morning, which can be blown into flame; or, if it should have gone out in one hut, they can nearly always fetch fire from another.

into as many pieces as there are eligible men in the family, and send them to the woman by the hand of the chief of the bearers[1] (who are chosen from outside the family). She may take one up from the ground and show it, saying, ' I want so and so.' The man so named becomes the heir. If the woman refuses all the men, she will have to repay the original marriage gifts which her husband made to her family, and often much more. If the man chosen refuses the woman, he sends her an arrow or a fowl, or some other small present, but usually an arrow, and tells her to marry some other man. If so, he gets no marriage gifts returned to him.'

Some of a man's property is, as we have seen, buried with him. Out of the rest, his successor has to pay the funeral expenses, including heavy fees to the undertakers, who, besides, have partaken of the offerings and the funeral feast. There may also be a prosecution for witchcraft to be paid for out of the estate, though this may be compensated by damages. If, however, the deceased had himself been prosecuted and had died of the ordeal, his heir has to pay damages to the bewitched person or his representatives.

There are certain well-understood causes of death which are not supposed to require any investigation, though, according to some, every death is put down to witchcraft. The witch is believed to kill a person, and then, when his relations have buried him, to send out messengers to find out where the grave is. When they come back, they tell their master that they have seen

---

[1] The 'undertakers,' or *adsukulu.*

the meat (the 'game'—*i.e.* the corpse), and say, 'Come along.' Then the owl 'which sits on the head of the chief' goes out and summons all the witches to the feast. The animals lead the way to the grave, a fire is made, and the chief asks who it was that killed the person they are about to eat. One answers, 'It was I,' and the chief tells him to 'bring the meat out.' 'So the man who killed him sounds a rattle and calls him by his early name'—the name he bore before he attended the mysteries, which has a compelling power over him — and he comes out. The wizard then reproaches him for real or imaginary insults and injuries—possibly there are unhealthy-minded persons who will brood for years over fancied wrongs, and when the man they are nursing a grudge against dies, imagine that they have killed him—and finally kills him over again. 'Then they take the meat and divide it, and take it with them to their village; the *mfiti* cooks it at night and eats it, and takes a pot and digs to conceal it in the deserted house of the deceased, and leaves and goes to his own house as if nothing had happened.'

If all the energy expended to prevent these proceedings counts for anything, it may well be believed that they never happen at all. When the circumstances of a death seem to warrant suspicion, the witch-detective, whose methods are described elsewhere, is sometimes called in, and the people pointed out by her are either killed at once or compelled to drink *mwavi*. But the ordeal is sometimes put in operation without resorting to her. Persons who feel themselves under suspicion may demand it in order to clear their character. So firmly do they believe that it will not hurt them if innocent, that no one, unless conscious of guilt, ever seems to shrink from the trial.

The Yaos hold that it should not be administered to a free person without grave cause—*i.e.* unless suspicion is definitely directed to some one person. The Angoni and Makololo chiefs, whose government (at least as regards the subject tribes) was more despotic, used to order wholesale *mwavi*-drinkings, trying a whole village or district to discover the supposed culprit. In these cases, the poison was often taken by proxy and given to fowls or dogs—each animal being tied by a string to the person whom it represented, and whose guilt or innocence was decided by its death or recovery. There was a *cause célèbre* of this kind at Chekusi's kraal, about twenty years ago. Chekusi's mother had been suffering from rheumatism, and had been treated for it by Dr. Henry, of the Livingstonia Mission. Shortly afterwards, unfortunately, she committed suicide in a fit of depression, and, naturally, things looked very black for the doctor. However, there were two other possible culprits, and a trial took place with three sets of fowls, one for the Europeans at Livlezi Mission, one, I think, for Mponda, with whom Chekusi was then more or less at war, and the third for the other suspected party. The proceedings were complicated by the number of victims demanded by the importance of the occasion: had one been allotted to each defendant, the decision would have been quite clear; as it was, some of each

set died and some recovered, and the issue was such
hopeless confusion that the case was dropped without
arriving at a verdict.

The poison used throughout the Shiré Highlands, on
the Lake, and by the Angoni appears to be the same;
it is the pounded bark of a tree known to science as
Erythrophleum guineense. Its effect is fatal within an
hour or two, unless it causes sickness; this symptom is
therefore held to be a sign of innocence. Its different
action on different people probably arises from the
strength of the dose being varied by accident or design.

When a trial of this sort is decided on, the *mapondera*,
or 'pounder,' is sent for. He prepares the poison in
the *bwalo*, before the assembled people, by pounding
the bark, steeped in water, in a small wooden mortar,
with a pestle which has a cover fixed round it to
prevent the liquid splashing out. The result is a red
infusion, said by those who have been fortunate enough
to taste it and recover, to be very bitter. This information I had from a man who complained that he
was not well, and to whom, finding that he seemed
to have feverish symptoms, I offered a dose of quinine.
After tasting it—and retiring out of sight to reject it
with decency—he declined any more, on the ground
that it was exactly like the *mwavi* he had been
compelled to drink a month ago. The usual dose is
about half a pint; the accused come up one by one
to drink, and then sit down on the ground to wait
till it takes effect. This, as stated, is usually within
an hour or two. In cases where public feeling is
very strong against the accused, the end is not always

waited for, but he or she is lynched as soon as the symptoms seem likely to be fatal.

It is said that the accused has a voice in the selection of the professional who is to mix the draught; but most natives believe so firmly in the infallibility of the *mwavi*-test, that in practice it matters little to them who compounds it. Of course, the *mapondera* has opportunities of diluting the dose, as his own inclinations or hints previously received from interested parties may prompt; and this is probably the reason why the greater number of those who submit to the test usually escape. I remember an occasion when several families escaping from the war which was going on between Chekusi's men and Bazale, near Lake Malombe, halted at a village near Ntumbi, where a child belonging to one of them died. They accused the people of the place of bewitching them, and called on them to drink *mwavi*, which was immediately done. One child of the village died; it is likely that it succumbed to a dose which was not strong enough to kill the adults. But the matter did not end here. The people who had demanded the ordeal were subjects of Chekusi's brother Mandala, who was also the over-lord of certain kraals in the neighbourhood, while the villagers who had drunk the poison were under the immediate jurisdiction of Chekusi himself. The latter thought that his rights had been infringed, and insisted that some of his brother's subjects should take *mwavi* in their turn. I do not know how many did so this time, but the number of deaths was two.

Two other cases came to my personal knowledge—

one a wholesale affair of the kind already referred to. Chekusi had been ill; and Mandala (apparently just then on exceptionally good terms with him) sent for a number of people to the royal kraal, and administered the ordeal to find out who had bewitched him. Among those who went from Ntumbi were two old men mentioned in a previous chapter—Pembereka and Kaboa. The former died—Kaboa either recovered or he did not drink the poison, which, however, is unusual, and, I fancy, unprecedented; and, if I understood him rightly, it is surprising that he should have been allowed to depart without further trouble. What he said to me was, 'I refused' (*ndakana*), which might, however, conceivably mean that his system had rejected the drug. The mourning for poor old Pembereka continued at his kraal for two or three days, and subsequently his family went up to Chekusi's to finish the mourning there and (we were told) to drink *mwavi*, but on what grounds I never made out: in any case there was no further fatality. As we have already seen, those who die by *mwavi* are not usually buried, but cast out to be eaten by wild beasts; we gathered from rumours which reached us that this was not done in Pembereka's case, but that he was buried at Chekusi's.

The other case was a local one: a young girl died suddenly — possibly of pneumonia or rapid consumption; she was delicate, but seemed in fairly good health when we last saw her, about three months before her death. Her father, the Ntumbi head-man, made a number of people drink *mwavi*, and one young

man died—*chifukwa wodiera antu*, as my informant
said—'because he was an eater of men.' It is possible,
however, that there might have been more deaths in
this case but for the action of an English planter who
heard of the matter in time and came to the rescue
with ipecacuanha.

A case which all the older residents in British
Central Africa will remember took place at Blantyre.
Mr. John Moir, at that time manager of the African
Lakes Company, got wind of the trial and arrived on
the scene when matters were already so far advanced
that it seemed best to act first and explain afterwards.
Accordingly, he began by kicking over the doctor's
mortar, and then set forth his views on the subject.
He succeeded in getting the proceedings quashed, but
—and this is the interesting feature in the story—the
rescued victim considered himself ever afterwards to
have a standing grievance against Mr. Moir. He was
a local head-man of some standing, and complained
that, as he had not been allowed the opportunity of
clearing his character, he was under a cloud and likely
to remain so for the rest of his life. His people were
leaving him and settling elsewhere—no one cared to
be associated with a person of such doubtful reputation
—in short, he was a ruined man!

The administration of the ordeal-poison is a very
solemn ceremony; commonly, as we have seen, it
takes place in the *bwalo*, or village forum, but Livingstone speaks of some Batoka head-men making a
pilgrimage to the graves of their ancestors for the
purpose.

'The ordeal by the poison of the muave is resorted to by the Batoka as well as by the other tribes; but a cock is often made to stand proxy for the supposed witch. Near the confluence of the Kafue the Mambo, or chief, with some of his head-men, came to our sleeping-place with a present; their foreheads were smeared with white flour, and an unusual seriousness marked their demeanour. Shortly before our arrival they had been accused of witchcraft; conscious of innocence, they accepted the ordeal. For this purpose they made a journey to the sacred hill of Nchomokela, on which repose the bodies of their ancestors; and after a solemn appeal to the unseen spirits to attest the innocence of their children, they swallowed the muave, vomited, and were therefore declared not guilty.'[1]

NOTE.—The Rev. H. Rowley says that the Mang'anja distinguished between deaths brought about by Mpambe (*i.e.* those resulting from old age or 'the ordinary diseases of the country'), and those caused by the *mfiti*. The former were buried; the latter, as being accursed, rolled in mats and hung up in trees. One cannot help suspecting some confusion here—more especially as violent deaths are reckoned as the work of the *mfiti*,—a word which this writer translates by 'evil spirit'—thus introducing another element of misconception. Dr. Hetherwick, in a communication received since this chapter has been in type, says: 'The Yaos lay their dead with their faces to the east. and with the knees bent to the chin. This is the invariable rule, and so the niche which they make in the side of the grave to receive the corpse is dug out on the *west* side of the pit. The turning of the face to the east is interesting. At old Kapeni's funeral one of his men went into the grave after the body was laid in its place, and fired an arrow up into the air. I have never found any explanation of this rite. It is not done on any other occasion that I have note of.'

---

[1] The *mapondera* is paid for his services after the conclusion of the trial, and those who recover, and so turn out to have been falsely accused, are entitled to liberal compensation. This has to be paid by the heir.

CHAPTER VIII

ARTS, INDUSTRIES, ETC.

Agriculture: Maize, tobacco, gardens, etc. Hunting, trapping. Ant-catching. Fishing. Weaving. Basket-making. Bark cloth. Ironwork. Wood - carving. Pottery. Salt.

THE principal crops cultivated in British Central Africa are maize, millet (of several kinds), rice, ground - nuts, beans, sweet potatoes, cassava, yams, pumpkins, several kinds of gourds, and tobacco. Bananas are planted near most villages in the Shiré Highlands, and are the staple crop of the Wan-konde ; they are less common west of the Upper Shiré. Cotton and sugar-cane are grown in some places; also the saccharine sorghum (the *imfe* of the Zulus); but no sugar is made—both kinds of cane are only used for chewing. Sesamum (*chitowe*) is grown in order to extract the oil from the seeds, and *chamba* (Indian hemp) for smoking. In villages near Blantyre, a few papaw-trees, pine-apples, and grenadillas are grown ; but most of the fruits eaten by natives are wild ones.

A certain number of plants are utilised which grow with little or no cultivation. Most villages are surrounded by castor-oil bushes; tomatoes (and, where they have been introduced, Cape gooseberries) grow like weeds among the other crops; so does a tiny kind of grain (*Eleusine*, I believe), like small bird-seed, which is called *maere*, and is so troublesome to husk and prepare, besides not being very palatable, that it is not gathered except in times of scarcity. Various plants which grow wild, or spring up like weeds in the gardens, are eaten as vegetables in time of scarcity; the commonest is a kind of Prince of Wales's feathers (*Amaranthus caudatus*), which when boiled is not unlike spinach.

Maize was probably introduced into Africa by the Portuguese, three hundred years ago. The Anyanja would seem to have obtained it from the Yaos, and the Yaos from the coast, if we may judge from the etymology of the name—in both languages, *chimanga*; Manga being the name for the coast. Nearly all Bantu languages have distinct words for it, showing, either that they did not derive it from each other, or that the name did not travel with the thing.

Sweet potatoes, tobacco, beans, and some of the minor crops are grown in, or close to, the villages, in among the huts of the more scattered ones, or outside the reed fences of the kraal enclosures. The tubers of the sweet potato are planted in flat mounds, about six feet by four or five, and the convolvulus-like stems and leaves trail over the ground. Cassava is sometimes planted close to the villages, sometimes in the regular gardens; it is grown from cuttings; a piece of the stem about a foot long, and cut off sloping at each end, is stuck into the ground and

M

grows into a handsome shrub about six feet high, with light green, palmate leaves. These are used as a vegetable, being boiled like spinach. This plant is supposed to have been introduced by the Portuguese; a great number of varieties are culti- vated; that usually seen is the sweet kind, which requires no special preparation, and can be eaten raw. Some of the others are buried for some time before being taken up, then steeped in water to get rid of the poisonous juice, and allowed to dry before being pounded.

Of beans there are endless varieties; one kind, often grown close to villages, is a small shrub with yellow flowers; these beans are gathered and eaten green.

Tobacco is grown both for home consumption and for sale. A good deal of attention is paid to the plants, the leaf-buds being pinched out to make the rest of the leaves grow larger. When ready, they are gathered, soaked in water till they turn brown, and spread in the sun to dry. The Yaos plait them into twists ; the Shiré Anyanja pound them with water, and make them up into balls; the Chipetas and Angoni make theirs into pyramids. Tobacco is used for smoking, but more frequently in the form of snuff. To make this, the leaves are dried by the fire in a potsherd, and then ground on stones. When tobacco is chewed, it is mixed with lime got by burn- ing snail-shells. Smoking is not a continuous pro- cess as with Europeans, but a large pipe is passed round, and each man takes a pull or two at it. This is the usual method of refreshment, when halting

GRINDING SNUFF

for a short time on a journey. Men will also smoke the intoxicating hemp (*chamba* or *dakha*), which they say is 'instead of food and drink' to them when they are tired, though they likewise admit that it 'catches their legs.' The plant grows about the villages without any special cultivation. Its use seems to be older than that of tobacco; it was smoked by the Bushmen before the Bantu penetrated into South Africa.

The gardens proper may be a short distance from the villages, or they may be three or four miles away. The people begin by hoeing the land close to their dwellings; when the soil is exhausted, they move farther out, and so on, from year to year. When the gardens come to be inconveniently far away, the village is moved ; and thus the population is continually shifting from place to place, and one sometimes finds sites of old gardens in what one had thought was untouched bush.

When a man has selected a site for a new garden, he marks the place, and bespeaks, or as the natives say, 'betroths' the ground, by tying some bunches of grass into knots, or, if there are trees on the spot, twisting some grass round their trunks. He is perfectly free to choose, so long as the land is not in cultivation, or has not been bespoken by some one else ; and, once marked, no one can interfere with it. The grass is then burnt off at the end of the dry season, and with the rains, in November, or the early part of December, the hoeing begins.

Where there are bits of alluvial soil close to a watercourse, which are either kept moist by the stream or can be easily irrigated, maize is sown during the dry season, so as to be gathered green early in the year when no other is to be had.

Some people break up the ground for their gardens during the winter or dry season, but the earth is then very hard, and most consider that it is no use doing so till after the rains have begun. If the garden is a new one, the ashes of the burnt grass (or the grass itself, if any has sprung up before the hoeing begins) are hoed into the soil for manure; if maize was grown in it the previous year, the dry stalks are carefully burnt for the same purpose.

The universal agricultural implement is the hoe, which, in this part of Africa, has a short handle, so that the person wielding it has to stoop, but also gains much more power for the stroke than one has with a long handle. The blade is leaf-shaped, rounded to a blunt point in front, and tapering to a spike at the back, which is driven into the handle, and, if it projects at the back, hammered down. The blade was formerly made by native blacksmiths, but is now generally bought at a trader's store and fixed into a handle by the purchaser, who chooses a stout piece of wood with a knob at the end— either a root of a tree, or a strong branch with a piece of the fork it springs from. Wooden hoes are still used in some remote places among the hills. They have very long, rather narrow blades, set into the handle at an acuter angle than the usual iron hoe, but, like it, suggesting the origin of the implement from the primitive forked branch with one of its

WOMEN WEEDING MAIZE-GARDEN

Note the pumpkins between the rows of maize

To face p. 181

ends cut short. Where hoes are unattainable, as in the case of refugees cultivating 'scratch' gardens in the bush in time of war, a still older instrument is used — the sharp-pointed digging-stick of bamboo. There are stories which seem to point to a time when this was in general use, and speak of the introduction of hoes.

Maize is sown in rows about six feet apart, the soil being gathered into heaps, and three or four grains sown on the top of each. I have seen a man and his wife doing this together, one making the holes with a pointed stick, while the other dropped the grains in. Pumpkins and gourds are sown on the same heaps with the maize, and spread out between the rows. The garden is then left alone unless the growing maize-plants require earthing up a little from time to time, till the rains are over, when it is time for the 'second hoeing,' to get rid of the weeds which have sprung up. 'The time of hunger' comes after the rains, when the last year's corn is eaten, and the new is not yet ripe—about March. This is not altogether due to improvidence, as some would have it, but partly to the difficulty of storing large quantities of provisions. The *nkokwes* hold just about enough for the year, and even so are tithed by rats and weevils which cannot be kept out ; and the insect-proof accommodation in the smoke of the *nsanja* does not suffice for much more than next year's seed-corn. Besides this, large accumulations, in a country likely at any time to be ravaged by war, are scarcely a sign of prudence, but rather the reverse.

It is at this hungry time that the pumpkins and gourds come in, and the first ears of green maize from the *dimba* patches of rich, damp soil by the stream-sides are eagerly looked for. Several sorts of cucumbers and marrows are cultivated, and some grow wild, or half wild ; one small round gourd is a really delicious vegetable, almost equal to our custard-marrows. But these are not always sufficient, or there may be an interval before they are ready, and the women ransack the country-side for wild herbs and roots which are not used except as a last resort, while the young people bring home all sorts of strange tit-bits in the shape of grasshoppers, caterpillars, beetles, and grubs. Between the scarcity and the green food, this is usually a season of sickness.

The maize grows to a great height in rich, alluvial soil like that of the Ntumbi plain, and the *mapira* is even taller. This is a different variety from the *amabele* of Natal, with its stiff, brush-like heads, generally standing about four feet; the ear of the *mapira* being a graceful, drooping plume. It is sown about the same time as the maize, but thinned out and transplanted in January. The weeding in both cases has to be kept up from time to time till the corn is ripe.

We have already mentioned how the crops are guarded by 'medicine'—a bundle of leaves, a snail-shell, a little horn on the top of an upright stick, or various other objects. While the corn is ripening, there are other dangers to be averted by less esoteric means. In most gardens, especially if at any distance from the village, and if there are any patches of brush within easy reach, you may see a platform mounted on poles, with a little hut or shelter on it. Here watchers are stationed day and night to drive away marauders—the baboons who come in troops, and the wild pigs, who are still more destructive, rooting up as well as gathering. In March one heard a continual drumming on whatever metal objects were available, to drive away the pigs; I think this was done in the villages as well as by the men in the watch-huts. One of the few offences for which boys are likely to get a really severe beating is letting the baboons get into the maize. The hippopotamus is very fond of maize, and gardens within reach of his haunts are protected by a reed fence—he is so wary that he will not go near what he thinks may be a trap—though he could tread it down in a moment. The women also frighten him off by making little sham traps out of the huge sausage-like fruits of the *mvunguti* tree.

Maize and mapira are ripe in May; the former is broken off by hand, and the cobs put into *mtanga* baskets; there is a special term for the operation of inserting them point downward so as to make the basket hold as many as possible. It is dried on the *nsanja*, over the household fire, before being put into the *nkokwe*. The mapira is cut with a large knife or a reaping-hook. These small sickles are much used for cutting grass; but I am not sure whether they are of recent European introduction or not; a straight knife is also used.

Beans and ground-nuts, with the *nsama*, which is very like a ground-nut and grows in the same way, the seed-vessel burying itself in the earth after flowering, are planted in patches by themselves beside the maize-garden.   These are boiled and eaten, green or ripe, and the ground-nuts are also used for oil.   They are pounded, boiled, and the oil skimmed from the top of the water.   Castor-oil is procured in the same way ; it is not used as medicine, but only for anointing the head and body.

Hoeing and weeding are sometimes got through more quickly, when time is pressing (as when the first rains have fallen) by means of a 'bee.'   The owner invites all his neighbours, men and women, and prepares large quantities of beer, with which they regale themselves after a hard morning's work.   Sometimes the pots are carried out to the garden, and the party consume the refreshment there.   Each person has a certain piece of ground allotted to him or her—a 'row to hoe,' and the work is got through with singing and mirth.   When the chief sends for a number of villagers to hoe his gardens, he entertains them royally with meat and beer.

After the harvest is gathered in comes the *mpakasa* season, which might be rendered 'autumn'; the deciduous trees lose their leaves; the grass is dry and ready for burning, and, as the people say, 'the wind blows and says *pi!*'   After this comes the real winter (*malimwe*), when people walk abroad and sit and drink beer, saying, ' At present there is no hoeing to do, only odds and ends of work about

WOMEN CARRYING BASKETS OF MAIZE

To face p. 185

the house'—though, even then, 'some break up the new hoeing-ground.' Then comes the time of the grass and bush-fires, when the air is full of flying soot, and then the *kokalupsya*—the driving rain which sweeps away the burnt grass — and then the last interval of waiting, when the new leaves show themselves in vivid green, red, and yellow, the thorn-trees burst into golden bloom and 'Mpambe thunders' in distant mutterings along the horizon.

The soil is exhausted by maize in two years, or three at the most; after that new ground is broken up, and the old is planted with beans and other less important crops for another year or two. This seems to have gone on for centuries, the forest closing up again over the deserted gardens, as if they had never been; it is this repeated cutting down, together with the bush-fires, which has changed so much of the primeval forest into straggling scrub.

HUNTING

None of the tribes of British Central Africa can be said to live by hunting, or even to make it one of their principal occupations. The nearest approach to a hunting tribe are the Apodzo, or Akombwi, of the Lower Zambezi, who are professional hippopotamus-hunters, and are sometimes spoken of as a clan, but as they speak a language of their own, they should perhaps be reckoned as a separate people.

Forty-five years ago, game seems to have been

scarce in the Shiré Highlands proper, though abundant near the Lake and west of the Shiré. The subsequent wars and famine allowed it to increase again ; and of late years some of the protected kinds have actually come back to their old haunts. The native who wishes to hunt now has to take out a gun-licence, and can no longer dig pitfalls for elephants, or set snares for buck, as he did in the old days.

No close time was recognised, but nature took care of that, for it is impossible to see or pursue animals through the thick grass of the spring and summer. Where game was at all abundant, hunting parties were organised : a long line of men would advance in a semicircle on the patch of grass or bush to be surrounded. The leader, who carried the ' medicines ' for luck, was in the middle, and with those on either side of him would wait till the ends of the two ' wings ' had met on the other side. When the circle was complete, the signal was given by whistling, and the hunters advanced all at once. These men would probably be armed with spears; perhaps a few of them with guns. The Chipetas and Mang'anja shoot a great deal with bows ; they do not seem to be first-class marksmen, though I have heard that some of the boys from the Katunga's district were very expert in bringing down birds flying. The only archer whose exploits I ever had the opportunity of witnessing seemed unable to hit a bird which I suppose to have been a white heron at a moderate distance. But it may have been an unlucky day

BOY WITH BOW

with him.   The bow was used as a weapon of war (with or without poisoned arrows) before the Angoni introduced the shield and stabbing spear. War arrows are a yard long and tipped with iron ; blunt cane or wooden arrows are used for shooting birds.   The iron arrow-heads are of a great many different patterns ; some are smooth, others have as many as half a dozen barbs below the point.

Many natives now have guns, usually flint-locks, which have come into the country through the Portuguese trade.   I remember examining one of these guns belonging to a Ntumbi villager ; it was immensely long in the barrel and had ' Tower ' and ' G.R.' engraved on the lock.   They imply the elsewhere obsolete powder-horn, which one sometimes sees very neatly carved, and where a more advanced stage of weapon has been reached, the percussion-caps are carried in the hollowed head of a club made of some hard wood, which receptacle has an opening fitted with a lid or stopper on one side, and a small hole at the top through which they can be shaken out one by one.

The Yaos observe a certain amount of ritual before starting on a hunting expedition, or, in fact, any journey ; this is fully detailed in *Africana*. The man intending to set out goes to his chief, who consults the oracle of the *ufa* cone on his behalf, and tells him to defer the journey, if the answer is unfavourable.   Dreams are also, as already stated, much relied on in deciding matters of this sort, and unfavourable omens, such as kicking against a stump,

or meeting a snake, may send the party back even
after it has started. If all is well, however, the chief
gives the applicant a talisman to keep him safe—
either a thread to be tied round his head or arm, or
a small vessel of oil to be carried with him. While
he is absent, his wife must not bathe, nor anoint
herself with oil, nor even wash her face, and if she
has a dream during this period, must be very careful about presenting an offering to the spirits.

The Angoni sometimes hunt with dogs—a better
class of animals than the miserable, yelping mongrels
which infest the villages. A boy who sold me a
pair of tusks of the bush pig (*Potamochoerus*, a smaller
and lighter animal than the European wild boar)
told me with great pride that the *nguluwe* had been
killed by his dog. This same dog, if I remember
rightly, once attended school with his master — I
suppose to keep him out of harm's way, as an impi
of the Machinga was supposed to be on the war-
path. He was black, about the size of a small
setter, with longer and rougher hair than most of the
village dogs (which look like remote and degenerate
descendants of fox-terriers, and are white or yellow,
or both mixed), and in shape he was more like an
Eskimo dog than anything else I can think of. He
had on a hide collar, and was led by a string, and
altogether seemed valued and well treated. Some
young men in one of these same villages told me
that they hunted elephants with dogs 'in Chekusi's
country,' and usually lost a great many. Men carry
whistles, made of a small buck's horn, to call dogs with.

Traps for game are of many kinds and varying
degrees of ingenuity. For large animals, such as the
elephant, hippo, or buffalo, there is the pitfall, dug
with sloping sides, and sometimes planted with sharp
stakes at the bottom, which is such a frequent cause of
accident to unwary travellers. It is covered over with
reeds and the ground made to look as natural as possible. Old disused pits are no less dangerous, because
the grass and shrubs grow over them and hide them from
view. They are dug right in the track of the animal in
a place where it is found to pass often—as in going
down to a stream to drink. In former times, fences
(sometimes extending over miles of country) were
made to guide buck into these pits.

Another trap for lions or leopards is made by erect-
ing two parallel fences of stout stakes. A heavy log is
supported at the further end between the fences and
the bait placed beneath it, so that it cannot be seized
without pushing aside the slight support; the animal
is then killed by the falling log. Smaller traps are set
for the different kinds of wild cat, and baited with
mice. Another trap often set for hippos or elephants
is a heavy log hung vertically above the pathway, with
a poisoned spear fixed in its lower end; the animal
treads on a catch which releases the string holding the
weighted spear. The poison for spears and arrows is
in most cases strophanthus.

Going along one of the paths leading through the
bush, one sometimes notices a curious little arrangement of sticks and string, like a narrow gate, about
eighteen inches high. This is a *msampa* trap, designed

to catch a buck by the leg, or smaller animals, which run close to the ground, by the neck. A cord with a running noose at one end is made fast by the other to the top of a springy sapling, which is bent down and kept in position by an easily released catch; the noose is then stretched open between the upright sticks, but so as to slip off easily as soon as the animal treads on the catch, when the sapling flies up and immediately tightens the cord.

Several kinds of smaller traps are set for field-rats and mice; one is a long narrow funnel, woven of slips of bamboo, with the ends pointing inwards at the mouth, so that a rat can get in but not out again; the stretching of the slips narrows the entrance, and there is no room to turn round. Some of these traps are woven of *mapira* stalks or palm fibre. It might be supposed that any mouse could easily gnaw its way out; but the trap is not set and left; it is placed in the creatures' run, and the grass is beaten to drive them into it, when they are at once taken out and despatched. Sometimes the animal is driven into a trap like this by a dog.

Another mouse-trap is made of a hollowed pumpkin, or the fruit of the *kigelia* (*mvunguti*) tree, which looks like a huge woody cucumber. It is baited with roasted maize or ground-nuts, and has a noose at the opening kept stretched by a bent stick, much on the same principle as the *msampa*.

The Apodzo, already mentioned, hunt the hippopotamus from canoes. Three go out at a time, with two men in each—one to paddle, and one to throw the harpoon. This consists of a strong barbed head, loosely inserted into a wooden handle to which it is attached by a stout cord, wound closely round the whole length, and uncoiling when the weapon is thrown; so that, when the wounded brute dives, the wood floats and shows his whereabouts. When he has been struck three times, the ropes are gathered up and twisted together, being then strong enough to hold him, and slowly hauled in till he can be despatched with spears.

Although not to be reckoned as hunting, the capture of wild honey, and of swarming white ants (neither an unimportant item in the native larder), may be mentioned here. The wild bees (some kinds of which, but not all, are stingless) make their nests in hollow trees, which are frequently pointed out to passing hunters or travellers by the small bird known as the honey-guide. They make a fire, cut a hole in the tree large enough to pass the arm through, smoke the bees out with lighted wisps of grass, and carry away the honeycombs in pieces of bark. The River people hang hives on trees—small cylindrical boxes made of bark, in which the bees build,—and remove them when full.

White ants, when they swarm, are fat yellow insects, an inch or more in length, which fill the European with unconquerable loathing, when they make a sudden irruption into the house, blunder into the lamps, crack the glasses, and get down the back of your neck in the dark. It is the small and much more insignificant workers who do the damage in houses, eating woodwork and plastering walls with their galleries; but they do not excite the same antipathy. The native, however, regards the *inswa* in a very different light ; in fact, one of the Blantyre catechists has been known to use them with great effect in a sermon, as a simile for the delights of this world! Sometimes a large ant-heap is found close to or actually among the huts of a village ; it never struck me at the time to ask whether this was accidental, or whether the responsible person had purposely located his abode close to this desirable game preserve. Passing by such a place one day soon after the rains had begun, I found two or three youths busy catching termites. They had dug in the heap a short trench, which, as they had roofed it over with grass, looked for all the world like a grave; and into this the swarming insects collected. At one end was a round opening with a cover, which was lifted off from time to time, and the *inswa* taken out by handfuls. They are roasted over the fire in an earthen pot, 'like coffee,' said my informant.

FISHING

Fish are caught with rod and line, nets, traps, and weirs, and sometimes speared. There are two kinds of fish-spear—the *momba*, with a straight point for striking the fish, and the barbed *chikolongwe*, or gaff, for hooking it out. Weirs are usually made at the mouth of a stream ; a fence is built right across with only one opening left in it, and behind it is placed a large *mono*, or basket-trap, constructed on the principle of a lobster-pot, and perhaps five feet long. The weir in the illustration is at Ngofi, on the eastern side of Lake Nyasa.

Smaller traps of the same kind are sunk in the water, like lobster-pots. Nets are sometimes set overnight and anchored with a couple of stones, the upper edge being kept on the top of the water by a line of floats. Other nets are cast from canoes; sometimes they are hauled in and the fish scooped on board with the canoe-balers, sometimes the ropes are taken on shore and the net hauled up on the beach like our seines. This is done with the largest kind of net, requiring twenty men to handle it. Another is chiefly used at night: the net is lowered between two canoes, while a third is paddled towards it with a lighted torch on board to attract the fish. The men alternately show the torch and knock loudly on the sides of the canoe, which seems to daze the fish and drive them towards the net. Hand-nets are also used, like shrimping-nets, with handles working over each other scissor-wise, but kept in place by a cross-bar which is not in the European implement. Nets are generally made of the *Bwazi* fibre. Net-making and canoe-patching are (or were) the two great industries of Likoma island; and the whole lakeside population is more or less engaged in fishing.

Fishing with rod and line may often be seen on the Shiré, where, in some places, small platforms are built out from the bank, so that the angler can cast his hook in deep water and free of reeds or bushes. The hook is large, not barbed, but bent in towards the shank, to make it more difficult to slip off; it is made

N

of iron wire and sharpened on a stone. The bait is usually maize-paste. After throwing the line, the angler strikes the top of the water sharply a few times with his rod, to agitate it, and call the attention of the fish. Poison is sometimes put into a pool to stupefy the fish, when they come to the surface and can be gathered out of the water by hand; a species of euphorbia, and a large shrub (*ombwe*) with bean-like pods and white blossoms, are used for this purpose, and can often be seen growing in the villages.

CANOE-MAKING

Canoes are made wherever there are trees of sufficient size growing where they can be brought down to the water without too much difficulty. 'The tree,' however, 'may be chosen far up on the hills, in which case it is drawn down by great numbers of men with ropes of thick creepers. A great thickness of bottom is left for the purpose, and rollers of bamboo or stick are spread across the path to facilitate the dragging.' The commonest form of canoe is the 'dug-out,' made from a single log of *mbawa* or some other hard wood, but there are some made of a large sheet of bark sewn at the ends. Hewing out a canoe with axe and adze is slow work, and it is no wonder that it is considered matter for rejoicing and brewing of beer when finished.

If the vessel is for the chief's own use, he often attends, to see how it is progressing and cheer up his men with libations of *moa*. There is not much variety in the shape; but some have incurved gunwales like

CANOES AT LIWONDE'S (UPPER SHIRÉ)

those in the illustration, some straight. The paddles
are short, with oblong blades, about the size and shape
of an ordinary spade. In low water, the canoe is pro-
pelled with punting-poles, which are always necessary
because the level of the river changes very quickly and
sand-banks shift their places from season to season.
Canoes are kept at the regular crossing-places of rivers
by men who will ferry passengers over for a consideration. When not in use, the paddles and poles are
carefully hidden, to prevent the canoe being summarily
'borrowed.' The largest canoes are, perhaps, thirty
or forty feet long, and have ten or twelve paddlers,
who work sitting, and sing in time to their strokes.

WEAVING

We have already said that spinning, weaving, and
sewing are considered emphatically men's work, as
they were by the ancient Egyptians. The material
spun is most frequently cotton, though, in the Chipeta
country, south-west of the Lake, the fibre of the *bwasi*
(*Securidaca longipedunculata*) is more in use. This
fibre is very strong, and is used for fishing-nets; but
native cloth, whether cotton or *bwasi*, is not often seen
now, since European material (very inferior to it in
quality) has been easier to obtain. The spinning-
wheel is unknown, and the process of twisting the
thread by hand and then spinning it on the *njinga*, a
wooden spindle with a whorl or reel of tortoise-shell
(or hard wood), is a very leisurely one. Three or four
bobbins full of thread are used to 'set' the loom,

which consists of four posts driven into the ground and connected by cross-bars. It is set up in the open space near the owner's hut, or perhaps in the *bwalo*. The web is never very large; two yards long by a yard in width appears to be the outside. The process has often been described, and can be seen in the illustration. There are also two excellent photographs of it in Sir H. H. Johnston's book.

Sewing is now done almost everywhere with European needles, which are very much in demand. Nine times out of ten, the requests of your carriers desiring extra tips, or of casual beggars (whom, however, I never found either as numerous or as troublesome as frequently represented), were for needles or soap (*sopo* or *sabao* according as British or Portuguese influence predominated in the experience of the speaker). Native needles and awls are either iron, or sharpened bamboo splinters; I have once or twice seen these, but the large ones, for thatching, are still in common use. Many men sew very neatly; they have an ingenious way of mending holes in their calicoes which is not like our darning, but consists in button-holing round the edge of the hole and continuing round and round inward, till it is filled up. Some seemed to aim at decorative effect, as in darning a blue cloth with red thread. The more artistic kinds of sewing, and such flights as the cutting out and making of Arab shirts, have probably been learnt on the coast, or from men who have been there; but the men, in general, are neat-fingered and take to these things almost instinctively, while to their wives, who are gathered into

1. Mat-making   2. Native Loom

To face p. 196

sewing classes at the missions, by way of making them
'womanly,' they are mostly pain and grief. One of a
husband's duties is to sew his wife's calico; if he
neglects this it is held to be a sufficient ground for
divorce. It is curious to notice the sort of convention
that has grown up about these things. Originally, I
suppose, these and similar occupations were looked
on as light and elegant relaxations for gentlemen who
came back weary from the wars, or from hunting, or
from a six months' trip to the coast, and so gradually
became exclusively appropriated to them. I once in
my ignorance asked an old woman if she could make
me a basket, and she replied in a slightly shocked tone
that it was *nchito ya amuna*—men's work. I imagine,
though I never heard the point raised, that it would be
little if at all short of improper for a man to set about
making pots.

The word *ruka*, 'to weave,' is used both for the
weaving of cloth and the making of mats and baskets;
but in these last there is a certain distinction observed,
ruka being applied to what is properly woven or inter-
plaited, while another word, *pika*, describes the plaiting
of the *nkokwe*, where the strands all run one way, and
are twined in and out between the uprights, but the
rows are not linked into one another. There is also
a kind of mat made with bundles of reeds laid side
by side and connected by strips of cane twined in
and out between them in pairs. This process is called
by English basket-makers 'pairing,' as distinct from
'weaving.'

Baskets are of many kinds, each with its own use

and name, and it is characteristic of the native habit of mind (one illustrated in all primitive languages), that there is no *general* term for a basket pure and simple without reference to its kind or use. This, I fancy, touches on the old controversy between Nominalists and Realists. But that the Bantu are not incapable of the degree of mental abstraction implied in general notions is shown by the fact that they have words for 'tree' and 'bird,' quite irrespective of the species of either, all of which have their own proper names.

One of the commonest kinds of basket is the *mtanga*, used for bringing in maize from the harvest-field, for carrying provisions or anything else that will go into it (being of convenient size and shape for carrying on the head), and, very often, for storing things inside the hut. It is made of flat slips of bamboo, woven at first as if for a mat; when a square of a little more than a foot across is finished, the slips are turned up, the corners rounded, and the upright part of the basket woven in a circle, which is finished by cutting off the ends at the top and enclosing the rim between two thin bamboo hoops, sewn on with strips of bark. *Mtangas* are made in several sizes, being both larger and smaller than the above; the diameter is always about equal to the height. They are very strong and serviceable, and Europeans find them useful in many ways. The *mtungwi* is a double basket with flat wooden rims, one of which fits into the other; it is made of split bamboo, like the *mtanga*, but the slips are narrower, and both halves are rounded,

Making "Mtanga" Basket

BOY WITH CRATE OF FOWLS

To face p. 199

instead of beginning as a square. The rims are of white wood, often charred or otherwise blackened, and ornamented with patterns cut out on it with a knife. Small flat baskets (*nsengwa*), from four to eight inches across, are used as plates, or to bring eggs, or other small articles for sale. They sometimes have an ornamental rim, worked in herring-bone pattern with a certain fibrous root, alternated with the rind of cane. The large flat baskets used for winnowing or sifting are eighteen inches or two feet across, and three or four inches deep in the middle; they slope more from the rim than the *nsengwa*, which is flat-bottomed. Bags of different shapes and sizes, which men wear round their necks on a journey, are woven out of palm-fibre. A much rougher construction is the coop or crate made for the transport of fowls, which is sometimes round, sometimes cylindrical.

The universal sleeping-mat, made of the *bango* reed (*Phragmites*), is sewn rather than woven; the edge of the mat is formed of a length of peeled bamboo, to which strings are fastened at regular intervals; then these are passed through the split reeds by means of a bamboo needle. The yellow, shiny surface of the canes makes these mats very attractive when new, but they splinter easily, and do not last long as a floor-covering in European houses. They will roll up tightly, with the upper surface outward (not the reverse way, as the curves of the canes are all on one side), and are so carried on a journey, as the Angoni have them in Plate 23. Finer and softer mats are made of palm-fibre; these are really woven, as are also the *fumbas*, or sleeping-bags, used by the River natives as a protection against mosquitoes; they are woven round two ends and one side, leaving the other side open. The man gets in, draws the edges together, turns over so as to get the opening underneath him, and sleeps soundly, untroubled by ventilation, or the lack of it. Of course, the fabric is not close enough to exclude the air, but a person unaccustomed to it would find his breathing seriously impeded, and I have never been able to understand how natives are able to sleep wrapped head and all in blankets, and looking more like chrysalids than anything else.

The making of bark-cloth is another vanishing industry; but formerly it was the only fabric known in many districts where cotton was not cultivated, and the other fibre-plants not utilised for weaving. The bark used is that of the fig-tree, or the *myombo* (*Brachystegia*), which has a leaf like the ash. The hard outer bark of the tree is first taken off, and then a large sheet of the inner carefully removed, by first cutting a long upright line, and then two parallel circles. It is scraped, and then beaten with a mallet made of ebony or some other hard and heavy wood, which has its face deeply scored with lines crossing one another, so as to present almost a toothed surface. It is folded, hammered, folded to a smaller compass, and hammered again, till it is beaten out to a yard in width and a tolerably even thickness. It is usually of a terra-cotta colour, but sometimes

dyed black by steeping in a certain kind of mud
found in the swamps. This dye does not always
last, but wears off and leaves the cloth pale grey.
The dyeing is done before beating. There is also
white bark-cloth, which I have not seen; it is made
by burning off the hard bark from the tree, which
heats and bleaches the inner. Good bark-cloth is
very soft and pliable, and very warm in cold weather.
Even after the introduction of English cloth, women
were often seen wearing bark-cloth above their calico
on cold or wet days. As already remarked, it continues to be worn ceremonially in the mysteries.

IRON-WORK AND WOOD-CARVING

The Mang'anja, like the Mashona and other Makalanga tribes, have been distinguished from time im-
memorial as workers in iron. The Zulus do not
appear to have practised this art to any great extent,
though it was handed down in certain families, who
probably learnt it from the Makalanga. It is not
common among the Baronga, and M. Junod, in giving
a woodcut of a knife in a carved sheath (of the kind
very common on the Zambezi and elsewhere), which
he obtained from a travelled native, remarks that it is
'pièce rare et qu'on m'a dit provenir de la tribu
des Bandjao'—a distant tribe in the north-west; it is
quite possible that this was really a Mashona knife.
The Zulus do not appear to have a distinct word for
a knife, either calling it *umkonto* (a weapon, or tool in
general), or using the Dutch word *mes*.

Livingstone, when first visiting the Shiré Highlands

in 1859, found that ' Iron ore is dug out of the hills, and its manufacture is the staple trade of the southern highlands. Each village has its smelting-house, its charcoal-burners and blacksmiths. They make good axes, spears, needles, arrow-heads, bracelets, and anklets, which are sold at surprisingly low rates; a hoe over two pounds in weight is exchanged for calico of about the value of fourpence.' In 1876 there was a smelting-furnace within a few hundred yards of Blantyre station, and 'a smithy in an old hut beside the station was daily patronised.' The furnaces have mostly disappeared, and the smiths do not often make hoes or axes, preferring to hammer scraps of imported iron—for instance, pieces of the hoops from packing-cases—into small knives or the like. I made a rough sketch of the smithy beside the *bwalo* at Ntumbi; it was in a very dilapidated condition, and I never saw the smith at work there, though he sold me a small razor of his own manufacture, which is now in the Ethnological Museum at Cambridge. The forge contained the usual fireplace, with a ridge of earth banked up round it, rather higher than the ordinary fireplace in a hut. On the further side of the hollow were two upright clay-pipes, into which the two openings of the goat-skin bellows were fixed when at work; they communicated below with another pipe opening into the midst of the embers. A split bamboo is used as tongs, and the smith keeps a pot of water beside him to quench the ends when they take fire. The anvil is a flat stone, and a large stone is used as the forge-hammer;

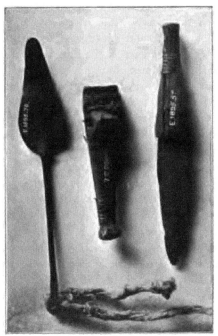

1. "Mbengo" ("Angoni Handkerchief") and Nyanja Sheath-Knife
2. Yao Knife, with Handle of Hippopotamus Ivory

In the Ethnological Museum at Cambridge

To face p. 203

iron hammers are used in later stages of the process. The characteristic Nyanja knife is two-edged, with carved wooden handle and sheath, as shown in the illustration.   The one shown in the illustration is not a very elaborate specimen, but they are sometimes beautifully carved, and of all sizes, from six inches and under to about a foot, but the tiny ones some-times seen are only made for sale to travellers as curios, on the Lower Shiré and Zambezi.   These knives serve every possible purpose of a pocket-knife, and are worn round the neck, or under the left arm, by a string passing over the right shoulder, or, if small, tied on the upper left arm.   The sheath is made with a projecting ear or loop for the string to pass through.

The Yaos prefer another style of knife, with one edge, and two or three grooves on the blade; the specimen in the cut has a handle of hippopotamus ivory.

The illustration shows another product of the smith's art—that known as an ' Angoni handkerchief'; it is worn round the neck, and used (with a vigour calculated to strike amazement into the unsophisticated beholder) to remove the results of toil from the forehead, or even to perform the ordinary office of a handkerchief for the nose.

Wood-carving is of a primitive sort, though often very neatly done.   The patterns on the knife-sheaths above mentioned mostly consist of triangles, chevrons, and lozenges, and are not nearly so elaborate as some specimens of Mashona and Zambezi work.   Indeed, the former seem, at least in some cases, to have origi-nated in unskilful copying of the interlaced pattern usually called Celtic, which is found in some of the latter, and probably introduced in the first instance by the Portuguese. The carving on blackened wood, which is very popular among the Yaos, is confined to the same elementary designs, and is done with very little relief, and no attempt at modelling of surface, the only object being to show the white figures on the dark ground.

Pillows or neck-rests of the Mashona or ancient Egyptian pattern are in use, but I never saw one being made, nor came across a new one. But it must be remembered that the people of the Shiré Highlands were, ten years ago, comparatively unused to the experience of a settled life, in which you can begin an important piece of carving with a reasonable prospect of being able to finish it. The country west of the Shiré has not been quite free from alarms and excursions for even so long as that. Quaint figures of birds are sometimes attempted by adventurous artists, but these are not very common, and I do not even remember coming across a stick with the top carved into the likeness of a human head, except the *tsanchima* staff mentioned in a previous chapter, which must have been of considerable age.

POTTERY

There are many kinds of pots—large water-jars, the large cooking-pots used for making porridge, and the small ones for boiling its accompaniments. The women, having procured the right kind of earth, break it up on a stone and knead it with water till it attains the proper consistency; then they mould a round lump, make a hole in the middle and work away at it with their hands and now and then a bamboo splint. No wheel or mould is used. Sometimes an incised pattern is made while the clay is soft. When finished, the pot is stood in the shade for a day; then they put it out into the sun, and when dry, burn it in an open wood fire. I am nearly sure, however, though, most unfortunately, I did not make a note of the fact at the time, that I once saw something like a small oven in use for the purpose. Pots not expected to stand the fire are considered fit for use after drying in the sun, and will hold water satisfactorily, though apt to grow soft if kept continuously wet. Smaller pots are sometimes coloured red by mixing oxide of iron with the clay; sometimes they have quite a good glaze, and the red surface is variegated with black bands. A large water-jar always stands inside the hut, which is filled up every day when the women fetch water from the nearest stream. They carry a large earthen or calabash jar on their heads; on the River this is balanced on a thing called a *ngoti*, which is a little wooden stand, with a saucer-shaped depression above and one below, something like a flat double wine-glass (the frontispiece will give a better idea of it than any description), the upper concavity fitting the jar, and the lower one the head. I suppose this eases the pressure on the head, like the grass rings or pads (*nkata*) used by all who carry heavy loads; but at first sight it seems as if it would add to the difficulties of carriage.

A long-handled gourd is carried along as a dipper,

to ladle the water into the jar, and after it is full, a few
leaves, or a twist of grass, are put on the top to keep
the water from spilling. I have seen flat wooden
crosses used (I think in Cornwall) for the same purpose.

In places where there is danger from crocodiles, as
in some parts of the Shiré, the women carry a gourd
at the end of a long pole, so that they can dip the
water from the top of a high bank, and run no risk of
being seized. Accidents of this kind have frequently
happened to women stooping at the water's edge to
fill their jars. The crocodile seems to turn round and
knock people over with a swing of his tail, if he cannot
get near enough to seize them with his jaws. A letter
written in English by a native a few years ago, related
a tragic occurrence of this sort — how a man, going
down the river with his wife, and camping for the night
on a sand-bank, awoke in the morning to find that 'the
woman had gone away with a crocodile!'

SALT-MAKING

Salt is so much in demand, for reasons already
adverted to, in this part of Africa, that its production
is an important industry. Its principal centre is near
Lake Chilwa, but inferior salt is made in places at a
distance from that lake, for home consumption, by
burning various grasses and other plants. In either
case the process is the same. The ashes, or the salt
earth dug up from the banks of the lake, are put into
a flat basket, preferably an old, worn *nsengwa*, and
water slowly poured on and allowed to drain through
into a pot placed beneath to receive it. 'The water

so strained through is saltish,' says the Rev. H. Barnes, speaking of Likoma, 'and is used with food to flavour it. In some parts this water is boiled till it is boiled away, and the result is a very white salt.' Sometimes the water is allowed to evaporate without boiling; I do not know if this is done at Chilwa, but the salt brought from thence is distinctly grey—certainly not white. People come in small parties from a distance, and live at the *kulo*, or salt-pit, where the earth is dug, till they have finished making all they want. The process is a slow one; it usually takes a month to make eighty pounds of salt, as large numbers of people do not engage in the work at once. They pack it in matting bags holding about twenty pounds' weight apiece, and carry it down to Blantyre and elsewhere for sale. A 'salt *ulendo*' is always sure of a speedy sale for its wares.

People who make salt at home—it is generally the women—do not, as a rule, take the trouble to boil or evaporate it, but use the liquor as it is for cooking.

Besides Lake Chilwa, there are some places near the mouth of the Ruo, whence salt is obtained, and some is said to come from the neighbourhood of Lake Nyasa, but this last is bitter and more like saltpetre. Sir A. Sharpe describes the process of salt-making in the saline swamps of Mweru, in very much the same way as the above, only the apparatus is different—'funnels made of closely woven grass rope' taking the place of baskets. Evidently these funnels or strainers are specially made for the purpose, showing that the industry is more specialised.

CHAPTER IX

LANGUAGE AND ORAL LITERATURE

Structure of the Bantu languages. Riddles. Songs. Music and dancing. Story-telling.

THE languages spoken in British Central Africa belong to the great Bantu family, which, as is now known, occupies (with a few exceptions) the whole continent of Africa south of a line drawn from the Gulf of Cameroons to the mouth of the Tana River on the east coast. Those spoken within the Protectorate are Nyanja, Yao, the Lomwe dialect of Makua, Tonga, Tumbuka, Nkonde, and a Zulu dialect spoken by the Angoni clans. In Northern Rhodesia we may mention Bisa, Bemba, Luba, and Lunda as the principal languages.

All the Bantu languages are as closely related together as English, Dutch, German, and the Scandinavian dialects. There are several points about them which are extremely interesting to the comparative philologist. They have no grammatical gender—the same pronoun is used for a man and a woman; and, accordingly, most natives who learn English come to grief on this point, like Winwood Reade's interpreter who asked: 'What you say when him son be girl?' On the other hand, nouns are divided into eight or ten classes, each with its own plural inflection, and adjectives and pronouns agreeing with it as they agree with each of the three genders in Latin. This agreement extends also to the verbs.

The Bantu languages further differ from those with which most of us are familiar, in that their inflections are indicated, not by suffixes, but by prefixes—a fact which first meets us in the various and perplexing forms assumed by the names of tribes and countries. Thus *Myao* is 'a Yao' (man or woman), *Wayao* is 'Yaos,' and *Chiyao* the Yao language. Each noun-class has its own prefix (sometimes much atrophied or even dropped altogether) for singular and for plural, and though these prefixes vary greatly in the different languages, they are always recognisable as having come from the same original, just as we know that the English *oak*, the German *Eiche*, the Dutch *eik*, and the Danish *eeg* are all derived from one primitive form. The inflectional prefixes of adjectives and verbs are derived from the noun-prefixes, though not always identical with them in form ; and the pronouns are modifications of the prefix. In fact, broadly speaking, the prefix may be called a pronoun, and the group of languages under consideration are sometimes called the prefix-pronominal languages.

The careful reader may think that a somewhat Hibernian assertion has been made above—viz. that the prefix is recognisable even where it has been dropped ; but this is in fact the case : the pronoun, which *must* be inserted before the verb, always shows what the lost prefix of the noun has been. Thus we have in Nyanja the word *njoka*, 'a snake'; it has no

O

prefix as it stands, but when used in a sentence we find it takes the pronoun *i*: *njoka i luma*, 'the snake bites.' Now in Zulu, which has kept its prefixes better than Nyanja, we find that 'snake' is *inyoka*.

This principle of agreement, by which all the words governed by the noun repeat its prefix in some form or another at their beginning, is called the *alliterative concord*, and may be illustrated by the following sentences :—

NYANJA

Mtengo watu u-li wotari, u-dza-gwa.
Tree   our it is high it will fall.

The pronoun for the class to which *mtengo* (anciently *umtengo*) belongs is *u*, which is quite clearly seen before the verbs 'to be' and 'to fall.' In the possessive pronoun and the adjective, it is a little disguised, because it becomes *w* before another vowel (*watu* = *u* + *atu*).

The plural of this is :

Mitengo yatu i-ri yetari, i-dza gwa.

Here the pronoun is *i*, or, before a vowel, *y*. *R* and *L* are interchangeable ; the verb 'to be' is usually *li* after *a* and *u*, *ri* after *i*.

Another class is thus exemplified :

Chiko changa chabwino chi-dza-sweka.
Gourd   my   good   it will be broken.

In the plural :

Ziko zanga zabwino zidzasweka.

YAO

Lu-peta a-lu lu-li lu-angu ngunu-lu-jasika, lu-enu
Basket   this   is   mine   not it is lost yours
'lu-la lu-jasiche. Here the prefix is *lu*.
that is lost.

('This basket is mine, it is not lost ; yours is lost.')

In the plural : *Mbeta asi sili syangu, nginisijasika, syenu 'sila sijasiche.* The plural prefix corresponding to *lu* is *izim (isim)*, or *izin*, and *p* following this prefix changes to *b*; hence *(isi)mbeta* is the plural of *lupeta*.

There are very few adjectives in the Bantu languages; their place may be supplied by a noun preceded by the possessive particle corresponding to the word 'of' : thus *chiko chabwino* is literally 'a gourd of goodness.' There are a good many verbs which can be used where we should use adjectives, as *ku ipa*, 'to be bad' (*ku* is the sign of the infinitive); *ku uma*, 'to be dry,' etc.

Verbs can express, by means of changes in the stem, a number of modifications in their meaning which we have to convey by separate words. These modifications are usually called 'forms,' but are really extensions of the principle of 'voice.' We have to be content with two voices—the active and passive, with traces of a middle; Hebrew has seven; some Bantu languages have as many as nine or ten; while, counting the secondary and tertiary derivatives, and the compounds, the late W. H. Bentley reckoned out over three hundred forms of one verb, *all actually in use*, in the language of the Lower Congo.

The aspirate exists neither in Yao nor Nyanja, and when heard in English words is often turned into *S*; thus the name Hetherwick becomes Salawichi. But the people west of the Shiré use it in words and names borrowed from the Zulus, and seem to find no difficulty with it. *L* and *R* are interchangeable, as already stated, or rather it would be more correct to say that the sound intended is really distinct from both and heard by some Europeans as *l*, by others as *r*. There are no very difficult sounds, except perhaps *ng* (pronounced as in 'sing' when it comes at the beginning of a word. There are no clicks in any language used in the region under consideration, except the Zulu spoken by some of the Angoni, and in this they tend to disappear. The accent is almost invariably on the penultimate.

The Bantu languages have, of course, no written literature—for we can hardly count the translations, etc., produced by missionaries and their pupils, or even the two or three native newspapers appearing in Cape Colony and Natal. But like most primitive tongues, they are rich in traditional tales, songs, proverbs, etc. Of the folk-stories we shall give some examples in the next chapter. Here are some specimens of Nyanja proverbs :—

'If you are patient, you will see the eyes of the snail.'

'Speed in walking in sand is even.' ('*Bei Nacht sind alle Katzen grau.*')

'You taste things chopped with an axe, but meat cut up with a knife you don't get a taste of.' (The sound of the axe directs passers-by to the place where the food is being prepared—perhaps inside the reed-fence of the kraal—when, of course, they must be asked to partake; had a knife been used, they would have heard nothing, and gone on.)

'If your neighbour's beard takes fire, quench it for him'—*i.e.* you may need a similar service some day.

'When a man or a reed dies, there grows up another.' ('*Il n'y a pas d'homme nécessaire.*')

'Sleep has no favourite.'

'Lingering met with liers in wait.'

Riddles, as already mentioned, are very popular. They are usually of the simple kind which describes some well-known object in more or less veiled and allusive language, something after the style of

> 'Walls there are as white as milk,
> Lined with skin as soft as silk,
> Within a fountain crystal-clear,
> A golden apple doth appear ;

but much more crudely expressed.

'I built my house without a door' is one which has the same answer as the above—viz. 'an egg.'

Others are:—

'Spin string that we may cross the river.'—A spider.

'The people are round about, their chief is in the centre.'—A fire, and the people sitting round it.

'I saw a chief walking along the road with flour on his head.'—Grey hair.

'Such an one built his house with one post only.'—A mushroom.

'A large bird covering its young with its wings.' —A house—referring to the roof with its broad eaves.

'My child cried on the road.'—A hammer.

'The sick man walks, but does not want to run, but when he sees this, he runs against his will.'—A steep hill (which forces people to run in descending it).

At Likoma they have a set form for riddle-contests, as thus: A. begins, 'A riddle!' The rest reply in chorus, 'Let it come!' A. 'I have built my house on the cliff!' All guess; if their guesses are wrong, A. repeats his riddle. If they still cannot guess right, they say, 'We pay up oxen.' A. 'How many?' They give a number. If A. is satisfied, he will now explain his riddle—'the ear' being the answer to the one given above. If any one guesses right, all clap their hands, and another player asks a fresh riddle.

Another popular amusement might be described as a 'debate.' Boys and grown men both delight in it, though with the former it is sometimes the prelude to a fight. One of a party sitting round the fire, or wakeful in the dormitory, will say, '*Tieni, ti chita mdkani*'—'Come, let us have a discussion,'—and will start it, perhaps, by asking whether a hippopotamus can climb a tree. The arguments for and against the proposition are then advanced with the greatest eagerness, till the point is settled, amid volleys of laughter, or the company tired out.

I have never, in Nyanja, come across any of the curious *itagu* ('catch-word compositions') which the Yaos delight in, and which are recited by two or more speakers. The following specimen of a duologue is given by Mr. Duff Macdonald :—

First Speaker.	Second Speaker.
Nda.	Nda kuluma.
Kuluma.	Kuluma mbale.
Mbale.	Mbale katete.
Katete.	Katete ngupe.
Ngupe.	Ngupe akane.
Kane.	Kane akongwe.
Kongwe.	Akongole chimanga.
Chimanga.	Chimanje macholo.
Macholo.	Gachole wandu.

It will be seen that the second speaker repeats the word given by the first (or something like it), and adds another to it, while the first in like manner catches up his last word, or part of it, sometimes giving it a different sense. It is almost impossible to translate this sort of thing, but the following composition on the same lines may serve to show how it is done.

A.	B.
Ten.	Tender and true.
True.	Truth shall prevail.
Veil.	Veil thy diminished head.
Head.	Head of the clan.
Plan.	Plant a new city, etc. etc.

Here, of course, there is no pretence of connection, but the *itagu* are really connected stories. The language of these *itagu* is very difficult; either because they are very old, or because words are purposely distorted.

Songs are numerous, and continually improvised afresh as wanted, though many old traditional ones are current, some of which are embodied in tales, and sung in chorus by the audience when the narrator comes to them. Natives nearly always sing when engaged in concerted work, such as paddling, hauling a heavy log, carrying a hammock, etc. They sometimes sing in unison, but not unfrequently in parts. Very often one sings the recitative, another answers, and others add the chorus. There is no metre, properly so called, in the songs, but there is a sort of rhythm, and they usually go very well to chants. Both Yao and Nyanja are exceedingly melodious languages, and it is possible, though not easy, to write rhymed verses in them, especially in trochaic metres, which violate no rule of accent or construction. Many, if not most, however, of the European tunes which have been adapted to native words in mission hymn-books are hopelessly unsuitable, and the result, as regards the accentuation of the words, is sometimes nothing short of grotesque.

No systematic study has yet been made of the native melodies by means of phonographic records; a few of the Nyanja and Chikunda songs have been written down, more or less tentatively by ear, and a good many Chinamwanga tunes have been noted down by Mrs. Dewar, of the Livingstonia Mission. These last, which are all associated with stories, come from a district outside the bounds of the Protectorate, about half-way between Nyasa and Tanganyika.

In general the character of all Bantu music is much

the same; the singing has a curious, monotonous, droning effect, which, however, is not without its charm, when heard amid the proper surroundings. It is sometimes said that all the melodies are in the minor key; but this is a mistake. M. Junod, who has made a very careful study of the music of the Baronga, says that the effect which gives rise to this impression is produced by the songs beginning on a high note and descending; and this turns out, on examination, to be the case with many of those collected by Mrs. Dewar, though the height of the opening note is often only comparative. As a specimen, I give the melody (as written down by Mrs. Pringle of Yair) of the famous canoe-song *Sina mama*.

The meaning of the words (collated from two printed sources and my own notes) is: 'I have no mother, I have no father; I have no mother, Mary, I have no father; I have no mother, to be nursed by her; I have no mother—thou art my mother, O Mary!' This song is often heard on the Shiré; but, containing as it does, a faint echo of Romanist teaching, probably originated in one of the Portuguese settlements on the Zambezi.

Another Shiré boat-song is *Wachenjera kale*, which, when I heard it, I took for a very *à propos* improvisation, having, I suppose, utterly forgotten the following passage from Livingstone's *Zambesi Expedition*, which I must have read, but which struck me as quite new when I came across it a few months later. 'In general they [the men of Mazaro or Vicenti on the Lower Zambezi] are trained canoe-men, and man many of the canoes plying to Senna and Tette; their pay is small, and, not trusting the traders, they must always have it before they start. . . . It is possible they may be good-humouredly giving their reason for insisting on being invariably paid in advance in the words of their favourite canoe-song, "Uachingere [uniformity in spelling African words is, even now, not much more than a pious aspiration], uachingere kale," "You cheated me of old," or "Thou art slippery, slippery truly."' I prefer the former rendering; and, moreover, my men repeated the *Wachenjera* thrice. There seemed to be no more of the song.

A very pretty corn-pounding song heard at Blantyre is as follows :—

Gu ! gu ! ndikatinka nkasinja.
Mai ! tate ! Zandia, gu !
Mwanawe uliranji?
Kuchenjera kwa amako,
Kundikwirira pa moto,
Kuti ine ndipsyerere.

It is not easy to get a satisfactory translation of this, though the words, on the face of them, are not very difficult. '*Gu! gu!* (the sound of the pestle descending into the wooden mortar)—I am going to pound corn; father! mother! Zandia! *gu!* (I take Zandia to be a proper name). You, child, why are you crying? —They are clever (or, they cheated me) at your mother's—to cover me up on the fire that I might be burnt—Zandia!' The 'child' addressed is perhaps the corn in the mortar, which cries out and complains of being crushed ('burnt'), or it may be meant of some maize-cobs put down to roast while the pounding is going on, which may be heard popping and crackling.

Several songs I have taken down are full of allusions to local chiefs and events of which I did not succeed in getting the explanation; they show, at all events, how passing incidents are commemorated and kept in mind. One speaks of 'Mandala, who ran away from the flag' (*mbendera*—the Portuguese *bandeira*), and 'Gomani (*i.e.* Chekusi), who died (or, no doubt, "was kilt entirely"—he being still alive at the time of recitation) in the *dambo*.' This may refer to one of the many wars between Chekusi and Chifisi, or Bazale.

Some of the songs are difficult to understand, as, even if not very old, they abound in unfamiliar words and constructions, and also in local allusions, which need explanation to outsiders. One I have written down seems to be about Chekusi's marriage, and brings in the names of several chiefs. Another says that ' I have seen Domwe' (a mountain in Angoniland) —' Ntaja is dead,—we are ravaged this year.' Another obscure effusion, after stating that something or other is at Matewere's (a son of the famous Mponda), goes on to say that ' I refuse (him or them) the oxhide shield,' or, maybe, the oxhide to make a shield.

These are ' Angoni' songs, and recognised as such on the other side of the river, though the language is not Zulu, but ordinary Nyanja. The original text of the last named is this :—

Ta iye (?) ni ri kwa Matewere chinkumbaleza—Ga da o ho!
Ndimana ine, ndimana cha ng'ombe chikopa tu!

The rhythm of the songs is rather indefinite; it resembles that of some sailors' chanties—*e.g.* the well-known *Rio Grande*. They often consist of only a few words, repeated *ad infinitum*, with a refrain of meaningless syllables, sometimes mere open vowel sounds—as: *e, e, e, e, o, o, o, o—wo ya yo ho,* etc. In canoe-songs and the like, time is marked by the beat of the paddles, the rise and fall of the women's pestles, and so on ; at a dance, it is given by the drums. Some soloist usually leads off with an improvised line, which is either taken up and sung in chorus, or a response to it is so sung, and the principal performer continues till he has exhausted his idea. If the song ' catches on,' it is remembered and repeated, and passes into the common stock. Some dances have their recognised songs, as ' *Kanonomera e! e!* ' at the Angoni women's

THE DANCING-MAN

To face p. 221

kunju dance, and '*Leka ululusa mwana hiye!* (Stop winnowing, child!)—*e! e! e! e!—o! o! o! o!*' at the *chamba* dance.

Singing, music, and dancing, or other rhythmic action, are very much mixed up together, as is always the case in the elementary stages of those arts; and a combination of all three is practised by the itinerant poet known as the 'dancing-man.' Of his instrument, the *chimwenyumwenyu*, Mr. Barnes says that 'performers on it are rare and are most welcome guests in any village.' It is a primitive kind of fiddle, with one string and a gourd resonator, played with a bow, which, when made, has its string passed over the string of the instrument, and so can never be taken off. The man in the illustration, however, appears to be playing on the *limba*, which has six strings strung on a piece of wood across the mouth of a large gourd, and is played with both thumbs. The gourd is hung round with bits of metal or of shells, to jingle and rattle when it is shaken. The 'dancing-man' teaches the children the chorus of his songs, and then, 'carries on a dialogue of song with his audience, with the excitement and rhythm of an inspired improvisatore.' Another kind of *limba* is that shown in the illustration, which was obtained from some Atonga:—a shallow wooden trough with a handle at one end, and pierced at top and bottom with six holes, through which a cord is strung backwards and forwards, and tightened up by winding round the handle. Like the other kind of *limba*, it is played with the thumbs. But the word *limba* is of wide application; it (or its plural

malimba, *marimba*) sometimes denotes the xylophone
or 'Kafir piano' (Ronga *timbila*), while natives use it
for a harmonium, organ, or piano.

Other stringed instruments are the *pango*, resembling
the dancing-man's *limba*, but played with a stick or
plectrum instead of the thumbs; the *mngoli*, the body
of which is made like a small drum—it has one string
with a bridge, and is played with a bow; the *kali-
rangwe*, with one string and a gourd resonator, played
either with the fingers or a bit of grass; and the very
primitive one (*mtangala*) represented in the illustration,
which is played by women only, and is simply a piece
of reed, slightly bent, with a string fastened at one end
and wound on the other, so that it can be tightened up
at pleasure. One end of this is held in the mouth and
the string twanged with the finger, producing a very
slight but not unpleasant sound, which, as Bishop
Colenso remarked of a somewhat similar instrument
in Natal, 'gratifies the performer and annoys nobody
else.'

The *sansi* has a set of iron keys fixed on a wooden
sounding-box, and played with the thumbs; it has a
piece of metal fixed on the front of the box, to which
are attached small discs cut from the shells of the
great *Achatina* snail, so as to clash when shaken, like
the bells on a tambourine. A very similar instrument
has the keys made of bamboo.

A flute (*chitoliro*) is made out of a piece of bamboo
about a foot long, cut off immediately above and below
the joints, so that it is closed at both ends, and from
three to six holes bored in the side, some of which are

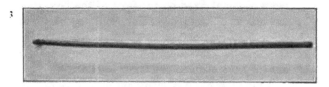

MUSICAL INSTRUMENTS

1. *Limba* (Atonga)   2. *Sansi*   3. Reed (*mtangala*)

From Specimens in the Ethnological Museum at Cambridge

closed with the fingers while playing. Bvalani, the boy with the coronet, used to play on this flute a pretty, though somewhat monotonous, little tune, consisting apparently of three or four notes, repeated over and over again; but neither I nor any other *msungu* has yet succeeded in getting a sound out of the one in my possession. It has one hole at one end, to blow into, and three at the other.

Whistles, made out of a small goat's or antelope's horn, and used for calling dogs and perhaps for signalling to each other on the road, are worn round the neck by Angoni and Chipetas; and Pan-pipes are made of reeds. Trumpets are made of gourds, sometimes fixed with wax on a long reed; the same word, *lipenga*, is used for a horn employed in the same way, or for a European key-bugle, or (in hymns) for the *Tuba mirum spargens sonum* of the Last Day. Some of the people near the south end of Tanganyika have huge trumpets cut out of a large tusk of ivory, like those used on the Upper Congo and elsewhere. One such is figured in Sir H. H. Johnston's book, p. 465.

The instrument above referred to as the 'Kafir piano' is, in a modified form, very popular throughout the Shiré Highlands and on the Lake, and may often be seen in the village *bwalo*. The Delagoa Bay *timbila* is portable (see the figure in M. Junod's *Chants et Contes des Baronga*, p. 27), with the wooden keys fixed on a flat frame—elsewhere, the frame is curved into the arc of a circle, so that the performer can easily reach all the keys when the instrument is slung round his neck. In both cases, resonators, made of gourds, or the hard shells of the *matondo* fruit, are attached to the keys. I once saw a very elaborately made and beautifully finished specimen which had come either from Delagoa Bay or Inhambane, and had polished iron keys padded with leather; but this was a sophisticated *timbila*, scarcely the genuine article. The Nyanja form of it, variously called *magologodo*, *mangondongondo*, *mangolongondo*, and *mangolongodingo*, usually has to be played *in situ*, or, if removed, must be carried away in pieces. Two logs of soft wood (banana-stems are the best), perhaps a yard long, are laid on the ground a certain distance apart, and on these are arranged six, or sometimes seven, crossbars (the Ronga 'piano' has ten) cut from the wood of certain trees, and carefully trimmed to shape. Sometimes they are merely laid on the logs, sometimes there are short pegs to keep them in place. The keys on the Ronga instrument are carefully tuned, and each one is cut away underneath in such a way as to make it give a different sound; but some of those I saw at Blantyre seemed to be merely rough bits of wood which fulfilled no condition beyond that of making a noise when struck. It is played by striking the keys with two sticks; the performer holds one in each hand and squats on his heels in front of it: sometimes there are two players, who face each other; the first leads, and the second is said to 'make a harmony with the one who is playing.'

But the drum is perhaps the commonest and most characteristic instrument, and the one which has been brought to the greatest perfection. There are

many different kinds, from the little *kandimbe*, a mere
toy for children, four or five inches across, and tapped
with the fingers, to the great *mpanje* and *kunta*, five
feet or more in length, or the *mgulugulu* war-drum,
which is beaten with sticks to call the people together.
None of them have two heads; the body is made of
a single piece of wood hollowed out, and the head
of goat-skin, or perhaps ox-hide; some small drums
(more like tambourines) are covered with snake or
lizard skin. The sound of the large ones can be heard
five or six miles away. Some are beaten with sticks,
some with the hand—either with the fist (as the big
mpangula, which is supported on a forked piece of
wood), or the open palm, or the fingers. Some of the
smaller drums are held against the chest and beaten
with the open hands, which gives a peculiar, soft,
booming sound; one kind is held under the arm;
another is laid lengthwise on the ground, and the
drummer sits astride it. Still another has legs like
a small round stool, and is beaten with two sticks as
it stands on the ground. The *mfinta* drum (large, but
not the largest kind) calls the people together when
the *mabisalila* is investigating a case of witchcraft;
it is also used in a dance where the performers carry
hoes and strike them together. There is a wonderful
variety in the notes; 'the smaller drums are made to
answer the big ones, the rapid and slower beats blend-
ing in the most perfect time. . . . There are skilled
drummers who go to the dances like a piper at a
Scotch wedding' (Scott).

Drums are tuned when necessary by leaving them

P

in front of a fire, or burning some grass inside them to
dry the skin and draw it tighter. The skin is fastened
on by small wooden pegs, and has a piece of rubber
fastened to the middle of its under-side.

Besides the drums, most dances require an additional
sound-producing agency in the shape of rattles. These
are worn on the arms and legs of the dancers, or shaken
in their hands. The commonest kind are made of a
hard-shelled fruit called *tseche*, about two inches or
less in diameter; it is allowed to dry till the seeds
shake about inside it, and then four or five are strung
on a stick, and several of these sticks attached round
the ankles of the dancers. Women never wear these
maseche at their *chamba* dance, above referred to; but
men always do at their corresponding one, called
chitoto.

The subject of dances is a large one, celebrating, as
they do, every important event in life, from birth to
death, besides ordinary merrymakings which have no
particular motive beyond cheerfulness and sociability.
In place of attempting to enumerate all the varieties,
which would be wearisome and convey no particular
impression, I shall content myself with extracting one
or two descriptions from my notes. 'Passing through
Mlomba's village (near Blantyre) found a grand
masewero[1] going on. The dancing man was performing, but not singing—calico turban on his head,
leather belt under his arms, with a great bunch of
long feathers stuck into it in front, some falling down
over his waistcloth, others reaching to his shoulders,

[1] Literally 'playing'—the word is used both for games and dances.

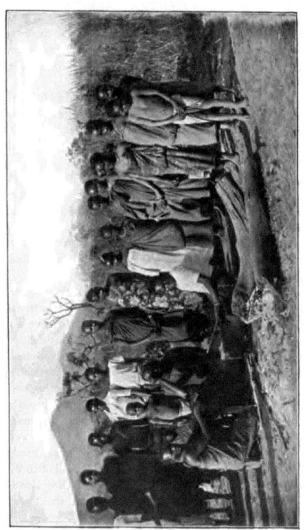

PREPARING FOR THE DANCE

a wild-cat skin hanging down his back, and dance-rattles on his legs. This dance is called the *tseche*. There were also six drummers: one sat on the ground and beat his drum (the kind with legs like a stool) with two sticks; the rest held theirs against their chests and beat them with both hands, the drum being supported by a piece of twine passing under it and looped over both wrists. They were well-made, muscular fellows, and danced pretty hard while drumming: this, it seems, is called the *nkonde*. Two younger boys came forward at intervals and danced *pas seuls*, and at the end a collection was taken up, chiefly in fowls.' Sometimes the beads contributed by a gratified audience are put into a hole in the gourd of the *chimwenyumwenyu*.

I remember the drums going all night long for the *chamba* dance at Ntumbi (which, by the bye, in spite of the name, has nothing to do with the smoking of the pernicious Indian hemp), and the ball was still in full swing between 7 and 8 A.M., when some of our boys and girls requested permission to go down before school hours and 'see the Angoni playing.'

Another dance which I witnessed at a Yao village near Blantyre, I am not sure whether to class as a diversion or a ritual solemnity. I think it was the latter, but not (as I was at one time inclined to suppose) the *chimbandi*, or 'great *unyago*,' which precedes the birth of a woman's first child (see Macdonald, *Africana*, i. 128), unless the latter has been considerably modified. In the first place, my friend Chewilaga, who appeared to play the principal part, had a baby

about six weeks old; in the second, so far from only
women being present, there were three men and a boy
working the drums, and one man among a few casual
spectators who gathered from outside; and there were
other points of difference. Eight or ten women (two
of them quite young girls) took part in the dance, led
by Chewilaga; they were all freshly anointed, almost
dripping with oil, and had on their best calicoes, and
(apparently) all their beads, and wore rattles on
one leg only. The drummers sat in a row on a form
made out of a split log: the three men held their
drums against their chests and beat them with their
hands; the boy had a four-legged standing drum,
which he beat with two sticks. The women—one with
a baby tied to her back—stood in front of the band
in a semicircle, 'marking time,' then formed in couples
and 'set to partners,' then marched round, in Indian
file, then bent forward from the hips, and all danced
together in a kind of jigging step; then formed in
semicircle again, and so *da capo*. The song (sung by
the dancers) consisted of a few words only, which I
failed to catch.

Some of the dances for amusement are confined to
one sex; in others, both take part. In one, partners
are chosen and led out into the middle; in another,
the man who beats the big drum leaves it at intervals
and dances alone in the centre of the ring, while every
one claps hands to fill up the gap.

The war-dance of the Angoni—executed, perhaps,
by hundreds of men leaping into the air at once and
beating their shields—is very striking; the Yaos and

Anyanja also have one, though the latter are not a particularly warlike race. 'One in the war-dance,' says a native account, 'comes and stretches his leg, stamping down his foot, *di !* and his gun, *di !* before his chief, saying, "Chief, we are here, none can come to kill you, for we are not dead yet."'

The *sinyao* dances have been already touched on in connection with the mysteries, and the mourning dances in the chapter on funeral ceremonies. The Rev. D. C. Scott thus describes the latter, and at the same time successfully conveys the impression produced by all: 'The heavy, deep *di ! di !* of the great bass drum, with silence succeeding, broken by the responsive wail and clapping of hands, then with the rapid call of the small *garansi* drum, and again with the deep hollow bass, and the never-ceasing circling of the dance, produces a weird sensation only possible in Africa.'[1]

[1] *Dictionary*, *s.v.* Masewera.

CHAPTER X

Methods of story-telling. Animal stories. *Brer Rabbit.*
Borrowed tales. Value of native folk-lore.

WE have mentioned that one of the great amusements,
both of children and grown-up people, is story-
telling—*ku imba ntanu.* This means literally ' to sing
a story,' and points to the way in which tales are
usually told. Most of them contain short pieces
which are sung, and are known to every one—so that,
when the narrator comes to them, the audience all
join in. Steere points out that these sung parts are
very common in the Swahili tales, and that the language found in them is older than what is usually
spoken, or than the rest of the story.

Another curious point is that, when a man is telling
a story late at night—say, beside the camp-fire or on a
journey—at every pause in his narrative the hearers
exclaim in chorus, ' We are all here!' As the tale
goes on, the responses become fewer and fewer, and
at last, when no one is left awake to answer, the
recitation stops.

The stories told by the Bantu of British Central
Africa are, broadly speaking, of three kinds. First,
we have legends about the origin of men and things,
such as we noticed in the fourth chapter, with which

may be grouped the traditions telling whence the different tribes came, and how they reached their present homes. About these last I shall have something to say in the next chapter. Secondly, we have the kind of animal story so well exemplified in *Uncle Remus*. And, thirdly, tales in which people, animals, and sometimes preternatural beings are mixed up together in a series of more or less marvellous incidents—like our own fairy stories, in fact. Some of these we can trace as imported; but they are none the less curious on that account.

The animal stories seem to be the commonest and best known among the Anyanja—at least, nearly all the stories I could induce natives to tell me were of this kind. The tales collected by Mr. Macdonald, and published in *Africana*, however, belong largely to the first and second classes. Some are like very faint and far-off echoes of the *Arabian Nights*; these have probably been heard on the coast by Yaos who have gone down with trading-parties, and retold in the villages on their return. An example of this kind is 'The Story of the Chief,' which will be given later on.

Every one knows the delightful *Uncle Remus* tales, and will remember the cunning and resourcefulness of 'Brer Rabbit,' who, with his family, 'wuz at de head er de gang when any racket wuz on hand, en dar dey stayed!' It is now generally agreed that these stories came from Africa; and wherever any Bantu folk-tales have been written down, there we are pretty sure to find Brer Rabbit, under one alias or another. The Anyanja call him *Kalulu*, the Yaos *Sungula*—generally

Che Sungula, 'Mr. Rabbit'; though naturalists remind us, by the bye, that he is not properly a rabbit but a hare. One comes across the Kalulu by himself in the bush, and he makes a form in the grass, not a burrow in the ground. If I can trust my recollection of him, he is a little smaller than an English hare.

I cannot help feeling surprised that some writers on African folk-lore have chosen to 'translate' *sungula*, or its equivalent in other Bantu languages, by 'fox,' because the character assigned to the hare is in their opinion more appropriate to the fox. By doing so, we spoil one of the most characteristic features in the stories, and, moreover, lose an important distinction; for the place given by the Bantu to the Hare is occupied in Hottentot folk-lore by the Jackal.

Of course the animals in *Uncle Remus* are not all the same as those in the African tales; as some of the latter do not live in America, better-known ones have been substituted for them. Thus the Elephant, the Hippopotamus, the Lion, and the Python have disappeared, so has the Crocodile ('Uncle Remus' lived in Middle Georgia, where there are no alligators); and I fancy that Brer Wolf and Brer Fox have taken the place of the Hyena, who sometimes gets the better of the Hare for a time, but is always worsted by him in the end. The Tortoise (a land and not a water tortoise, usually) is as clever as Brer Terrapin, but is more bloodthirsty and vindictive—a kind of Shylock. The Baboon (*nyani*) does not seem to have an American counterpart, and the Cat, the Cock, and the Swallow, though one does not see why, have also dropped out.

A somewhat puzzling creature in the Nyanja tales
is the Dzimwe, sometimes translated 'elephant,'
though the native explanations are rather hazy, and
leave one with the impression that he is a kind of
bogey—perhaps akin to Chiruwi. One boy actually
states that *dzimwe* (or, in the Likoma dialect, *jimwe*)
sometimes means 'an elephant,' and sometimes 'a
spirit.' In the present case, it seems more satisfactory
to take it as the former; though in one or two stories
we have the elephant under his proper Nyanja name
of *njobvu*. In neither case does he act up to his
reputation for wisdom, for in the end he is always
cruelly victimised by the Hare.

The latter's manners, I think, must have been
softened by his sojourn in the States; for only on
rare occasions—as when he puts an end to Brer Wolf
with the boiling kettle—are his actions really cruel.
We cannot say the same of the Kalulu ; yet it would
be a mistake to conclude, from the enjoyment with
which these stories are received, that the African
natives are a bloodthirsty and ferocious race. What
they enjoy is the cleverness with which the tables are
turned by the weaker party on the stronger, who
seemed to have him entirely in his power. And, after
all, generation after generation of English children
have been fascinated by *Jack the Giant-Killer*, without
being precisely horrified by the murderous stratagem
practised by Jack on the Cornish giant.

The native does not recognise such a clear distinction between animals and human beings as we
do. Animals do not speak, it is true, but, for all he

knows, there may be nothing to prevent their doing so if they choose. He believes (and acts on the belief) that certain human beings can change themselves into animals and back again. So, in telling stories about animals, he seems continually to forget that they are not human, or perhaps, rather, he assumes that their habits, abodes, and domestic arrangements are very much the same as those of his own people.

One of the most typical of the Kalulu stories is the following, told me by one of the Blantyre native teachers. Being an educated man, accustomed to composition and dictation, he was able to give it in a very clear and connected form; whereas it is difficult, and sometimes impossible, to make sense of those written down from the dictation of village children, who perhaps did not know the stories very well to begin with, and continually lost the thread when entreated to go slower or repeat a phrase.

'The Hare and the Elephant were once friends, and the Hare said, "Come, man, and let us go and look for food." And they went to a village and said, "We want to hoe for you, if you will give us food"; and the headman said "Good." And he let them hoe in his garden, and gave them some beans to eat there in the garden (in the middle of the day). And they went to the garden and cooked those beans. (They could make a fire as soon as they arrived, and put on the pot with the beans, so as to let them cook slowly while they worked.) When they had finished hoeing, the beans were done, and the Elephant said, "I am going to the water to bathe, do you look well after the beans, and

we will eat them together when I return." Then he
went away and took off his skin, and ran, and came to
the place where the Hare was. (We are to understand
that he was quite unrecognisable in this condition.)
When the Hare saw him, he was afraid, thinking that
he was a wild beast, and he ran away ; and the Elephant
ate up those beans, and went back to the water, and
put on his skin again, and returned, and said, "Have
you taken off the pot with the beans?" And the Hare
said, "No, my friend, there came here a terrible wild
beast, and I ran away, and it ate those beans." And
the Elephant said, "No, you are cheating me—you
ate those beans yourself—it was not a wild beast, no!"
And the next day they went again to hoe, and cooked
their beans. When the beans were nearly done, the
Elephant said to the Hare, "I shall go and bathe—we
will eat the beans when I return." And he did just
the same as before. When he returned and asked if
the beans were ready, the Hare answered, "The wild
beast came again to-day and has eaten the beans."
The Elephant said, "My friend, it is very deceitful of
you to eat the beans twice over, and not let me have
any!" And the Hare said, "Now, I am going to
make a bow—if it comes again I will shoot it." Next
day, they put on their beans again ; and the Elephant
took the bow which the Hare had made, and said, "You
have not made it well—give it to me; I will make it
right for you." And he kept on paring and shaving it,
a little here and a little there, till he had made it too
thin in one place, and said, "Now it is good ; if the wild
beast comes, you can shoot it." Then he went down

to the water, and took off his skin, and ran, and came where the Hare was. When the Hare saw that wild beast coming, he took his bow to shoot it, and the bow broke. So he ran away again, and the Elephant ate the beans, and came back as before, and asked, "Did you shoot the wild beast?" And the Hare answered, "No, my bow broke, and I ran away." Next day they put on the beans once more, and the Hare went aside and made his bow, and hid it. When the Elephant went away to bathe, the Hare took his bow and held it in his hand, and took a barbed arrow, and when the wild beast came once more, he shot him through the heart, and the Elephant said, "*Mai! mai! mai! mai!* (mother!) Oh! my friend, to shoot me like this, because of those miserable beans! I meant to have left some for you to-day, that you too might eat!" And the Hare said, "Ha! my friend!—then it was you who finished up those beans by yourself, and I thought it was a wild beast!" The Elephant said, "Ha! to shoot me with a barbed arrow!—you have hurt me, my friend!—and how shall I get this out?" And he tried to pull out the arrow, and died. And the Hare ate the beans by himself, and went home.'

Another story in which these two figure is given by Mr. Macdonald under the title of 'The Fox and the Hyena'; but this is in two parts—in the first, the Hyena plays a series of tricks on a long-suffering creature called the *mbendu*, apparently a kind of civet-cat; in the second, he tries to repeat these tricks on the Hare (for this is a case where 'fox' is used to translate *sungula*), and fails. In my version, the Hare is cheated at first, and learns by bitter experience; the closing incident, too, is different. The Hare and the Dzimwe went on a journey together, begging food (as native travellers do) at all the villages they came to. At the first, the Elephant said, 'Let us ask for sugar-cane and *bango* reeds' (which are uneatable); he then took the sugar-cane and gave the Hare the *bango*. At the next village he acted in the same way with millet and pebbles. At the next, the people had been cooking porridge; and the Elephant, in order to secure both the Hare's portion and his own, sent the latter back to gather some 'medicine' leaves from a tree he had noticed on the way, saying that the *nsima* would not be good without them. The Hare, however, produced some from his bag; he had run back on the road, just after passing the tree, saying that he wanted to look for an arrow he had dropped, and had then picked the leaves. The Dzimwe was so disgusted at being out-witted that he would not eat, but left all the *nsima* to the Hare. Next day, however, when they reached another village, he contrived to get him out of the way for a time, and, on his return, refused to share his porridge with him (an almost unheard-of thing in native manners), alleging that, in the interval, 'many strangers' had arrived, and eaten up all the cooked food in the village, so that there was barely enough for himself. The Hare then retired, stripped off his skin, tied *maseche* rattles to his legs, and came and danced at the door of the hut where the Elephant was eating. The latter, thinking that he was a *chirombo*, fled and left him to finish the porridge. Subsequently, he was induced, by his sister's baskets (the luggage she had brought from home), and fastened it firmly, and put his sister into the baskets, and sang :

> "*Chínguli chánga, nde, nde, nde,*
> *Mpérekezéni, nde, nde, nde,*
> *Kúli amái, nde, nde, nde,*
> *Chínguli chánga, nde, nde, nde.*'

That is, " My top! take her home to her mother!"

'It flew up and flew away over the Bush, and the hyenas followed ; but he repeated the same song again, and they flew on till they were just above their mother's village. Then he sang again, *Chínguli chánga* (and so on, as above), and the people heard it in the air over their heads, and looked up, and saw them ; and the *chinguli* came to a stop, and let them down right on top of the grain-mortar. And then the brother said, " My sister wanted to send me back because I had sore eyes ; but they would have eaten her at that village, and I have brought her home."' In another version, the mother follows this up with some more good advice, pointing out what she owes to her brother, and warning her ' never to do it again.'

A favourite Yao story is that of the python (*Sato*) who was befriended by a man when caught in a bush-

chínguli, which, moreover, I have never heard in any other connection. The usual word for this kind of top is *nguli,* or *nanguli* ; *chi* being the augmentative prefix. Another version says rather vaguely that ' he cut out a tree,' and made his sister go into it. Evidently the function of the *chinguli* is the same as that of the magic carpet in the *Arabian Nights.* In the Fiote story of ' Ngomba's Balloon,' given by Mr. Dennett, a basket of some sort seems to be endowed with magical powers. The song should be read phonetically (giving the vowels their German or Italian value), with the accents as marked : the *e* in *nde, nde, nde* (a meaningless refrain) is like that in our word ' end.'

Apparently the Hare meets his match in the Tortoise
—though the famous race is by the Anyanja related
as taking place between the Tortoise and the Bush-
buck (*mbawala*). On one occasion these two hoed a
garden together, and the Hare cheated the Tortoise
out of his dinner, as, on another occasion, the Elephant
cheated him. The Tortoise, however, had his revenge
a little later, when they were sowing ground-nuts; he
crawled into the Hare's seed-bag, as it lay on the
ground, and ate up the supply. The Hare took this
defeat so much to heart that he 'went away and cried.'

All over the world we find tales intended to explain
how animals came by this or that peculiarity which
is striking enough to catch the attention, but has no
obvious use. Thus, the Calabar people tell how the
Tortoise fell off a tree and broke his shell to pieces,
and had it stuck together again, so that the joins are
visible to this day; and the Hottentots say that the
Hare has a split lip because the Moon threw a piece of
wood at him. We know how Brer Rabbit lost his
long, bushy tail, through letting it hang in the water
while fishing. The Anyanja also think that the Hare
once had a long tail, and there is a story which relates
how he had a piece cut off it at every village he
passed through; but I have never been able to secure
it in detail. There is a Yao tale to the effect that
baboons are descended from a woman who ran away
to the Bush because the chief had killed one of her
children. She refused to shave her head (in mourning),
and hair subsequently grew all over her body.

The Spider, who on the Guinea Coast is the principal

figure in the animal stories, is, so far as I know, almost absent from Bantu folk-lore. One exception I have already referred to, in a Yao creation-myth; in another Yao tale he crosses a stream and makes a bridge for a chief to escape from his enemies. Here, however, he does not take a specially prominent part, being only one of four helpers provided by the spirit of the chief's elder brother. The Spider is very prominent in the folk-lore of the Duala, who have probably borrowed him from their western neighbours.

We have mentioned that the natives see nothing strange in men assuming the forms of animals—they believe that it happens every day. Their stories give us many instances of the converse process—animals taking human shape whenever it suits them. Thus a girl marries a lion who has turned himself into a man, and, finding out his real nature, runs away from him. Another I give as I have it written down.

'A person (a girl) refused (all) men; there came a baboon; he took off the skin from his body and was turned into a man. The Angoni woman married the baboon, and he hoed the crops, and his companions came from the Bush and ate the crops of his mother-in-law's garden, and (so) he went (with them) into the Bush.'

But a better example still is that of the 'Girl and the Hyena,' which Mr. Macdonald thinks is intended as a warning to girls not to be too fastidious in their choice of husbands, and to accept those first suggested to them, lest worse befall. It might equally well be a warning against marrying a stranger from a distance, and certainly shows the tie between brother

and sister in a very pleasing light. Here it is, as told me by Katembo at Blantyre.

'There was a woman who refused all husbands, and at last there came a hyena, and she said, " I want this one." (So they were married), and the husband said, " My wife, let us go home." Her brother, who had sore eyes, followed after them, and she (saw him and) said, " Where are you going ? " The brother crouched down and hid in the grass, and when they were out of sight he followed them again, till he came to the village. When his sister found he was there, she hid him in the hen-coop. When it was quite dark, a number of hyenas came outside the hut and sang :

" Here is meat, we will eat it ; but it is not fat enough yet."

'The girl was asleep, but her brother heard them, and as soon as it was light he went and told her that they meant to eat her. She would not believe it, so he told her to tie a string to her little finger that night before she went to sleep, and leave the end outside the hut, so that he could take it with him into the chicken-house. In the middle of the night the hyenas came again, and, when he heard them, he pulled the string and woke his sister ; so she, too, heard them singing :

" Here is meat, we will eat it ; but it is not fat enough yet."

'In the morning she said, "I heard them, my brother." Then he said to her husband, " Brother-in-law, lend me an adze, I want to make myself a big wooden top" (*chinguli*).[1] When he had finished it, he put it into

---

[1] I have never been able to discover any other meaning but this for

Q

Che Sungula, 'Mr. Rabbit'; though naturalists remind us, by the bye, that he is not properly a rabbit but a hare. One comes across the Kalulu by himself in the bush, and he makes a form in the grass, not a burrow in the ground. If I can trust my recollection of him, he is a little smaller than an English hare.

I cannot help feeling surprised that some writers on African folk-lore have chosen to 'translate' *sungula*, or its equivalent in other Bantu languages, by 'fox,' because the character assigned to the hare is in their opinion more appropriate to the fox. By doing so, we spoil one of the most characteristic features in the stories, and, moreover, lose an important distinction; for the place given by the Bantu to the Hare is occupied in Hottentot folk-lore by the Jackal.

Of course the animals in *Uncle Remus* are not all the same as those in the African tales; as some of the latter do not live in America, better-known ones have been substituted for them. Thus the Elephant, the Hippopotamus, the Lion, and the Python have disappeared, so has the Crocodile ('Uncle Remus' lived in Middle Georgia, where there are no alligators); and I fancy that Brer Wolf and Brer Fox have taken the place of the Hyena, who sometimes gets the better of the Hare for a time, but is always worsted by him in the end. The Tortoise (a land and not a water tortoise, usually) is as clever as Brer Terrapin, but is more bloodthirsty and vindictive—a kind of Shylock. The Baboon (*nyani*) does not seem to have an American counterpart, and the Cat, the Cock, and the Swallow, though one does not see why, have also dropped out.

fire. He appealed first to a passing herd of buck to stop and save him, but they, considering that he had just eaten one of their number, not unnaturally refused. Then a man passed by with a hoe in his hand, and, on being assured that the python would not devour him, hoed up a piece of ground all round him, and thus saved him from the fire. The grateful python told him to come back in four days' time, which he did, and found that it had changed into a young lad, who took him home, entertained him with plenty of beer, and finally presented him with two pieces (1 piece = 16 yards) of calico and a magic bottle, which was to be opened in presence of his enemies.

When the man went home, he found there was war; his family had fled, and the enemy were occupying the village. He opened his bottle, and they were immediately annihilated. He then went to hoe in the gardens, leaving his bottle and other property in his hut. Another detachment of the enemy arrived—they took possession of the village and all that was in it, pursued him to his garden, and took him prisoner. He was tied up, with his neck in a gori-stick, with a view to being killed next day. During the night he felt a rat gnawing his feet, and asked it to go to the chief's house and bring the bottle. The rat did so, and the man said, ' I will pay you in the morning.' When the people were all assembled, and the man was brought out into the *bwalo* to be killed, he opened his bottle. ' The people who sat there when he held it up were dead and gone '—there was no one there! So he rewarded the rat with two cows.

Che Sungula, 'Mr. Rabbit'; though naturalists remind us, by the bye, that he is not properly a rabbit but a hare. One comes across the Kalulu by himself in the bush, and he makes a form in the grass, not a burrow in the ground. If I can trust my recollection of him, he is a little smaller than an English hare.

I cannot help feeling surprised that some writers on African folk-lore have chosen to 'translate' *sungula,* or its equivalent in other Bantu languages, by 'fox,' because the character assigned to the hare is in their opinion more appropriate to the fox. By doing so, we spoil one of the most characteristic features in the stories, and, moreover, lose an important distinction; for the place given by the Bantu to the Hare is occupied in Hottentot folk-lore by the Jackal.

Of course the animals in *Uncle Remus* are not all the same as those in the African tales; as some of the latter do not live in America, better-known ones have been substituted for them. Thus the Elephant, the Hippopotamus, the Lion, and the Python have disappeared, so has the Crocodile ('Uncle Remus' lived in Middle Georgia, where there are no alligators); and I fancy that Brer Wolf and Brer Fox have taken the place of the Hyena, who sometimes gets the better of the Hare for a time, but is always worsted by him in the end. The Tortoise (a land and not a water tortoise, usually) is as clever as Brer Terrapin, but is more bloodthirsty and vindictive—a kind of Shylock. The Baboon (*nyani*) does not seem to have an American counterpart, and the Cat, the Cock, and the Swallow, though one does not see why, have also dropped out.

A somewhat puzzling creature in the Nyanja tales is the Dzimwe, sometimes translated 'elephant,' though the native explanations are rather hazy, and leave one with the impression that he is a kind of bogey—perhaps akin to Chiruwi. One boy actually states that *dzimwe* (or, in the Likoma dialect, *jimwe*) sometimes means 'an elephant,' and sometimes 'a spirit.' In the present case, it seems more satisfactory to take it as the former; though in one or two stories we have the elephant under his proper Nyanja name of *njobvu*. In neither case does he act up to his reputation for wisdom, for in the end he is always cruelly victimised by the Hare.

The latter's manners, I think, must have been softened by his sojourn in the States; for only on rare occasions—as when he puts an end to Brer Wolf with the boiling kettle—are his actions really cruel. We cannot say the same of the Kalulu; yet it would be a mistake to conclude, from the enjoyment with which these stories are received, that the African natives are a bloodthirsty and ferocious race. What they enjoy is the cleverness with which the tables are turned by the weaker party on the stronger, who seemed to have him entirely in his power. And, after all, generation after generation of English children have been fascinated by *Jack the Giant-Killer*, without being precisely horrified by the murderous stratagem practised by Jack on the Cornish giant.

The native does not recognise such a clear distinction between animals and human beings as we do. Animals do not speak, it is true, but, for all he knows, there may be nothing to prevent their doing so if they choose. He believes (and acts on the belief) that certain human beings can change themselves into animals and back again. So, in telling stories about animals, he seems continually to forget that they are not human, or perhaps, rather, he assumes that their habits, abodes, and domestic arrangements are very much the same as those of his own people.

One of the most typical of the Kalulu stories is the following, told me by one of the Blantyre native teachers. Being an educated man, accustomed to composition and dictation, he was able to give it in a very clear and connected form; whereas it is difficult, and sometimes impossible, to make sense of those written down from the dictation of village children, who perhaps did not know the stories very well to begin with, and continually lost the thread when entreated to go slower or repeat a phrase.

'The Hare and the Elephant were once friends, and the Hare said, "Come, man, and let us go and look for food." And they went to a village and said, "We want to hoe for you, if you will give us food"; and the headman said "Good." And he let them hoe in his garden, and gave them some beans to eat there in the garden (in the middle of the day). And they went to the garden and cooked those beans. (They could make a fire as soon as they arrived, and put on the pot with the beans, so as to let them cook slowly while they worked.) When they had finished hoeing, the beans were done, and the Elephant said, " I am going to the water to bathe, do you look well after the beans, and

we will eat them together when I return." Then he
went away and took off his skin, and ran, and came to
the place where the Hare was. (We are to understand
that he was quite unrecognisable in this condition.)
When the Hare saw him, he was afraid, thinking that
he was a wild beast, and he ran away; and the Elephant
ate up those beans, and went back to the water, and
put on his skin again, and returned, and said, "Have
you taken off the pot with the beans?" And the Hare
said, "No, my friend, there came here a terrible wild
beast, and I ran away, and it ate those beans." And
the Elephant said, "No, you are cheating me—you
ate those beans yourself—it was not a wild beast, no!"
And the next day they went again to hoe, and cooked
their beans. When the beans were nearly done, the
Elephant said to the Hare, "I shall go and bathe—we
will eat the beans when I return." And he did just
the same as before. When he returned and asked if
the beans were ready, the Hare answered, "The wild
beast came again to-day and has eaten the beans."
The Elephant said, "My friend, it is very deceitful of
you to eat the beans twice over, and not let me have
any!" And the Hare said, "Now, I am going to
make a bow—if it comes again I will shoot it." Next
day, they put on their beans again; and the Elephant
took the bow which the Hare had made, and said, "You
have not made it well—give it to me; I will make it
right for you." And he kept on paring and shaving it,
a little here and a little there, till he had made it too
thin in one place, and said, "Now it is good; if the wild
beast comes, you can shoot it." Then he went down

to the water, and took off his skin, and ran, and came where the Hare was. When the Hare saw that wild beast coming, he took his bow to shoot it, and the bow broke. So he ran away again, and the Elephant ate the beans, and came back as before, and asked, "Did you shoot the wild beast?" And the Hare answered, "No, my bow broke, and I ran away." Next day they put on the beans once more, and the Hare went aside and made his bow, and hid it. When the Elephant went away to bathe, the Hare took his bow and held it in his hand, and took a barbed arrow, and when the wild beast came once more, he shot him through the heart, and the Elephant said, "*Mai! mai! mai! mai!* (mother!) Oh! my friend, to shoot me like this, because of those miserable beans! I meant to have left some for you to-day, that you too might eat!" And the Hare said, "Ha! my friend!—then it was you who finished up those beans by yourself, and I thought it was a wild beast!" The Elephant said, "Ha! to shoot me with a barbed arrow!—you have hurt me, my friend!—and how shall I get this out?" And he tried to pull out the arrow, and died. And the Hare ate the beans by himself, and went home.'

Another story in which these two figure is given by Mr. Macdonald under the title of 'The Fox and the Hyena'; but this is in two parts—in the first, the Hyena plays a series of tricks on a long-suffering creature called the *mbendu*, apparently a kind of civet-cat; in the second, he tries to repeat these tricks on the Hare (for this is a case where 'fox' is used to translate *sungula*), and fails. In my version, the Hare is cheated at first, and learns by bitter experience; the closing incident, too, is different. The Hare and the Dzimwe went on a journey together, begging food (as native travellers do) at all the villages they came to. At the first, the Elephant said, 'Let us ask for sugar-cane and *bango* reeds' (which are uneatable); he then took the sugar-cane and gave the Hare the *bango*. At the next village he acted in the same way with millet and pebbles. At the next, the people had been cooking porridge; and the Elephant, in order to secure both the Hare's portion and his own, sent the latter back to gather some 'medicine' leaves from a tree he had noticed on the way, saying that the *nsima* would not be good without them. The Hare, however, produced some from his bag; he had run back on the road, just after passing the tree, saying that he wanted to look for an arrow he had dropped, and had then picked the leaves. The Dzimwe was so disgusted at being out-witted that he would not eat, but left all the *nsima* to the Hare. Next day, however, when they reached another village, he contrived to get him out of the way for a time, and, on his return, refused to share his porridge with him (an almost unheard-of thing in native manners), alleging that, in the interval, 'many strangers' had arrived, and eaten up all the cooked food in the village, so that there was barely enough for himself. The Hare then retired, stripped off his skin, tied *maseche* rattles to his legs, and came and danced at the door of the hut where the Elephant was eating. The latter, thinking that he was a *chirombo*, fled and left him to finish the porridge. Subsequently, he was induced, by a stratagem not detailed in my version, to strip off his own skin, which the Hare hid while his back was turned. 'And he said, "Who has taken my skin?" and since he was without a skin, he died of the heat.'

Brer Rabbit's methods of disguise are less drastic. 'He slip off en git in a mud-hole, en des lef' his eyes stickin' out'; and when Brer B'ar passed by and said, 'Howdy, Brer Frog, is you see Brer Rabbit go by?' answered, without turning a hair, 'He des gone by.' He plays the same trick on Mrs. Cow; but this time by hiding in a 'brier-patch.' In a Basuto story, he cuts off both his ears and pretends to grind meal on a flat stone; the hyenas in pursuit of him fail to recognise him, and ask him where the Hare has gone.

The trick by which the Hare induced the Elephant to destroy himself, is repeated with endless variations in other stories. In fact, it is found in all countries and all ages. The Cornish giant, already referred to, is one of the best known examples, and no doubt the men who chipped flints in Kent's Hole laughed themselves into fits over something of the same sort. In one Nyanja story the Swallow invites the Cock to dinner, and pretends to fly into the pot where the pumpkins are cooking. In reality he disappears into the shadows of the *nsanja*, and then shows himself up aloft, afterwards alleging that his temporary presence in the pot has greatly improved the flavour of the pumpkins. The Cock, when returning the invitation, tries the same experiment, and is cooked most effectually. In another tale, the *ntengu* bird treats the wildcat in the same way.

Apparently the Hare meets his match in the Tortoise
—though the famous race is by the Anyanja related
as taking place between the Tortoise and the Bush-
buck (*mbawala*). On one occasion these two hoed a
garden together, and the Hare cheated the Tortoise
out of his dinner, as, on another occasion, the Elephant
cheated him. The Tortoise, however, had his revenge
a little later, when they were sowing ground-nuts ; he
crawled into the Hare's seed-bag, as it lay on the
ground, and ate up the supply. The Hare took this
defeat so much to heart that he 'went away and cried.'

All over the world we find tales intended to explain
how animals came by this or that peculiarity which
is striking enough to catch the attention, but has no
obvious use. Thus, the Calabar people tell how the
Tortoise fell off a tree and broke his shell to pieces,
and had it stuck together again, so that the joins are
visible to this day ; and the Hottentots say that the
Hare has a split lip because the Moon threw a piece of
wood at him. We know how Brer Rabbit lost his
long, bushy tail, through letting it hang in the water
while fishing. The Anyanja also think that the Hare
once had a long tail, and there is a story which relates
how he had a piece cut off it at every village he
passed through ; but I have never been able to secure
it in detail. There is a Yao tale to the effect that
baboons are descended from a woman who ran away
to the Bush because the chief had killed one of her
children. She refused to shave her head (in mourning),
and hair subsequently grew all over her body.

The Spider, who on the Guinea Coast is the principal

figure in the animal stories, is, so far as I know, almost absent from Bantu folk-lore. One exception I have already referred to, in a Yao creation-myth; in another Yao tale he crosses a stream and makes a bridge for a chief to escape from his enemies. Here, however, he does not take a specially prominent part, being only one of four helpers provided by the spirit of the chief's elder brother. The Spider is very prominent in the folk-lore of the Duala, who have probably borrowed him from their western neighbours.

We have mentioned that the natives see nothing strange in men assuming the forms of animals—they believe that it happens every day. Their stories give us many instances of the converse process—animals taking human shape whenever it suits them. Thus a girl marries a lion who has turned himself into a man, and, finding out his real nature, runs away from him. Another I give as I have it written down.

'A person (a girl) refused (all) men; there came a baboon; he took off the skin from his body and was turned into a man. The Angoni woman married the baboon, and he hoed the crops, and his companions came from the Bush and ate the crops of his mother-in-law's garden, and (so) he went (with them) into the Bush.'

But a better example still is that of the 'Girl and the Hyena,' which Mr. Macdonald thinks is intended as a warning to girls not to be too fastidious in their choice of husbands, and to accept those first suggested to them, lest worse befall. It might equally well be a warning against marrying a stranger from a distance, and certainly shows the tie between brother

and sister in a very pleasing light. Here it is, as told
me by Katembo at Blantyre.

'There was a woman who refused all husbands, and
at last there came a hyena, and she said, "I want this
one." (So they were married), and the husband said,
"My wife, let us go home." Her brother, who had sore
eyes, followed after them, and she (saw him and) said,
"Where are you going?" The brother crouched down
and hid in the grass, and when they were out of sight
he followed them again, till he came to the village.
When his sister found he was there, she hid him in the
hen-coop. When it was quite dark, a number of
hyenas came outside the hut and sang:

"Here is meat, we will eat it; but it is not fat enough yet."

'The girl was asleep, but her brother heard them, and
as soon as it was light he went and told her that they
meant to eat her. She would not believe it, so he told
her to tie a string to her little finger that night before
she went to sleep, and leave the end outside the hut,
so that he could take it with him into the chicken-
house. In the middle of the night the hyenas came
again, and, when he heard them, he pulled the string
and woke his sister; so she, too, heard them singing:

"Here is meat, we will eat it; but it is not fat enough yet."

'In the morning she said, "I heard them, my brother."
Then he said to her husband, "Brother-in-law, lend me
an adze, I want to make myself a big wooden top"
(*chinguli*).[1] When he had finished it, he put it into

[1] I have never been able to discover any other meaning but this for

Q

his sister's baskets (the luggage she had brought from home), and fastened it firmly, and put his sister into the baskets, and sang :

> "*Chínguli chánga, nde, nde, nde,*
> *Mpérekezéni, nde, nde, nde,*
> *Kúli amái, nde, nde, nde,*
> *Chínguli chánga, nde, nde, nde.'*

That is, " My top ! take her home to her mother ! "

' It flew up and flew away over the Bush, and the hyenas followed ; but he repeated the same song again, and they flew on till they were just above their mother's village. Then he sang again, *Chínguli chánga* (and so on, as above), and the people heard it in the air over their heads, and looked up, and saw them ; and the *chinguli* came to a stop, and let them down right on top of the grain-mortar. And then the brother said, " My sister wanted to send me back because I had sore eyes ; but they would have eaten her at that village, and I have brought her home."' In another version, the mother follows this up with some more good advice, pointing out what she owes to her brother, and warning her ' never to do it again.'

A favourite Yao story is that of the python (*Sato*) who was befriended by a man when caught in a bush-

---

chinguli, which, moreover, I have never heard in any other connection. The usual word for this kind of top is *nguli*, or *nanguli*; *chi* being the augmentative prefix. Another version says rather vaguely that ' he cut out a tree,' and made his sister go into it. Evidently the function of the *chinguli* is the same as that of the magic carpet in the *Arabian Nights*. In the Fiote story of ' Ngomba's Balloon,' given by Mr. Dennett, a basket of some sort seems to be endowed with magical powers. The song should be read phonetically (giving the vowels their German or Italian value), with the accents as marked : the *e* in *nde, nde, nde* (a meaningless refrain) is like that in our word ' end.'

fire. He appealed first to a passing herd of buck
to stop and save him, but they, considering that he
had just eaten one of their number, not unnaturally
refused. Then a man passed by with a hoe in his
hand, and, on being assured that the python would not
devour him, hoed up a piece of ground all round him,
and thus saved him from the fire. The grateful python
told him to come back in four days' time, which he did,
and found that it had changed into a young lad, who
took him home, entertained him with plenty of beer,
and finally presented him with two pieces (1 piece = 16
yards) of calico and a magic bottle, which was to be
opened in presence of his enemies.

When the man went home, he found there was war;
his family had fled, and the enemy were occupying the
village. He opened his bottle, and they were immediately annihilated. He then went to hoe in the
gardens, leaving his bottle and other property in his
hut. Another detachment of the enemy arrived—they
took possession of the village and all that was in it,
pursued him to his garden, and took him prisoner.
He was tied up, with his neck in a gori-stick, with a
view to being killed next day. During the night he
felt a rat gnawing his feet, and asked it to go to the
chief's house and bring the bottle. The rat did so,
and the man said, 'I will pay you in the morning.'
When the people were all assembled, and the man was
brought out into the *bwalo* to be killed, he opened his
bottle. 'The people who sat there when he held it up
were dead and gone'—there was no one there! So he
rewarded the rat with two cows.

Animal stories sometimes vary in having one or more of their characters replaced by human beings: thus there is one in which the Antelope sets a trap and catches a Leopard in it. He spares the Leopard's life, but meets with no gratitude, for the latter eats all his children, and then his wife. He appeals for help to a number of animals in succession, without getting it, till the Hare takes the case in hand, and induces the Leopard to put his head once more into the trap, and show how he was caught. Once in, the Hare advises the Antelope to kill him. Now the same story is told to explain why there should be a standing feud between crocodiles and men. The Crocodile behaved very much in the same way as the Leopard, and finally jumped on the man's back and made him carry him. The Hare intervened, heard the whole story, and then asked the Crocodile to show him how he got into the trap, with results as above.

The Yao tale of the Hyena and the Bees is a version, with animal actors, of a story which, in various shapes, is probably found throughout the whole of Bantu Africa. The Basuto tell it of a girl called Tselane, who was carried off by a cannibal. He put her into a bag, which he threw over his shoulder, and started for home. On the way he stopped at a hut, which turned out to be her uncle's, and laid down his sack while he went in to rest. Tselane's relatives discovered her plight, let her out, and put in a dog and a quantity of venomous ants in her place. Consequently the cannibal, when he had shut himself up in his hut to enjoy his feast alone, died a miser-

able death. In the Yao story, the Hyena steals the
fox's (or jackal's) cubs, and puts them into a bag ;
but the mother contrives to substitute a swarm of bees
for them before he carries them off. 'So the Hyena
and his brethren died.'

There is a rather curious Nyanja story, introducing
a being very like the *Chiruwi* mentioned in Chapter
III. Some children went out into the Bush to gather
masuku fruit. While they were out, it came on to
rain, and the stream which they had crossed easily was
full when they reached it on the way home, and too
deep to ford. While they were considering what to
do, there came along 'a big bird, with one wing, one
eye, and one leg,' and carried them over, strictly
charging them to tell no one at home that it had done
so. One boy, however, told his mother what had
happened ; the rest all denied it, and asked people not
to listen to him, saying they had crossed in the ordinary way. Next time they went to look for *masuku*
they forded the stream, and some of them held out a
branch to the boy who had talked, to help him over ;
it was rotten, and broke, and he was swept away
by the current. They called out after him, ' You
told.'

Mr. Macdonald gives a story which in some respects
reminds one of Grimm's ' Frau Holle,' though not so
much as does a Ronga one given by M. Junod under
the title of *La Route du Ciel.* Both of these, though
differing greatly from one another, are evidently the
same tale. In the Yao one, a woman who has been
persuaded by a trick to throw her baby into the water,

and has seen it swallowed by a crocodile, climbs a tree in her distress, and says, ' I want to go on high.' The tree grows up with her and carries her to a strange country, where she meets, first, leopards, then the *Nsensi* (a large kind of water-rat, or perhaps a bird), and lastly, some great fishes, who all show the way to Mulungu. When she reached 'the village of Mulungu,' she told her story. 'Then Mulungu called the crocodile, and it came. Mulungu said, "Give up the child," and it delivered it up. The girl received the child and went down to her mother. Her mother was much delighted and gave her much cloth and a good house.'

Her wicked companions were now envious, and, wishing to enjoy like good fortune, began by throwing their babies into the water. They climbed the tree and reached Mulungu's country, but gave rude answers to the leopards, the *nsensi*, and the fishes. 'Then they came to Mulungu. Mulungu said, "What do you want?" The girls said, "We have thrown our children into the water." But Mulungu said, "What was the reason of that?" The girls hid the matter and said "Nothing." But Mulungu said, "It is false. You cheated your companion, saying, 'Throw your child into the water,' and now you tell me a lie." Then Mulungu took a bottle of lightning, and said, "Your children are in here." The girls took the bottle, and the bottle made a report like a gun. The girls both died.'

In the Ronga version, likewise, the wicked sister is killed by lightning. ' Le ciel fit explosion et la tua.'

is cheated at first, and learns by bitter experience; the
closing incident, too, is different. The Hare and the
Dzimwe went on a journey together, begging food (as
native travellers do) at all the villages they came to.
At the first, the Elephant said, 'Let us ask for sugar-
cane and *bango* reeds' (which are uneatable); he then
took the sugar-cane and gave the Hare the *bango*. At
the next village he acted in the same way with millet
and pebbles. At the next, the people had been cooking porridge; and the Elephant, in order to secure both
the Hare's portion and his own, sent the latter back
to gather some 'medicine' leaves from a tree he had
noticed on the way, saying that the *nsima* would not
be good without them. The Hare, however, produced
some from his bag; he had run back on the road, just
after passing the tree, saying that he wanted to look
for an arrow he had dropped, and had then picked the
leaves. The Dzimwe was so disgusted at being out-
witted that he would not eat, but left all the *nsima*
to the Hare. Next day, however, when they reached
another village, he contrived to get him out of the
way for a time, and, on his return, refused to share his
porridge with him (an almost unheard-of thing in native
manners), alleging that, in the interval, 'many strangers'
had arrived, and eaten up all the cooked food in the
village, so that there was barely enough for himself.
The Hare then retired, stripped off his skin, tied *maseche*
rattles to his legs, and came and danced at the door of
the hut where the Elephant was eating. The latter,
thinking that he was a *chirombo*, fled and left him to
finish the porridge. Subsequently, he was induced, by

of them were poor. And the father brought three
tusks of ivory to give to his three poor sons. The
sons then said, " Let us go to the coast, let us buy
goods." And they called up men to carry their
goods. Then they set off on their journey and came
to the coast. When they arrived, they built a grass
house and slept there one day. In the morning one
of them set off with his tusk to buy goods, but his
brothers did not know that he had gone to buy goods.
And he bought a precious glass for looking into every
land.

'Then the second one set off and bought a mat for
flying with into every land. Then the third bought a
medicine for making people dead or alive. But each
of these did not know that the others had gone to buy
goods.

'Afterwards, he who had the glass began to look
into it. When he looked, he saw that in the land of
his home there had died his friend. Then he told the
others that there was a mourning, and they asked,
"How do you know that at our home some one has
died ? " And he answered, " Because I looked in my
glass." Then he gave them the glass that they might
look, and they saw their friend dead. Afterwards they
began to grumble, saying, " If only we had medicine
for flying " ; and the second brother produced his mat.
The others said, " Make us fly that we may reach our
home to-day, that we may be at the funeral, because
he was a friend of ours." And he placed them on the
mat, and they flew, and came to their village on the
same day.

'When they arrived, they again began to grumble, saying, "If only we had medicine to make this man alive, we would make him alive." Then came the one who had medicine for making alive, and made the man alive again.

'But afterwards there arose a dispute as to whom the man should belong. The one who had the glass said, "He is mine, because I saw him." The one who had the mat answered, "I flew and conveyed you." Then answered he who had the medicine, saying, "Did I not come and make him alive?" But the one with the mat said, "Could you have brought the man to life without him who carried you there?" The sons were then about to quarrel and came to the father, bringing the man with them. And the father said, "You have all done foolishly, because you bought precious things which take away all peace; you wished to excel beyond all men, but you have failed."'

This story, it was found on inquiry, had long been known to several of the Domasi villagers. We see that the trading voyage has become the usual journey to the coast, and the magic carpet a mat; the claiming of the man as a' slave (regardless of the fact that he is previously spoken of as a friend to be mourned), is a local touch. On the Lower Congo (see Dennett, *Folk-Lore of the Fjort*) we find a tale which is evidently the same as this, of two wives who between them brought their husband back to life. It is found in M. Junod's collection under the title of *Les Trois Vaisseaux*; we have also a Swahili version, and one from the Kru coast in West Africa. The excellent moral

figure in the animal stories, is, so far as I know, almost absent from Bantu folk-lore. One exception I have already referred to, in a Yao creation-myth; in another Yao tale he crosses a stream and makes a bridge for a chief to escape from his enemies. Here, however, he does not take a specially prominent part, being only one of four helpers provided by the spirit of the chief's elder brother. The Spider is very prominent in the folk-lore of the Duala, who have probably borrowed him from their western neighbours.

We have mentioned that the natives see nothing strange in men assuming the forms of animals—they believe that it happens every day. Their stories give us many instances of the converse process—animals taking human shape whenever it suits them. Thus a girl marries a lion who has turned himself into a man, and, finding out his real nature, runs away from him. Another I give as I have it written down.

'A person (a girl) refused (all) men; there came a baboon; he took off the skin from his body and was turned into a man. The Angoni woman married the baboon, and he hoed the crops, and his companions came from the Bush and ate the crops of his mother-in-law's garden, and (so) he went (with them) into the Bush.'

But a better example still is that of the 'Girl and the Hyena,' which Mr. Macdonald thinks is intended as a warning to girls not to be too fastidious in their choice of husbands, and to accept those first suggested to them, lest worse befall. It might equally well be a warning against marrying a stranger from a distance, and certainly shows the tie between brother

because, though he is speaking of the Delagoa Bay
natives, it will also apply to other Bantu tribes.

'Every young man, every girl, knows one or two
tales which he or she is always willing to repeat.
Sometimes, even, they are expected to amuse the
company with a story, told by way of forfeit, when
they are the losers in a game. Beginners often get
confused and break down. They mix up the incidents,
or lose the thread of the narrative. "That is too
much for you!" (literally, "that has overcome you,")
says the audience, and a more skilled reciter then takes
the stage. Next time, the novice will acquit himself
better. Besides, when the young people have come to
an end of all they know, there remain the old women,
who are the real repositories of tradition. Some of
them know ten, twenty, or thirty tales, and I know
more than one who could go on the whole evening,
every day for a fortnight, without completely exhaust-
ing her stock. . . . Children exercise their memory
in this way, and accustom themselves to speak in
public; and it is perhaps to this custom that the South
African races owe their extreme facility in expressing
themselves.'[1]

[1] *Chants et Contes des Baronga*, pp. 70-71.

CHAPTER XI

Totemistic clans. Kinship counted through women.
The paramount chief: his powers. Succession to the
chieftainship. Administration of justice. Crime and
punishment. Slavery.

BOTH Yaos and Anyanja trace descent through the
mother, and cannot marry within their own clan, which
is, of course, the mother's. The Yao clans are still
clearly known and named. Mr. R. S. Hynde says:
'The Yaos are divided among themselves into sub-
tribes, stocks, or totemistic clans,[1] each with its own
distinctive name, *e.g.* the Amwale, the Asomba, the
Apiri clan. If you question them on the subject, they
will usually be able to tell you this clan name, unless
the person questioned be a slave, who, from various
causes, may not know it.' *Somba* means 'a fish,' and
mwale 'a girl'; *piri* in Nyanja is 'a mountain,' though
I have been unable to discover its significance as a
Yao word. Thus, if Mwepeta, of the *Somba* clan,
marries Ndiagani, of the *Mwale*, their children will
be *Mwale*, and none of them can marry a *Mwale*.
Their nearest relation and natural guardian will be
their mother's brother, who (if the grandfather is dead)

[1] Each of these clans appears to have a *mwiko* with regard to some
animal, but the subject has not yet been sufficiently investigated.

fire. He appealed first to a passing herd of buck to stop and save him, but they, considering that he had just eaten one of their number, not unnaturally refused. Then a man passed by with a hoe in his hand, and, on being assured that the python would not devour him, hoed up a piece of ground all round him, and thus saved him from the fire. The grateful python told him to come back in four days' time, which he did, and found that it had changed into a young lad, who took him home, entertained him with plenty of beer, and finally presented him with two pieces (1 piece = 16 yards) of calico and a magic bottle, which was to be opened in presence of his enemies.

When the man went home, he found there was war; his family had fled, and the enemy were occupying the village. He opened his bottle, and they were im-, mediately annihilated. He then went to hoe in the gardens, leaving his bottle and other property in his hut. Another detachment of the enemy arrived—they took possession of the village and all that was in it, pursued him to his garden, and took him prisoner. He was tied up, with his neck in a gori-stick, with a view to being killed next day. During the night he felt a rat gnawing his feet, and asked it to go to the chief's house and bring the bottle. The rat did so, and the man said, 'I will pay you in the morning.' When the people were all assembled, and the man was brought out into the *bwalo* to be killed, he opened his bottle. 'The people who sat there when he held it up were dead and gone'—there was no one there! So he rewarded the rat with two cows.

The Yao chief, Kapeni, belonged to the Abanda clan, and was succeeded on his death, not by any of his sons (who, of course, were not Abanda), but by the son of his sister, born of the same mother. Had any younger sons of his mother survived, they would have had the preference; but half-brothers or sisters (children of the same father, but not of the same mother), are not counted as relatives—except that they cannot marry. According to the Yao system of descent, a man should be able to marry his father's sisters, but this is seldom done, and is, in fact, considered very wrong; but he may marry their daughters. Where *chilawa* prevails, however, these too are forbidden—they are really reckoned as sisters.

Native terms of relationship are often very puzzling. *Mbale* is a word which may be applied to a brother, sister, cousin, or relative of almost any sort—sometimes even to a friend. There is no word for 'sister' or 'brother'; but there are words meaning 'elder brother (or sister)' and 'younger brother (or sister)'; and these are never used apart from their possessive pronouns. There is a word which means 'sister' when used by a brother, and 'brother' when used by a sister, but is never applied to one of the same sex as the speaker. A man will call all his father's brothers 'father,' and all his mother's sisters 'mother'; and the term 'grandparents' may include all the great-uncles and great-aunts.

Mr. Duff Macdonald well shows the process by which a family may grow into a small state. A man wishing to found a new village asks permission of his chief—

which in most cases is readily granted—and moves out
into the bush with his wives and children. Temporary
shelters are built, and then the man cuts down the trees,
while his wives hoe up the ground for gardens; and,
when these are ready, and planted, more permanent
dwellings are erected. If there are daughters old
enough to marry, the village is soon enlarged by the
sons-in-law who come and build their huts there. The
new chief may be accompanied by his younger brothers,
or by friends who call themselves by that name, and
place themselves under his authority. As the new
settlement grows in power and importance, it will be
joined by others, and may grow wealthy by trading.

In general, the Bantu have everywhere much the
same system of government: the same features can
nearly always be traced, even when modified by local
circumstances. The Anyanja, when they first became
known to Europeans, lived in small villages (as they
do now), each under the control of its own head-man.
A district, containing a large number of villages, was
ruled by a sub-chief: such were Chinsunzi and Kan-
komba, in the Shiré Highlands, in 1861; and over the
whole country was the Paramount Chief, or *Rundo*
(*Lundu*), who at the same period was Mankokwe.[1]
Mankokwe's dominions appear to have extended from
Lake Chilwa to the Shiré, and down the latter river
as far as the Ruo; below the Ruo was another paramount chief, Tingani. Above the confluence of the

---

[1] According to one authority, the unit is the *mzinda*, which comprises
all the villages having the same *unyago* or *nkole*. Others merely translate *msinda*, 'head village,' or 'capital'; but it seems to be the capital
not of the *Rundo* but of the sub-chief.

Shiré and the Zambezi, between Kebrabasa and Zumbo, were two other independent Nyanja chiefs, Sandia and Mpende. All these chiefs seem at one time to have been 'united under the government of their great chief, Undi, whose empire extended from Lake Shirwa to the River Loangwa; but after Undi's death it fell to pieces, and a large portion of it on the Zambezi was absorbed by their powerful southern neighbours, the Banyai.'[1] This process has been repeated over and over again in the history of Africa. The Anyanja, being an agricultural (and on the whole a peaceable) people, kept up no national life outside their little village communities, but tended more and more to what German historians call *Particularism*. Consequently, they were unable to withstand the shock of an invasion; and their organisation, such as it was, went to pieces before the onslaught of Yaos, Makololo, and Angoni.

Women chiefs are mentioned several times by Livingstone as ruling in various parts of this region: Chikandakadzi, near Morambala (her position with regard to Tingani is not stated); Nyango, who seems to have ranked as *Rundo* in part of the Upper Shiré Valley, and Mamburuma, near Zumbo on the Zambezi; also Manenko and Nyamosana in the Lunda country. More recently, we find Nalolo, a sister of Liwanika, occupying the position of a chief in the Barotse country. The present Kazembe appears to be a woman. Sebituane, the Makololo chief, appointed his daughter as his successor, 'probably,' says Livingstone, 'in imitation

[1] Livingstone, *Zambesi*, p. 198.

of some of the negro tribes with whom he had come
into contact.' She, however, soon resigned what proved
a distasteful position; for her father, unwilling that
she should transfer her power to a husband, directed
her not to marry, but to contract any number of temporary alliances.   It may be, however, that this feature
of the situation was due, not so much to Sebituane's
Bechuana ideas of the husband necessarily being 'the
woman's lord,' as to some lingering Rotse and Lunda
traditions of polyandry; and a writer in the *Livingstonia
Missionary Magazine* characterises the present Kazembe
as 'a thoroughly bad woman—a woman of Samaria
over again,' which may be due to a misunderstanding
of a very peculiar institution.

It is impossible not to connect these scattered indications with those afforded by the Yao system of
kinship, and marriage customs, as to the state of
things in an earlier period of which we have no
record.

The Yao tribal organisation is in itself much the
same as that of the Anyanja, but it was more
closely knit, owing to the exigencies of war; and the
relations of the conquerors to the conquered tribes
must be distinguished from those which obtained
among themselves.   But it must be remembered that
the Yaos were not an aggressive tribe, organised for
conquest, under a chief like Tshaka or Mziligazi.   In
their own country—between Lake Chilwa and the Upper
Rovuma—they seem to have been both a pastoral and
an industrial people.   'Yao-land proper,' says Archdeacon Johnson, 'had plenty of smelting-furnaces,

R

cattle, and peas and beans, plenty for man and beast.'
They cultivated 'down both sides of the Lujenda, till
the valleys were full of Indian corn, and settlement
extended its fields to those of the next settlement.'
The Machinga, who occupied this country, were dis-
lodged by the Alolo (Makua) from the south-east, who
themselves expelled from the north by the (Zulu)
Magwangwara, drove them into the country of the
Mangoche, forcing the latter into the Shiré Highlands.
This was the so-called invasion of 1861.

There are five branches of the Yao nation : the
Makale, near the sources of the Rovuma ; the Nama-
taka (or Mwembe people), on the hills west of the
Lujenda ; the Masaninga, Mangoche, and Machinga.
The last three were the tribes who entered the Shiré
Highlands. Their chiefs seem to have been quite
independent of one another ; Kapeni of Sochi was
perhaps the most powerful.

The chieftainship is hereditary, and passes, as already
stated, to the deceased's younger brothers in succession,
or, failing those, to the eldest son of his sister. The
new chief takes, at the same time, his predecessor's
official name, so that there is always a Kapeni, or
Malemya, or Mponda, as the case may be. The Angoni
chiefs, however, observe the Zulu rule of inheritance,
and are succeeded by the eldest son of the principal
(or 'official') wife, who is the one married after accession
—earlier ones do not count.

But there are some chiefs who have not succeeded
to their position by right of birth, but attained it
by superior cleverness and energy. Such a man may

even be a slave, as was said to have been the case with Chibisa, who, in the early sixties, had much more real power than his neighbour Mankokwe, the Rundo of the Shiré Highlands. This man began by representing himself as possessed by the spirit of Chibisa, a deceased ₁prophetess of note among the Nyungwe tribe, near Tete, whose name he assumed. The Nyungwe believed him, and he gradually obtained a complete ascendency over their chief, Kapichi, finally inducing part of the latter's people to secede with him and settle at the foot of the Murchison Cataracts. His history may be read in the Rev. H. Rowley's *Story of the Universities' Mission*, where it is related how, at last, he fell in battle, fighting Terere, though without mention of the sand-bullet which killed him— the only thing against which he had no charm.

The unexpected rise of a man like this has often been the agency in breaking up Bantu 'empires' like that of Undi. But the new power is seldom permanent, as it does not often happen that such parvenu chiefs leave behind them successors of equal ability; while, having no backing but their own immediate followers, they lack that support of custom and tradition which in normal times will keep a mere average ruler in his place, so long as he does not forfeit it by any act of his own.

The customary order of succession is sometimes set aside, not so much by the tribe collectively (though it, too, being represented by the head-men, has a share in deciding the question), as by the household of the late chief. As both wives and slaves have a personal interest in the appointment of the successor, it is but just that they should have a chance to express their objections, if any. When Malemya of Zomba died, in 1878, his slaves, and many of his head-men, disliked the obvious heir, his younger brother Kumtaja, while the widows openly preferred a nephew, Kasabola. The head-men announced that, if Kumtaja were appointed, the people of the chief's village would all leave and go to live elsewhere. Kasabola, accordingly, was installed, and took the name of Malemya, while Kumtaja left, taking with him such head-men as would go, and founded a new village not far off. Malemya, finding him an inconvenient neighbour, called in the Angoni, who came and raided Kumtaja's village in August 1884. He fled first to Lake Chilwa, and then to the Upper Shiré, where he died some years ago.

When the new chief is appointed, some little time is allowed to pass before he is formally inducted. The day is then fixed for him to assume his official title (literally, 'to enter the name'), after which his old name is never heard again. He is lectured on his duties to his people—which are held to consist chiefly in exercising hospitality, and not beating them too much ; and, if he is a Yao of certain families, he is invested with the *lisanda*, a white head-band with hanging ends. Some Yao chiefs are not entitled to wear the *lisanda* ; while, on the other hand, the right is enjoyed by some minor head-men who belong to the privileged families. It is henceforth worn on all solemn occasions—and sometimes at beer-drinkings— and the chief's first appearance in it is hailed with songs of rejoicing. The proceedings, as might be expected, end with feasting.

On the Lake a special oblong house, with one side open, is built for the chief's investiture. The insignia of royalty are here, a red blanket, and a red fez, called *chisoti cha sindi*—both probably imported.

The chief's powers are not despotic;[1] he is not supposed to act without consulting his head-men, who represent the general views of the tribe ; and he seldom disregards their opinion to any serious extent. Should he persist in doing so, his career would either come to a sudden and violent end, or his people would leave him to seek some more congenial ruler, and he would find himself lord of deserted villages. This is a recognised and constitutional remedy for grievances, and no chief refuses an asylum to such refugees; indeed, it is to his interest to welcome them. Fugitive slaves, on the other hand, are often returned to their masters.

The village head-man settles all local matters, usually with the assistance of the elders or heads of families, who are called his 'younger brothers.' He consults them before engaging in war, or undertaking any public work, such as constructing a stockade round the village ; but he cannot summon them to work on his own private account, nor exact tribute from them. He settles any disputes among them, but if they are not satisfied with his decision, they can appeal to

---

[1] ' The chief may often have less influence than powerful head-men, and we have known cases where he contented himself with grumbling when his head-men acted contrary to his desire ; and in many criminal trials he is eclipsed by the sorcerers and pounders of poison ' (*Africana*, i. 155).

a higher head-man, or sub-chief, or to the chief himself.

Graver matters are reported by the head-man to the sub-chief, and by him, if necessary, to the chief. The latter holds the head-man responsible for any wrong-doing of his people which may come to his ears, just as the chief in his turn will be held responsible for any aggression of his head-men against outsiders. So far is this principle carried that, when a man has been injured by an inhabitant of a certain village, he and his friends are quite satisfied if they can catch any other man belonging to the same village, whom they will either put to death or hold to ransom till reparation is made.

The *mlandu* and the *ordeal* are the two great judicial institutions of Bantu Africa. With the ordeal we have partly dealt elsewhere, but there will be a little more to say about it presently.

Mlandu is a word which may be variously rendered as 'lawsuit,' 'complaint,' 'discussion,' crime,' and other-wise, according to the context. It is the same thing known as a 'palaver' in West Africa, and an *indaba* by the Zulus. Civil cases are thus settled. The head-man and his 'younger brothers' take their seats in the *bwalo*, and, as a rule, the whole village is assembled, the men sitting on one side, and the women —a little apart—on the other. The accuser speaks first, then the accused, and the various members of the council give their opinions in turn. The speeches are often long and eloquent, and the case may extend over days or even weeks before the head-man gives his decision, or, as the natives say, 'cuts the case.' If no decision is come to, or if either party wishes to appeal, the case is transferred to a higher court, and 'the *mlandu* spoken' before the sub-chief or the chief. An important case of this sort is sometimes attended by hundreds of people. The successful party in the suit makes the judge a present out of the damages. Matrimonial cases are settled before a court of this kind—if, for instance, a wife feels herself aggrieved and returns to her relatives. She is represented before the court by her 'surety.' The husband may also bring an action for divorce in this way.

Criminal charges, too, in the first instance, are brought before the chief's or head-man's court. A man caught stealing may, by native law, be killed, and his death entails no prosecution. He may be caught alive, and would then be put into a slave-stick for safe-keeping, till ransomed by his friends; and killed, or kept as a slave, if no ransom were forthcoming.

When a theft has been committed, without suspicion falling on any particular person, the diviner or the *mabisalila* is consulted, and the person pointed out by him or her accused before the court. The prosecutors demand restitution of the stolen goods; the defendant pleads not guilty, and offers to drink *mwavi* to prove it. His friends, if they believe him innocent, will demand the ordeal on his behalf; if they have misgivings, they will be afraid to run the risk, convinced, as they are, that the guilty party invariably dies, and knowing that, in such a case, they will have to pay the full value of whatever was stolen. If guilty, a man will probably confess rather than risk the ordeal—he, or his relations, will have to make restitution and pay a fine besides, the head-man of his village being held responsible. These payments also have to be made for him, if his confidence in the judgment of the ordeal turns out to have been misplaced—his death, in the native view, conclusively proving his guilt. If, on the other hand, he survives, the accusers have to pay over a fine to him, and the sorcerer is assumed to have been mistaken. Some try a second sorcerer, but he must not point out the man just acquitted, as no man can be made to drink *mwavi* twice on the same charge.

Theft, if brought into court at all, is always punished by a fine; but sometimes the thief is handed over as a slave to the injured party. Other ordeals are sometimes used besides the *mwavi*—plunging the hand into hot water, or touching red-hot iron—but the principle is the same: injury to the hand proves guilt. It will be noticed that the head-man is held responsible for thefts committed by his villagers, in accordance with the principle already stated. (He may, in fact, be the receiver of the stolen goods.) If he refuses to take the matter up when it is brought to his notice, war may be the result.

A murderer, if caught red-handed, may be killed by the friends of his victim; or they may put him in a slave-stick till slaves have been paid over for his ransom. Some of these are sometimes sacrificed to the *manes* of the victim. If the actual slayer cannot be caught, a man from the same village may be captured and held to ransom in the same way. In some cases, no distinction is made between accidental homicide and murder; sometimes a gun which has been the cause of an accident is seized instead of the owner, and held till he pays several slaves for it. Sometimes, however, the view is taken that the man or his gun may have been bewitched, and steps are taken to find out and punish the person who has done this. The man who kills his own slave, or even his younger brother, or other ward, is not amenable to justice, but—unless he can protect himself by a charm —he is afraid of the mysterious *chirope* which over-takes those who shed blood within the tribe. The chief, to whom he goes if he has committed such a murder, procures the charm for him from his own medicine-man, and uses it himself as well, ' because of the blood that has been shed in his land.'

Adultery is theoretically a capital crime with most Bantu tribes; that is, the man may be (and frequently is) shot or speared by the husband; the wife is frequently let off with a warning the first time, but for a second offence either killed or divorced and sent back to her relatives, who in such a case must return whatever present was made at the marriage. Sometimes she drinks *mwavi*, and is, of course, accounted guilty if she dies. But in practice, the matter is often arranged by paying damages, or the guilty man may be sold into slavery. Still there can be no question that (where they have not been corrupted by outside influences, or their customs and institutions disorganised by war, etc.) they look on it as a very serious affair.

Slave wives are more summarily dealt with, and are

often either killed or sold. I have seen one 'Angoni'
woman who had had her nose and ears cut off, but
seemed to be living on in her husband's (or master's)
family, as before,—though evidently doing most of
the heavy work. But such cases are not common,
except perhaps among the coast Arabs, who have
large slave harems and rule them by terror.

From what has already been said, it will be seen
that in ordinary procedure formal executions are not
common; if the criminal has not been killed red-
handed, or if he does not undergo the ordeal, the trial
usually ends in a fine, or in his being handed over as a
slave to his accusers. But where the chief orders a
man to be executed, he is usually stabbed or has his
throat cut. Sometimes a wizard is shot at once on
being detected by the Mabisalila, and sometimes,
when convicted by the ordeal, the crowd fall upon him
and lynch him without waiting for the poison to do its
work: an outbreak of panic ferocity which has its
parallel, in a more deliberate form, in the records of
English and Scottish witch-trials.

Witches were in former times sometimes burned
alive by the Yaos; but Mr. Macdonald says that in
his time this was only done if they refused the *mwavi*
test, which was not likely to happen. It was done
also by the Anyanja at Likoma, and the stake where
these executions took place stood on the site of the
present Cathedral. But by far the greater number of
cases were left to be decided by the issue of the poison.

At one time, the Yaos used to torture the person
pointed out by the witch-detective by squeezing his

head between two pieces of wood, till he pointed out where the horns were buried ; but in later times the Mabisalila found the horns (as already described) as well as naming the witch. But I do not think that this, or judicial torture to extort confession of ordinary crime, is common.

An act of sacrilege held to be penal is when a free man sets fire to grass or reeds near a lake supposed to be the abode of a tutelary spirit, in which case he would be thrown into the lake. This perhaps would be rather a sacrifice than an execution.

Imprisonment as a punishment is scarcely known, and indeed scarcely possible, though, as has been said, men are sometimes detained in the slave-stick till ransomed or otherwise disposed of. It is a small log with a fork at one end, long enough for the other end to rest on the ground when a man's neck is inserted into the fork and secured with an iron pin. Slaves are confined in these sticks on the march (as in the familiar picture in Livingstone's *Zambezi Expedition*), or when they are likely to run away,—or sometimes as a punishment. Debtors, adulterers, and thieves may be put in the slave-stick till their debts or fines are paid up. Slaves, when thus confined, sometimes have the other end of the stick fastened up to a tree, so that they can do their usual work of pounding corn, or the like, There is also a form of stocks called in Yao *ugwalata*. consisting of a hole in the verandah-part of a hut, through which a man's arm or leg is passed, and secured so that he cannot draw it back. Slaves are sometimes severely beaten.

The Makololo chiefs approach more nearly the idea of an irresponsible despot than any others in this part of Africa ; but this is owing to a special set of circumstances, and they cannot be taken as typical. It is the more necessary to bear this in mind, because the chapter of horrors which Mr. Macdonald gives under the heading, ' A Slave Government,' may seem to contradict some of the statements we have made. These chiefs, then, were placed in a very exceptional position. They were a small minority of warriors in the midst of an unwarlike population whom they regarded with contempt, but who were strong enough to make them think they must secure their position by ruthless severity. Some of them had actually been slaves themselves, though the only Makololo among them, Ramakukane, was of good family. Cruelty is not a Makololo trait, though Sebituane and Sekeletu could act with firmness and even harshness when the occasion seemed to demand it. But some unusually barbarous punishments seem to have been used in the Barotse valley where the Makololo had settled, and to which some of these chiefs belonged by birth. They may have brought some of these customs with them ; and their becoming possessed of virtually unlimited power, while at the same time their footing was but a precarious one, did the rest. None of them was subject to the others ; they were far enough apart to be quite independent ; but they acted together in face of a common enemy. It is a pleasing fiction that their despotism was on the whole of a benevolent character, and voluntarily submitted to by the Mang'anja, who

welcomed them as protectors against the Yaos; but
this illusion is dispelled by a closer acquaintance with
the facts. Even before the departure of the Livingstone expedition, they had begun to tyrannise over
the Shiré population; but it was only after that event
that their power became fully established. Several of
them were undoubtedly men of fine qualities; but a
careful examination of their careers before and after
(roughly speaking) 1861, leads to the conclusion that
some at least must have degenerated sadly.

They took advantage of the famine of 1862-3 to
enslave the Mang'anja, and 'their power increased
every day till they could claim all on the Lower Shiré
for their subjects.' They had no council of head-men,
and though each village had a head-man, he was not
a responsible local ruler, but a mere taskmaster
appointed by the chief. Forced labour and oppressive
tribute were exacted. No woman had a 'surety,' as
with the Yaos, but the chief disposed at will of his
subjects' daughters—assigned them to husbands of his
own choosing, or took them into his harem, as he felt
disposed. Wholesale *mwavi*-drinkings took place, at
which no one was allowed to refuse the cup; and
judicial torture was frequent.

The ordinary tribute paid to chiefs varies in different
tribes, but is not in general excessive. In some parts,
when an elephant is killed, the chief claims 'the ground
tusk'—*i.e.* the one which touches the ground when it
falls; elsewhere this is not insisted on. Presents are
usually expected from strangers passing through the
country, but they get something in return; and a chief

(though in practice he may fall short of the ideal) is always supposed to be generous. Yao local head-men send their chief a percentage of the ivory when they kill elephants, and (if they live near enough) a haunch of any large animal (such as an eland) which they may shoot. It is also the custom for them to invite him to a beer-drinking at least once in the year. Sometimes the chief sends for the village head-men, or orders them to find men, to do some work for him at his village— hoeing, or building huts. This was frequently done by the Angoni chiefs, who also (as has been said before) made periodical levies of their subjects' sons to herd their cattle, and of their daughters for the harem.

There is no regular priestly class. The professional diviners and medicine-men to a certain extent occupy the same position, and a Yao chief sometimes appoints a 'sacrificer,' whose duties are of a somewhat miscellaneous character. Besides taking the omens before a battle, he has to carry the banner and lead the army —the chief himself, like David in later life, not going into action. (He stays behind to 'supply powder and deal with deserters.') The 'sacrificer' tastes the beer offered to the chief's guests, to show that it is not poisoned, and beats one of the drums at witch-dances, where he represents the chief, if the latter is unable to be present. Whether he is the same as the chief's medicine-man is not clear.

But the strictly religious functions of a priest, as we have seen, are performed by the chief on behalf of his tribe, by the head-man for the village, by the father for the family, and (in private matters) by the individual for himself.

We have seen how the chief presides over, or at least takes part in, public prayers for rain; but the Yaos and Anyanja do not at present seem to have anything corresponding to the 'feast of first-fruits' among the southern Bantu, where the chief ceremonially 'tastes' the first of the new crops before the people are allowed to gather them. There are traces of such a rite among the Yaos, and I am inclined to think that the Angoni keep up something of the kind, or did a few years back, because I was informed at one of the Ntumbi kraals, about the beginning of the harvest season, that the father of the family was away at Chekusi's, 'eating maize,'—an expression of which I did not at the time grasp the probable bearing. The Zulus keep the *ukutsh-wama* with great solemnity, and the Angoni would have brought the custom with them from the south, though I do not know how they observe it in detail.

The chief is supposed to be the owner of all the land, but in strictness he cannot alienate it without the consent of the tribe. It seems, however, as if, apart from European or Arab influence, the idea of permanent property in land scarcely existed. No one is supposed to own land except so long as he actually cultivates it; and, owing to the method of agriculture, it is abandoned every few years. Any member of the tribe can make a fresh garden where he likes, provided no one else has bespoken the ground; but a stranger would require the chief's permission to settle. The chief's land is well defined, and has recognised boundaries, but there seem to be no definite limits to the territory occupied by a tribe.

The Mang'anja used to recognise certain animals as *nyama ya lundu*, 'king's meat,' not allowed to be eaten by the people in general. Among these were the *nkaka*, or scaly ant-eater, whereof the Rev. D. C. Scott was on one occasion invited to partake by Ramakukane, and a certain kind of large frog or toad called *tesi*, said to be very delicate eating.

It remains to speak of slavery, which has always been, in varying proportions, a feature of Bantu society. The outside slave *trade* does not so much concern us here, as (in this part of Africa, at any rate) it is entirely an exotic thing, introduced and fostered by the Portuguese on one side and the Arabs on the other. And though this has been largely, if not wholly, done away with (it is certain that there was some smuggling going on, twelve years ago), yet domestic slavery, which is very difficult for governments to interfere with, still continues in fact, if not in name, and will only die out gradually. The proportion of slaves to free people is probably not large—unless all the Anyanja subject to the Angoni are counted as slaves —which is not, strictly speaking, correct; they are rather in the position of serfs or villeins.

Slavery may be a matter of birth; the children of slaves, or of a slave mother and free father, are slaves also. Some slaves are persons taken prisoners in war, or sold (probably to pay a debt) by father, grandfather, or elder brother. Others may have been condemned to

slavery as criminals, or bewitchers, or possessed of
'the evil eye,' and these are sold to some one at a
distance—to get rid of them. Or they may be seized
on account of a debt they cannot pay ; or, lastly, they
may voluntarily become slaves, in time of famine, in
order to get food.

The owner has the power of life and death over
his slaves, but subject to the moral restraint already
mentioned. Slaves may be beaten—sometimes cruelly
—or confined in *gori*-sticks, at the will of their masters,
but as a rule they are kindly treated, and, in fact,
to an outsider, are often indistinguishable from the
family. In speaking of or to them, the master says
mwana ('child'), or *mnyamata* ('boy'), rather than
kapolo ('slave'). Some of the families at Nziza and
Ntumbi had Yao slaves who must have been captured
in the raids across the Shiré a few years before, and
who seemed quite contented with their lot.

Slaves are employed about the usual work of a
house and garden: the women are generally the
master's junior wives, and share the household labours
among them ; the men sometimes relieve them of part
of the heavy work, such as pounding corn, or fetching
wood and water, but are also engaged in more strictly
masculine pursuits. They are supplied with guns and
go out hunting ; they spin, weave, sew, make baskets,
etc. ; and sometimes they are sent to carry loads for a
trading party, or accompany their master to war. A
man may even send a confidential slave to the coast to
trade on his account. A chief often gives considerable
authority to his principal slave, who may attain a

S

position of great importance, and cases are not unknown where such a slave has become a chief.

People kidnapped from another tribe may be, and
sometimes are, ransomed by their friends. After a
fight it is common to send word that such and such
prisoners have been taken, so that a ransom may be
sent. It does not seem to be possible, in practice, for
a slave to redeem himself; but once free, there are no
special disabilities attaching to his position. A slave
who runs away places himself under the protection of
another master, if he can find one to shelter him; but
if he can escape being caught, he *may* achieve freedom
for himself, as, apparently, Chibisa did. But in general
a masterless slave does not find the highroad a safe
place, and hastens to put himself under some one's
protection.

Slaves are not distinguished by any special mark,
badge, or dress. They may possess property (such as
cloth, guns, and ivory), as their owner frequently
allows them to keep part of what they earn. They
may even, in some cases, own other slaves. The
master gives the slave a wife—usually a slave woman,
but occasionally he may let him marry his daughter.
The case of a free woman marrying a slave husband
is, however, rare; and he is likely to be superseded
at any time.

On the death of a slave-owner, such of his slaves as
are not chosen to accompany him (and this, as we
have seen, is by no means universal) pass into the
possession of his heir. If a slave dies possessed of
property, it all goes to his master.

The Machinga, at Mponda's on the Upper Shiré, made a raid on Ntumbi and Nziza, in May 1894, for the purpose of capturing women and children, but the men of the place frustrated this attempt, and took two prisoners, who were sent up to Chekusi's, but released (I believe) after their guns had been taken from them. There is reason to believe that they had been more successful on previous occasions, not so very long before, and that the women in question had been smuggled across the Shiré, and, as there was no safe opportunity of sending them down to the coast, bought by various Yaos in the Shiré Highlands, who set them to work in their gardens, and, if inquiry was made, passed them off as their wives. In Livingstone's time even the Anyanja, who have themselves suffered so much from the slave-trade, at times kidnapped people and sold them to the Portuguese. There is a special word for this (*fwamba*), and though practised it seems to have been always more or less reprobated—or at any rate felt to be wrong.

CHAPTER XII

TRADITIONS AND HISTORY

Probable origin of the Yaos. The Makalanga. Undi.
Migrations of the Angoni. The Tambuka.

THE Yaos believe themselves to be descended from
the same stock as the Anyanja, Anguru, and Awisa,
while they count the Angoni as a different race, and
do not profess to know whence they came. These
four tribes, therefore, must have kept together till
a much later period than that at which the Zulus
separated from the main stock of the Bantu. The
Yaos imagined the tribes with whom they acknowledged kinship to have started with them from
Kapirimtiya, and gone in different directions.

The story of how Mtanga improved the Yao
country in the beginning by moulding it into hills and
valleys, seems to bear out the opinion that the moun-
tainous region of Unangu was the early home of the
race; but how ong they lived there, before the raids of
the Magwangwara sent them forth on their wanderings,
is hard to say. Dr. M'Call Theal says : ' There is not a
single tribe in South Africa to-day that bears the same
title, has the same relative power, and occupies the
same ground as its ancestors three hundred years ago.
The people we call Mashona are indeed descended

from the Makalanga of the early Portuguese days, and
they preserve their old name and part of their old
country; but the contrast . . . is striking.'

The more one studies the wars and migrations of the
Bantu tribes, the more one is reminded of the state of
things in our own island between (roughly speaking)
500 and 1000 A.D. We are apt to forget the length of
time over which this process extended, and that though
the Bantu, so far as we can tell, began it later, there
seems no valid reason why it should not, in their case,
have a similar termination. However, as we have to
do with facts, not speculations, it seems futile to discuss
a point which only posterity will have an opportunity
of deciding.

The Makalanga speak much the same language as
the various tribes comprehended under the general
name of Anyanja, and may, at one time, have formed
a homogeneous body with them. The kingdom of the
Makalanga, as described by the Portuguese writers,
would almost seem to have been something more than
an ordinary African state; but their way of describing
everything, so to speak, in terms of Europe, is somewhat misleading. Probably it was not unlike the
' empire ' of Undi at a later date and fell to pieces much
in the same way. These decentralised agricultural
tribes either fell victims to internal quarrels, or to
aggressive action on the part of some warlike neighbour—or, very possibly, to both together.

It is not known when the Zulus moved southward
into the territory they now occupy, and where they
must have been settled for some generations before the

beginning of the nineteenth century, as the graves of at least four kings (some say eight), of earlier date than that epoch, are still to be seen at Mahlabatini, in the valley of the White Umfolozi. In 1687 they, and tribes allied to them, seem to have been in peaceful occupation of Natal and Zululand, living so close together that migration on a large scale was impossible. Yet, about the same time, the Amaxosa, or 'Cape Kafirs,' who are very closely related to them, seem to have been pressing on to the south; and they reached the Great Fish River soon after the beginning of the eighteenth century. However this may be, the Zulu king Senzagakona had, about 1800, risen to a position of some importance, though still subject to Dingiswayo, chief of the Umtetwas in Natal. His son, Tshaka, succeeded in 1810, and, after Dingiswayo's death, assumed a paramount position, his career resembling that of Napoleon, or rather (since he may be said to have consolidated, if not erected, a nation), Theodoric or Charlemagne. But what chiefly concerns us here is the *northward* migration of the Zulus which took place in his time. Umziligazi, one of his captains, quarrelled with him and fled, taking his clan with him. These are the people now known as the Matabele, having settled in the early thirties between the Limpopo and Zambezi.

Another chief, Manukosi, seceded about 1819, and invaded the country about Delagoa Bay, gradually subduing the Tonga tribes. This branch of the Zulus is called Gaza; their last king, Gungunyana (Manukosi's grandson), was deposed by the Portuguese in 1896.

The Angoni (Abanguni) were originally the tribe of

ANGONI WARRIORS

Zwide, the son of Yanga. He, too, rebelled against Tshaka (about 1820), and was defeated ; his people fled north—the only direction open to them—under Zwangendaba, and, according to a native account, came first into the Tonga country, where they fought with the people, and took many captives, then into the Basuto country (meaning probably the Bapedi of the Eastern Transvaal), where they did the same, and thence to the Karanga (Makalanga) country. Here they were overtaken by Ngaba, one of Tshaka's captains, with whom they fought two battles, and then fled, crossing the Zambezi in 1825. The date is fixed by the tradition of an eclipse, known to have occurred in that year ; and in the terror of that mysterious darkness, so inexplicable to the native mind, Zwangendaba's son, Mombera, was prematurely born. This is the Mombera whose funeral was described in an earlier chapter. He was a man of great shrewdness and force of character, and remained to the last, in spite of some passing misunderstandings, a staunch friend to Dr. Laws and the Livingstonia missionaries. He refused to be a party to sending his own or his people's children to school on the ground that they would soon become wiser than their parents, and so learn to despise them. If the missionaries liked to try their hand at teaching the grown men, they were welcome to do so; and Mombera, not content with this negative permission, took reading lessons himself, with praiseworthy assiduity. Unfortunately, he began too late in life, and though he mastered the alphabet quickly enough, he failed, in spite of all his efforts, to grasp the principle of combining letters into syllables.   He would not, however, allow the blackboard used by his instructor (the Rev. J. A. Smith, now of Mlanje) to remain at his kraal, for fear of magic.

A curious tradition about the crossing of the Zambezi was given by the Ntumbi head-men, who said that, when the Angoni reached the river and found no canoes to take them over, their chief, Chetusa, struck the water with his staff, and it divided to let them pass.   Then he struck it again, and it returned to its place.   It is only fair to add, that this account was written down by one of the Blantyre teachers, and, if not unconsciously coloured by him, may possibly contain an echo of his own narratives. On the other hand, he had been but a short time in contact with them, and these older and more responsible men, while well up in the traditions of their own people, were less likely to have been impressed by 'the stories of the white men.'

This account then goes on to state that they went north, and came 'to Magomero,' and fought two days with the Atonga, 'who dwell there to this day'; and the Atonga 'clasped their feet,' *i.e.* submitted, and acknowledged them as chiefs.   The name of Magomero is given by the Blantyre people to the Konde country at the north end of the Lake, as well as to the place of that name, near to Lake Chilwa. As the word seems to mean 'the slopes,' it may be of frequent occurrence.   They then passed round the north end of the Lake, and turned south again. Harry Kambwiri's written account says nothing of this, but it is evidently to be understood, as the next fact mentioned is that they crossed the Rovuma. Crossing the Lichilingo, and another stream called the Luli, they came to Mwalija's, where there were cattle, and intended to push on thence to the Lujenda, but 'found a desert without water,'—so they returned, lifted Mwalija's cattle, and struck off south-westward, wishing to return whence they came. They reached the Shiré at Matope (the regular crossing-place, a few miles north of the Cataracts), and wished to settle there; but one Sosola cheated them into going on by showing them a basket of cow-dung, and saying that cattle had passed by, but were now in the Chipeta country. The raiders' instinct at once rose to the bait, and they crossed to Mponda's, and went on north-westward to Mount Chirobwe. Finally, they settled near Domwe Mountain, somewhat to the north of it, and while there fought with Mpezeni, son of Zwangendaba, and defeated him. 'Mpezeni's people ran away,' and this must have been when they settled in the old Undi country (near the present Fort Jameson), where Mpezeni died a few years ago.

It is interesting to note that, in 1903, Madzimavi, a son of Mpezeni's, but not the one chosen as his successor, applied to the Native Commissioner for permission to take the name of Zwangendaba(Sungandawa, as spelt in the official document), on the ground that his grandfather's spirit had appeared to him in a dream, and ordered him to do so. His request was refused, after discussion with the principal chiefs, a majority of whom seemed to be of the opinion that such a step on

Madzimavi's part was only preliminary to declaring himself independent, if not ousting his brother altogether.

Champiti, the Ntumbi head-man, who seemed to be between forty and fifty years of age, a tall, thin man, of a type common both among the Mashona of the south and the Wahima of Uganda, said that his father came from the south and crossed the Zambezi, with many of his people. They passed by the district where he was then living, 'but none of them died by the way,' and went on to the north, and round the top of the Lake. This might very well be, even if Champiti's father had been grown up in 1825—and he need not have been, as it seems to have been a wholesale migration of families. Or he might have been impressed as a mat-carrier for the army; every Zulu warrior was attended by several of these boys, usually under ten years old. Champiti himself was born somewhere on the northward march. He mentioned passing through a country called Bena, up in the north, where the people 'had no clothes and howled like dogs'; they had cattle there with long horns—the length of the walking-stick he carried (about four feet). The Wabena, at the present day, live in German East Africa, some sixty or seventy miles to the north of Lake Nyasa, though in accordance with Dr. Theal's principle, stated above, they may have been anywhere in the middle of last century. But the absence of clothes, and the possession of long-horned cattle—if not the howling like dogs—would equally well fit the Wankonde.

Coming south again, Champiti's people lived at
Matengo, wherever that may have been, till he was
the age of a small boy whom he pointed out to me—
say, at a rough guess, eleven or twelve. Pembereka
and Kaboa, whom I have had occasion to mention
more than once, accompanied the party when they
left Matengo, after which they passed Zomba, Lake
Chilwa, and Blantyre, and 'crossed a big river with a
great deal of sand in it'—evidently the Shiré at, or
above, Lake Malombe. After this they seem to have
settled pretty much where we found them.

The above is sufficient to show that the 'Angoni'
are a very mixed multitude ; there were probably no
Zulus in this particular band ; and we find in another
account that Chiwere, one of the leading chiefs, was a
Senga, who detached himself from the main body
because his people, being regarded as a subject race,
had been 'treated badly' by the Zulus. And, while
those who crossed the Shiré from the east brought
some new elements back with them, they left some
of their own forces behind in the shape of those
'Magwangwara,' who have been thorns in the sides of
Yaos and Anyanja ever since.

Other bands, under different names, penetrated still
farther north, some of them even reaching Lake Victoria.

The date of the crossing referred to is fixed at 1867,
or soon after, by the late Mr. E. D. Young, who, reaching Chibisa's with the Livingstone Search Expedition,
in August of that year, found that the ' Mazitu ' were
encamped on the hills at Magomero. They had taken
the place formerly occupied by the Yaos in the estima-

tion of the Anyanja, and the former foes united to
oppose them.   The Makololo, too, began to regard
them as a serious danger, and expelled their old
adversary, Mankokwe, from his position near Tyolo,
lest he should make common cause with the Angoni.
The latter were at this time occupying the left, or
eastern, bank of the Shiré, and negotiating with the
Anyanja to be ferried across, while the Machinga
Yaos were in possession of the right bank, from the
Cataracts to the Lake.

The Angoni are variously known as Mazitu, Mavitu
(Maviti), and, in more northern regions, as Magwangwara, Wamachonde, and Ruga-Ruga.

From this time forward, Chekusi's Angoni raided
Yaos and Anyanja impartially for some years.   The
former fled to the hill-tops, the latter to islands in the
Shiré.   When the invaders retired, they came from
their hiding-places and cultivated their gardens in the
plains, but only to have their crops swept off by fresh
raids, as soon as they were ripe, and (as we have
previously mentioned) their women and children
carried off as slaves beyond the river.   These raids
occurred with unfailing regularity, till the settlement
of the Mission party at Blantyre in 1876.   There was
an alarm in July 1877, but the invasion did not
take place, probably owing to the presence of the
Europeans.

The last of these raids took place in 1884, but was
brought to a peaceable conclusion.   The Rev. D. C.
Scott, accompanied by Mrs. Scott and Dr. Peden,
visited Chekusi's kraal and succeeded in coming to a

friendly understanding with that chief; and thenceforth the only Angoni hosts to cross the river were gangs of porters, or of men seeking work on the plantations. Chekusi died subsequent to the proclamation of the British Protectorate in 1891; his son was executed by the British administration after the 'rising' of 1896; and Mandala, whose village, after the delimitation of 1901 was found to be in Portuguese territory, was taken prisoner and died on the march to Tete. Mpezeni's son and successor is a minor, and Mombera has been succeeded by a chief who has but little real authority, so that the prestige of these Zulu clans is now a thing of the past.

We have already seen how the Makololo came to be settled on the Shiré.

The Tambuka, or Tumbuka, according to their own account, 'came from the north,' where they were one tribe, ruled over by one chief, named Chikulamayembe. This was in some indefinite time long ago, before the Angoni had come. When they separated, they were living on the Rukuru river, where it flows through a natural arch of rock. Here 'they worshipped a hill called Chikangombe; there is there a hot spring which they worshipped also.' They split up and went in different directions, living much as the Mang'anja of the Shiré Highlands did before they were displaced by invaders. 'They lived separately. One said, "I am chief," and another said so also. They did not build big villages, but small ones of a few huts, containing their slaves, wives, and others.' When they elected a chief, they anointed him with lion's fat. 'Chikulamayembe' seems to mean 'giver of hoes,' and this chief was so called 'because they saw his kindness and bounty to the poor. When a person had no hoe, he came to the chief and asked one, and he got it.' Hoes are used as money by some tribes—as by those of the Upper Congo, and formerly by the Baronga of Delagoa Bay.

Chikulamayembe's people moved on from the Rukuru to the hill Zabula, which appears to have been regarded with superstitious awe. 'The old people of the tribe thought this hill could give rain.' Here another separation took place, and, soon after, they were attacked by the Angoni. 'The Tambuka had many cattle and goats,' says the native account, 'but the Ngoni hearing that they had cattle came and fought with them. The Ngoni killed the Tambuka, took their cattle, and sent them to their chief Zwang-endaba. Thus the Tambuka failed to withstand the Ngoni, through their living apart and being scattered.' For a time the invaders carried all before them ; then they met with a temporary check, being defeated by three Tambuka chiefs in succession. The last of these, Chigamuka, inflicted such a crushing blow on them that, 'to-day, if a Tambuka reminds a Ngoni of Chigamuka, the latter will strike him, because the Ngoni died and were beaten there.'

They recovered, however, after a time, and resumed their career of conquest. 'To-day,' said Dr. Steele's informant, in 1893, 'they are the masters of the Tam-buka, Tonga, Chewa, Bisa, and Senga. There is no chief of the Tambuka, but the Ngoni alone.

The records of these wars and migrations are necessarily very imperfect. They serve, however, to explain the great mixture of types which attentive observation shows us in most tribes of the Bantu race. Probably, if we may judge by analogy from similar processes in the past, the ultimate result will be the building up of several distinct nationalities, each with a well-marked type of its own, and institutions modified by so much of European culture as they can receive and assimilate. But such speculation belongs to the future. Our business here is only with the present, and our attempt has been to give some notion of these people as they now are, or (in cases where they have been influenced by contact with Europeans) as they were until lately.

NOTE.—It appears that there were really two Zulu migrations, the second one led by Ngola, Chekusi's predecessor. It was the latter who fought with Mpezeni's people, as stated on page 281, and Champiti's account must probably be taken to refer to them. It seems that at one time they even reached the sea at Mozambique.

BIBLIOGRAPHY

OF THE PRINCIPAL WORKS MADE USE OF IN THE
FOREGOING PAGES

LIVINGSTONE, DAVID, *Narrative of an Expedition to the
Zambezi and its Tributaries, and of the Discovery of
Lakes Shirwa and Nyassa*, 1858-1864. London, John
Murray, 1865. (Original unabridged edition.)

ROWLEY, Rev. HENRY, *Story of the Universities' Mission to
Central Africa*. London, 1866.

MACDONALD, Rev. DUFF, *Africana*, 2 vols. London, Simpkin,
Marshall and Co., 1882.

JOHNSTON, Sir H. H., K.C.B., *British Central Africa*.
London, Methuen, 1897.

SCOTT, Rev. D. C., *Cyclopædic Dictionary of the Mang'anja
Language*. Edinburgh, Blackwood, 1892.

BARNES, Rev. H. B. (U.M.C.A.), *Nyanja-English Vocabulary*.
London, S.P.C.K., 1902.

Occasional Papers for Nyasaland (Likoma, 1893), afterwards
The Nyasa News (Likoma, 1893-95). This periodical
contains a large amount of exceedingly valuable information. Some use has also been made of two other
magazines—*Life and Work in Central Africa* (Blantyre),
and *The Aurora* (Livingstonia Mission, Bandawe).

ADDENDA

I. P. 74-5.—The Spider absent from Bantu folklore. This statement requires some modification. Since writing the above, I have examined a number of Duala animal-stories collected by Herr Wilhelm Lederbogen, formerly of the Government School at Kamerun. The Duala are the most north-westerly Bantu tribe, and have probably borrowed some of their folklore from their Efik neighbours. As in most of the West Coast stories, moreover, the place of the Hare is taken by a small species of antelope, to which the English-speaking natives of Sierra Leone have, for some occult reason, given the name of Cunnie Rabbit. (It is curious that a Duala native, when telling a story in German, also called the creature a hare, but explained that 'it is not like [the hares] here, but has little horns.'—See Elli Meinhof, *Märchen aus Kamerun.*) Mr. Dennett also gives a Lower Congo story of 'How the Spider won and lost Nzambi's Daughter.'—(See *Folklore of the Fjort.*)

II. P. 155-6.—This mode of burying those who have died of smallpox is not invariable, or else the practice has been modified of late years. A more recent native account says: 'In this case a small reed is stuck into the side of the grave. Along this reed the disease will creep and so escape from the body into the open air. For they say that if they do not thus allow the disease to escape, "they will only plant the disease in the ground, and epidemics will be frequent."'

The same authority states that a difference is made in case of violent death: 'One who has died from the effects of a gunshot wound or the thrust of a spear is buried at

T

once without the ordinary delay of a day or two waiting for the relations to arrive. The body is not allowed to be at the village even for one night, but is buried at once. Nor do the *awilo* in this case dig the grave to any depth. They say that if they dig deeply they will be stabbed. One killed by a wild beast is treated in similar fashion.'—(*Life and Work in British Central Africa*, Dec. 1905, p. 4.)

The writer of the above is apparently a Yao. He does not specify whether these remarks apply to Yao or Anyanja; but as, in other passages, he is careful to point out where the practice of the two tribes differs, we may no doubt understand him as referring to both.

III. P. 279.—Mombera. Dr. Elmslie (*Among the Wild Ngoni*, Edinburgh, 1901) gives an interesting picture of this chief. ' Mombera had a dual character. He was at his best in the early part of the day, before he became intoxicated, and so by sunrise people with cases to be judged went to see him. Then his affability and generous behaviour were pleasant to see, but toward afternoon, when the beer he continually sipped began to act, his civility was at an end for the day.' . . . Many natives, in later life, when they find their digestive powers weakening, come to depend on the nourishing *moa* for their principal sustenance, with results (when, like Mombera, they can command unlimited quantities) as above.

' When sober, he delighted to play with his children, and manifested a very pleasing interest in them and their mothers. . . . He had a great interest in old people, of whom he had always a great number living in huts within the seraglio. He treated them with respect, and provided for them from his own table. If he was shown anything new and strange, he would generally have it shown to the old people, and while they knelt before him in due respect, one could notice with pleasure their trustful attitude and how he would heartily respond to any observation of wonder they might express. . . . He said they would have to report to the ancestral spirits how many new and wonderful things had now become known to the people. . . .

'. . . He was neither cruel nor bloodthirsty. He discountenanced the poison ordeal which was adopted from the Tonga slaves, believing rather in their own trial by boiling water, which at most only maimed the person and did not destroy life as the *mwavi* did. He was considered to be "too soft" by the more degraded and fiery dispositions, and had no delight in condemning to death. Only two instances of the death-penalty being inflicted by Mombera came under my own observation during all the years I lived under him. In one case he caused a man to be put to death for cattle-stealing, after having pardoned him for the same offence. . . . The other case was where a member of the royal family killed a slave who had run away from him and put himself under the protection of another master. . . .' (Pp. 115-117.)

GLOSSARY

(*Unless otherwise stated, the language is Nyanja*)

Abusa, plural of *mbusa*, a herd-boy.

Adzukulu, grandchildren, also spelt *ajukulu* and *asukuru*. But it usually means the relatives or friends who make all the arrangements for burying a deceased person.

Afiti, plural of *mfiti*, a wizard.

Amabele (Zulu), 'Kafir corn'—*Holcus sorghum*.

Amadhlozi (Zulu), plural of *idhlozi*, ancestral spirits, when they appear in the form of snakes.

Amatongo (Zulu), ancestral spirits manifesting themselves in dreams.

Antu, plural of *muntu*, a person.

Awilo (Yao). See *Adzukulu*.

Bango, a very common kind of reed—*Phragmites communis*.

Bwalo, the village place of assembly or 'forum'; it is also used (see p. 122) for the unmarried men's house.

Bwazi, a shrub (*Securidaca longipedunculata*) and the fibre procured from its bark.

Bwebweta, v., to rave or talk nonsense, as if possessed by spirits.

Chagwa, lit. 'it has fallen'; name of a game. See p. 113.

Chamba, Indian hemp; also name of a dance.

Chifukwa, lit. 'a fault,' but used as a conjunction—'because.'

Chikolongwe, a barbed fish-spear, or gaff.

Chikonyo, a cob of maize.

Chimanga, maize.

Chinamwali, the initiation ceremonies for girls.

Chinangwa (Yao), cassava.

Chipini, a metal ornament, like a stud, worn by women in the nose.

Chipongwe, impudence.

Chire, the bush.

Chiri, a steep bank.

Chirombo, a wild beast, a monster; also an insect or a weed.

Chirope, madness caused by shedding blood. See p. 67.

Chitalaka, red porcelain beads, white inside.

Chitowe, sesamum, the seed of which is used for making oil.

Dambo, a plain, or open grass-land in the Bush.

Dimba, a patch of alluvial soil beside a stream.

Dzombe, a locust.

Fumba, a sleeping-bag made of matting.

Garanzi, a small drum, beaten quickly.
Gome (*nyumba ya*), a square house.
Gowero, boys' house in a village.
Gwape (*gwapi*), the klipspringer —*Oreotragus saltator.*

Imfe (Zulu), a kind of sorghum with sweet juice (*S. saccharinum*); Nyanja *msale.*
Inswa, 'white ants,' or termites.
Isigcogco or *isicoco* (Zulu), head-ring worn by men when of an age and standing to be called to the chief's council.

Kokalupsya, the early rains which sweep away the ashes of the burnt grass and scrub (*lupsya*).
Kombe, the strophanthus creeper; the arrow-poison made from it.
Kondo, keloids, or scars made by cutting, as tribal marks or for ornament.

Lisoka (Yao), the spiritual part of man; a ghost.
Lobola, v. (Zulu), properly, to arrange a marriage 'by agreeing to deliver a certain number of cattle' to the girl's father or guardian.
Lululuta, v., or *luluta*, 'to utter the cry called *ntungululu* on the return of men from war or hunting, or any other exciting occasion. The sound is produced by vibrations of the tongue intermitting the cry or whistle by the lips.'

Lundu (*Rundo*), paramount chief.
Lupsya, burnt grass, etc. See *Kokalupsya.*

Mabisalila, the witch-finder woman. See p. 89.
Maere, a small kind of millet— *Eleusine.*
Makani, a debate or discussion.
Malimwe, the winter.
Mankwala, medicine.
Mapira, Sorghum vulgare.
Mapondera, the man who pounds the poison for the *mwavi* ordeal.
Maseche (plural of *tseche*), rattles made from the hard-shelled fruits of a certain tree.
Masuku, the fruit of the *msuku* tree —*Napaca kirkii.*
Matekenya, plural of *tekenya*, the jigger—*Sarcopsyllus penetrans.*
Matondo, fruit of the *mtondo* tree.
Mbawa, the mahogany - tree— *K'haya senegalensis.*
Mbidzi, a zebra.
Mbulu, the wild dog—*Lycaon pictus.*
Mchombwa, the game of *msuo* or *mankala.*
Mdzi, a village. Also *mudzi.* Zulu *umuzi.*
Mdzodzo, a kind of black ant emitting an offensive smell.
Mfiti, a wizard.
Miiko, plural of *mwiko*, which see.
Mlandu, a 'case,' discussion or trial.
Mlungusi, a kind of thorn-tree.
Moa, native beer.
Momba, a straight fish-spear.
Mono, a basket-trap for fish.
Moto, fire.
Mpakasa, autumn; the beginning of the dry season.
Mbeza, a kind of caterpillar.

Mpkiyu (Tonga), a kind of medicine for effecting the transformation of people into animals.

Mpingo, the ebony-tree—*Diospyrus*.

Mpini. See *Konde*.

Mpira, india-rubber, or a ball made of it.

Msale. See *Imfe*.

Msampa, a kind of trap.

Msuku, the tree *Napaca kirkii*.

Msuo. See *Mchombwa*.

Mtanga, a kind of basket.

Mtumbamtumba, a large kind of black and white, strong-smelling ants.

Mvula, rain. Yao *ula*.

Mvunguti, a tree (*Kigelia*) with large cucumber-shaped fruits, 1 to 2 feet long.

Mwavi, the poison prepared from the bark of *Erythrophleum guineense*; the ordeal in which it is used.

Mwiko, a prohibition of some particular food to an individual or family.

Myombo, a tree like an ash—*Brachystegia longifolia*.

Muinda, the head village of a district.

Namwali, a girl who has been initiated.

Nchito, work. *Nchito ya amuna*, 'work of men (males).'

Ndiwo, anything eaten as relish with porridge.

Ng'ama, red oxide of iron.

Nguluwe, a bush-pig.

Njinga, a reel or spindle.

Nkaka, the scaly ant-eater, Pangolin.

Nkalango, a thicket; a clump of trees left standing to shelter the graves.

Nkata, a grass ring or pad used in carrying loads on the head.

Nkokwe, a corn-bin or granary made of basket-work.

Nkole, the initiation ceremonies (the word used at Likoma). See *Unyago*.

Nsanja, the shelf or stage above the fireplace in a Nyanja hut.

Nsengwa, a small round basket.

Nsima, porridge made of maize or *mapira* meal.

Ntengu, a small blackbird.

Nyanja, a lake or river.

Nyasa (Yao), a lake or river.

Nzama, a kind of bean, resembling a ground-nut.

Peka, v., to make fire by drilling.

Pelele, a lip-ring worn by women.

Rundo. See *Lundu.*

Sonkwe, a kind of hibiscus, from which fibre is obtained.

Tengo, the bush.

Tsanchima, a masked performer in the *sinyao* dance.

Ufa, flour.

Ulendo, a journey; also a party making the journey, a caravan.

Unyago (Yao), the initiation ceremonies for young people. See *Nkole*.

Wodiera, an eater, literally '(one) of eating,' contracted from *wa ku diera*.

Zikonyo, plural of *chikonyo*, which see.

Zinyao, the dance at the mysteries, in which the performers dress up with masks, etc., as animals.

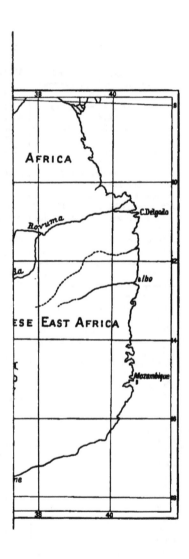

INDEX

ABANDA (Yao clan), 160, 253.
Abstinence from certain foods, 94-6.
Achikunda (Chikundas), 24, 61, 95.
Achipeta, 25 ; their tobacco, 178 ; their country, 281.
Adultery, 152, 265-6.
Agnatic descent (*chilawa*), 253.
Ajawa. *See* Yaos.
Alolo (Anguru), 24, 32, 33.
—— their tribe marks, 39.
Alunda, 25.
Alungu, 25.
Ancestral spirits, 48 *et seq.*, 54, 62-66.
Angoni, 24, 29, 34, 35.
—— their prayers and sacrifices, 53.
—— harems of chiefs, 132.
—— chiefs order wholesale *mwavi*-drinkings, 170.
—— war-dance, 228.
—— migrations, 278-285.
—— raids, 283-4.
Animals as witches' messengers, 84, 169.
—— in folklore, 231 *et seq.*
—— reserved for chiefs' eating, 272.
Ants, white (termites), 22, 191 ; used as food, 137, 192.
—— omens drawn from, 94.
Ant-eater, 17, 272.
Anyanja, 24 *et seq.*, 277.
—— subject to Angoni, 29, 35, 272.

Anyanja conquered by Makololo, 37, 268-9.
—— their worship, 63.
—— their chiefs, 'old gods of the land,' 51, 58.
—— villages, 99 *et seq.*
—— betrothal and marriage customs, 130 *et seq.*
—— burial, 156, and Ch. VII. *passim.*
—— tales, 231, 233, 238 *et seq.*
—— system of kinship, 253.
—— tribal organisation, 255-6.
—— raided by Angoni, 283-4.
Apodzo, hippo-hunters, 190-1.
Arrows, 187.
Astræa, myth of, 75.
Atonga, 33.
—— their beliefs, 56, 58.
—— burial customs, 157 *et seq.*
—— conquered by Angoni, 280.
Awankonde, 22, 34.
—— their beliefs, 62.
—— prayers, 63.
—— marriage ceremonies, 131.
Awemba (Babemba) 25, 71.
—— human sacrifices, 160.
—— corpses of chiefs mummified, 163.

BABEMBA. *See* Awemba.
Babies, 102 *et seq.*
Baboons, 17, 121, 183.
Bachelors' house, 122.
Ball-game, 113.

Printed by T. and A. Constable, Printers to His Majesty
at the Edinburgh University Press

Lightning Source UK Ltd.
Milton Keynes UK
UKHW021946021222
413123UK00009B/386